Lessons Learned:

Practical Advice for the Teaching of Psychology

Edited by:
Baron Perlman
Lee I. McCann
Susan H. McFadden
University of Wisconsin-Oshkosh

American Psychological Society
1010 Vermont Avenue, NW
Suite 1100
Washington, DC 20005-4907
(202) 783-2077 ◆ Fax: (202) 783-2083
www.psychologicalscience.org

Second Printing 2001

Published by
American Psychological Society
1010 Vermont Ave., NW
Suite 1100
Washington, DC 20005-4907

International Standard Book Number: **0-9626884-2-8**
Library of Congress Catalog Number: **99-62277**

Production Editor (second printing): Brian Weaver

AMERICAN PSYCHOLOGICAL SOCIETY

www.psychologicalscience.org

Acknowledgments

M any people have supported us in the creation and editing of the Teaching Tips column and the publishing of this book. We thank Alan Kraut and Lee Herring for their support for the idea of the column. Both Lee Herring and Elizabeth Ruksznis, former editors of the *Observer*, and Sarah Brookhart, its present editor, and Brian Weaver, the production editor for this book, have provided excellent stewardship. Columns we believed were close to perfect when submitted were improved. Our relationship with them could not have been better.

We must thank Doug Bernstein from the University of Illinois, who through his superb work overseeing the National Institute for the Teaching of Psychology, has provided a forum that sustains us year after year. Charles Brewer, former editor of the journal *Teaching of Psychology*, has helped us with our teaching, our writing, and has inspired interest in the process of and research on teaching.

Most importantly, we thank the contributors to the *APS Observer* Teaching Tips column. All have provided thoughtful writings and have tolerated our requests for more ideas and drafts with equanimity and a collegial spirit. Their willingness to spend the time and effort to contribute is greatly appreciated. We are pleased that several authors are from other countries, providing evidence that psychology truly is taught and valued around the globe.

Baron Perlman
Lee I. McCann
Susan H. McFadden
June, 2001

Table of Contents

Preface

*... in lecture halls, seminar rooms, field settings, labs, and even
electronic classrooms—the places where most people receive most
of their formal education—teachers possess the power to create
conditions that can help students learn a great deal—or keep
them from learning much at all.*

—Palmer, 1998

Origins of the *APS Observer* Teaching Tips Columns

In 1993, Lee I. McCann and Barry Perlman attended the 15th Annual
National Institute on the Teaching of Psychology (NITOP) conference cosponsored by the University of Illinois at Urbana-Champaign
and the University of South Florida. Neither of us had attended a teaching
conference before, but the presentations listed in the brochure were appealing and we had some teaching data to present. The conference was so stimulating that we have returned every year since to enjoy good conversation
with colleagues about teaching and to garner new ideas on how to teach
better.

One outcome of attending NITOP was our desire to share its focus on
teaching with others. Alan Kraut, executive director of the American Psychological Society (APS), was in attendance in 1994—when APS began
cosponsoring the conference—and we talked with him about an article we
had written for the *APS Observer* on how to obtain a first teaching job,
with advice on preparing and presenting one's teaching abilities and cre-
dentials. Was APS interested in an ongoing column about teaching? One
thing led to another, and conversations with Alan Kraut and Lee Herring,
then editor of the *Observer*, moved at a lively pace. Within a few months,
the Teaching Tips column was a reality, with one of our colleagues at University of Wisconsin-Oshkosh, Susan H. McFadden, joining us as a coeditor.

Since beginning the editing of Teaching Tips, we have found authors,
and some have found us. It is a fun and exciting process, and we continue
to learn a tremendous amount about teaching.

We wanted to present teaching information in a lively format, avoiding
the scholarly writing style to which most of us are accustomed. We hope it
is fun for authors to write in this manner and a pleasant change of pace for

readers.

The Book's Rationale and Purpose

Except for rare exceptions, all faculty teach, and teaching is receiving more emphasis and attention in the popular press, legislative bodies, and on college campuses. Campuses of all sizes are discovering or rediscovering either voluntarily, or in response to outside forces, the importance of good teaching.

In that spirit, we developed the Teaching Tips column with the goals of:

◆   Informing undergraduate, graduate, and future faculty (teaching assistants), about both the content and methods of teaching;

◆   Bringing a wide variety of teaching topics to the attention of teachers of psychology; and

◆   Enhancing the teaching of psychology, and thus improving the quality of the education our students receive.

Overview

This book is a practical presentation of the processes and issues involved in the teaching of psychology. It consists of eight sections, each composed of *APS Observer* Teaching Tips columns. One article by Sechrest et al. preceded Tips but was written in the same style and spirit, and is included. Contributions explore topics ranging from specific teaching tasks (e.g., writing a syllabus) to more general teaching issues (e.g., handling the difficult student). Authors were asked to supply recommended readings for the original columns and many have chosen to update them for this publication. Each column stands alone, although in the actual teaching of a course over a semester, many of the topics interconnect. After reading each column, readers should have several new teaching ideas to think about, and be able to implement those of interest.

The typical reader will be a college or university psychology faculty member, but the book is also useful for high school teachers of psychology. Faculty in other disciplines will find the book a valuable resource for their teaching as well. For new teachers, the book is a starting point. For the experienced teacher, it is a resource to consult. Additionally, teaching assistants and their supervisors in psychology and other graduate programs will find this book useful, as will new faculty and their mentors.

Recommended Readings and References

Palmer, P. (1998). *The courage to teach: Exploring the inner landscape of a teacher's life*. San Francisco: Jossey-Bass.

Part 1

Steps in a Teacher's Life

Chapter 1

How to Land that First Teaching Job

Baron Perlman
Susan H. McFadden
Lee I. McCann
University of Wisconsin-Oshkosh

Teaching is a major factor in faculty role definition—and teaching experience is an important hiring criterion—at hundreds of psychology departments in regional universities and liberal arts colleges across the nation. Teaching also is being emphasized increasingly at many doctoral institutions. Because instruction consumes almost two-thirds (64 percent) of faculty work time (Bowen & Schuster, 1986), we maintain that academic job applicants should consider how best to present their teaching experiences and ability.

Applying for the Position

The materials applicants provide to recruitment committees should communicate their preparedness to teach and their understanding of teaching and its place in higher education. An applicant should avoid being perceived as apathetic toward teaching or as viewing teaching as a secondary activity (or *necessary evil*).

An applicant should want to create the impression in others that he/she is a future academician who sees teaching as a serious and indispensable part of academic life. A concern for excellent teaching is not antithetical to being a first-rate scholar, and it may in fact be highly correlated with teaching skills. Displaying an ability to teach will not diminish your competitiveness for an academic position.

Demonstrate Your Teaching Awareness

To demonstrate teaching skills, candidates should present information on their teaching experiences. For example, candidates who have participated in a first-rate teaching assistant program and/or a graduate seminar on teaching should describe what they have learned from these experiences.

This article first appeared in the March 1994 APS Observer.

Document Your Teaching Abilities

If you are presently teaching, you should ask those writing letters of recommendation to observe your teaching. Search committees often read letters saying: "I have not observed Sam/Sally teach, but I am sure he/she will be an excellent teacher." Certainly your mentors would not say you exhibit promise to be an excellent scholar, if they had no familiarity with your scholarship! It is helpful if individuals writing recommendations can document their knowledge of your teaching philosophy and/or your efforts to improve teaching.

Develop a Teaching Portfolio

You may want to create a *Teaching Portfolio* to include in your application materials. This portfolio would include your teaching statement (described below), course syllabi, teaching evaluations from courses you have taught, and any other information related to teaching that the search committee requests.

The Teaching Statement—The teaching statement is of special importance, as it is the only chance you may have to detail your ideas and skills related to teaching. We urge job applicants to write a teaching statement, whether one is requested or not. In a recent recruitment, our position announcement requested statements for both teaching and research interests. Of 156 applicants, only 35 (22 percent) provided teaching statements (Perlman, Marxen, McFadden, & McCann, 1993).

To write an articulate and meaningful teaching statement, candidates must: (a) think about teaching and discuss it with others; and (b) read about the subject. If you have done this reading, you stand out among peers in the academic job hunt. A model of teaching, such as the one presented by McFadden and Perlman (1989), can help structure your ideas about teaching. Other sources might include the journal *Teaching of Psychology*, which for 20 years has been a forum for teaching information in our discipline. Another source would be the quarterly journal *New Directions for Teaching and Learning*. More generally, there are numerous books about the improvement of teaching (e.g., Eble, 1976; Lowman, 1984; McKeachie, 1994).

Candidates who are articulate about teaching—and who have given the art and craft of teaching some thought before arriving on campus for an interview—distinguish themselves as individuals motivated to serve the needs of students and to join collegially with faculty in the teaching enterprise.

Teaching Experience—You should have teaching experience. In addition to teaching at your home institution as a TA, you may want to consider ad hoc teaching at a nearby institution as you finish your doctorate. Responsibility for a complete course is important in learning what it means to teach. You may want to suggest submitting a videotape of your teaching to the recruitment committee.

Campus Visit

Teach a class. We urge finalists for an academic position who have been invited for a campus visit to request the opportunity to teach a class. Using a colloquium to evaluate teaching abilities and potential is a time honored tradition, but why not actual teaching? Prepare a lecture with requisite overheads and other teaching aids, and demonstrate your teaching ability while getting a chance to interact with the students you would be teaching if hired.

Meet with Students

We also urge candidates to ask to meet with undergraduates. You want to discover their perspectives on the psychology department, and what they need and value in teaching faculty. Their questions and your answers will give both you and the students information about the fit between your expertise and interests as well as the students' needs.

Ask About Mentoring

In addition, you should learn what kind of mentoring takes place regarding teaching. The academic Darwinian notion of "survival of the fittest" is being replaced at many institutions with mentoring programs. Becoming an expert teacher is a developmental process that takes years.

Talk with Department Faculty

Talk with department faculty about teaching. For example, what courses do they teach? What observations can they share with you about teaching? What is taught across the curriculum (e.g., ethics, scientific method, writing), if anything? Try not to focus too much on your needs or wants, but attempt to determine what is needed to best serve the students and department and to describe the contributions you could make.

Conclusion

We urge candidates to attend to teaching when applying for academic positions and during academic position interviews. Your subject matter expertise is not the equivalent of being, or having the potential to become, a good teacher. It is our experience in working with and mentoring new faculty that they often experience a shock during their first two years of teaching, finding that class preparation and teaching require much more time and energy than anticipated.

The unfortunate result is disillusionment, frustration, and dissatisfaction with academic life. Use both graduate school and the search process as preparation for a career as an academician who knows and cares about teaching.

Recommended Readings and References

Bowen, H. R., & Schuster, J. H. (1986). *American professors: A national resource imperiled.* New York: Oxford University Press.

Eble, K. E. (1976). *The craft of teaching.* San Francisco: Jossey-Bass.

Lowman, J. (1984). *Mastering the techniques of teaching.* San Francisco: Jossey-Bass.

McFadden, S. H., & Perlman, B. (1989). Faculty recruitment and excellent undergraduate teaching. *Teaching of Psychology, 16,* 195-198.

McKeachie, W. J. (1994). *Teaching tips: Strategies, research, and theory for college and university teachers* (9th ed.). Lexington, MA: D. C. Heath.

Perlman, B., Marxen, J., McFadden, S.H., & McCann, L. I. (1996). Applicants for a faculty position do not emphasize teaching. *Teaching of Psychology, 23,* 103-104.

Perlman, B., & McCann, L. I. (1996). *Recruiting good college faculty: Practical advice for a successful search.* Bolton, MA: Anker.

Chapter 2

As Time Goes By: Maintaining Vitality In the Classroom

Margaret A. Lloyd
Georgia Southern University

For beginning teachers, mastering the craft of teaching usually takes a back seat to mastering the content—it's enough just to stay one day ahead of the students! But experienced teachers know that being effective in the classroom isn't merely a matter of finally "getting down" both content and craft, and then forgetting about it. Rather, maintaining our vitality as teachers requires regular attention and care.

In our early years of teaching—if we're lucky—we discover mentors who guide our development. As we mature, we need to become our own mentors—devising our own ways of enhancing the quality of our teaching and solving the teaching-related problems that invariably arise. If you're an experienced teacher and feel it's time for a *tune-up*, the following tips may help.

Self-Mentoring Tips

Be Willing To Experiment!

One of the best ways to maintain a sense of excitement about teaching is to do something different. If you typically teach large classes, try a smaller one, or vice versa. Develop a new course or offer a seminar on a special topic. If you're a dynamic and effective lecturer, learn how to lead good discussions. Team teach a course. Incorporate more demonstrations and activities in your classes. Would cooperative learning strategies work in any of your classes?

Take Careful Notes About What Works And What Doesn't

We learn by experience, but sometimes we fail to take full advantage of our experience because we forget the lesson we learned! To solve this problem, write notes to yourself about what goes over particularly well and what *bombs* in classes. Keep a sheet of paper in the back of each course folder for notes about revisions you want to implement the next time you teach the class. At the end of the term, immediately review these notes and evaluate the course. Then, compile a list of the changes you want to make for next time, and file it for later reference.

This article first appeared in the November 1994 APS Observer

Seek Out New Ideas About Teaching

Keeping up with advancements in our discipline is familiar to us. We may be less knowledgeable about how to keep up on the craft of teaching. Luckily, there are numerous resources on instruction available.

Read journals on teaching—*Teaching of Psychology* is available; you receive a free journal subscription with a membership in the Society for the Teaching of Psychology (APA's Division 2), and you can join the Division as an affiliate member without having to join APA.

Utilize teaching resources—The Office of Teaching Resources in Psychology (OTRP) of the Society for the Teaching of Psychology distributes teaching materials (classroom activities, syllabi, annotated bibliographies, etc.). You can view the current list of resources by visiting the OTRP home page, ORTP Online (www.lemoyne.edu/OTRP/).

Read newsletters on teaching—There are several newsletters for teachers. *The Teaching Professor* has reduced rates for group subscriptions, and your department/division/college might want to subscribe. Or, there is *The Psychology Teacher Network* which is published by APA. It is free to members; and available to nonmembers for a small price.

Attend a conference or session devoted to teaching—Teaching conferences exist across the country, both regional and national. Teaching conferences provide a context within which to focus solely on teaching and to compare experiences and ideas with other teachers of psychology. Many people who have taught for years find it enriching to learn new teaching techniques and to talk with others who are also interested in teaching. The most widely known may be the annual National Institute on the Teaching of Psychology, held each January in St. Petersburg Beach, Florida. It is run cooperatively by the University of Illinois at Urbana-Champaign, the University of South Florida, and APS. APS also has a one day Institute on the Teaching of Psychology as part of its national meeting.

Other conferences include those sponsored by Ithaca College, Southern Indiana University, Texas Wesleyan University, Kennesaw State College, the College of DuPage, SUNY-Farmingdale, James Madison University, and the Lewis M. Terman Western Regional Teachers Conference. (My apologies to any conferences I have omitted.)

Consider other sources of new ideas—Read books about teaching (see the list of recommended readings for suggestions). Share teaching strategies with interested colleagues. Why not institute once-a-term departmental teaching workshops for those who are interested?

Get a Different Perspective on Your Teaching

A great way to see how you're actually coming across in the classroom is to have a class videotaped and view it for strengths and weaknesses. Many of us do this early in our careers, but it's helpful to do it later as well, because, over time, our perspectives on teaching change, as does our teaching. You'll see some good things ("Wow, that was a really lucid explanation!") and some bad ones ("I can't believe it—I must have said, 'OK?' 25 times in 50 minutes!").

Also, check for nonverbal messages that affect your students and the classroom atmosphere. You can get other perspectives by asking faculty with reputations for excellent teaching to observe your classes or a videotape. See what services your institution's Teaching Center offers.

Stay in Touch With Your Students

Do students return blank stares when you share a humorous anecdote that used to bring forth appreciative chortles and nods of understanding? I can still recall my shock at students' mystified looks when I mentioned the Bay of Pigs disaster while discussing a social psychology experiment! As we become more experienced as teachers, we also grow older. Sooner or later, we hit the point when we're the age of our students' parents. For better or worse, this means that students' perceptions of us change, and vice versa.

A big part of being a good teacher is to know *where your students are coming from* so you can connect the course material to experiences in their lives and use language to which they can relate. (If you have college-aged children or acquaintances, this gives you a small edge—although I know parents who would dispute this!) As we get more distant in age from our students, it's important to stay tuned in to their culture. Take a look at the demographic information and survey data on the attitudes of college freshmen in the Almanac issue of the *Chronicle of Higher Education* published every August. It's also helpful to know what books students are reading; the *Chronicle* usually carries a list of best-sellers on college campuses. And, if you're feeling really adventuresome, tune into MTV or some pop radio stations (stand well back from the speakers) to hear what they're listening to!

Regularly Seek Students' Suggestions for Improving Your Courses

Try conducting midterm evaluations on critical aspects of your courses. This strategy is especially helpful if you're trying something new for the first time, or if you discover that something that used to work in class no longer has the same effect. Giving midterm evaluations also allows you to make changes in a course, if you choose, while the students who made the suggestions can still benefit from them. Or, consider a small student committee to keep you apprised of how things are going in the course.

Cultivate a Positive Attitude and Maintain Your Enthusiasm

An essential part of teaching—especially these days—is motivating students to be interested in the material. Enthusiasm and optimism are contagious. After teaching the same ideas for a long time, we may find our excitement about the material diminishing. Also, sometimes we wrongly assume, because certain concepts are common knowledge to us, that students are also familiar with them. From this perspective, it is like being forced to tell a joke realizing that the audience already knows the punchline. But, if we can key in on what we find interesting about the material, students are likely to get excited about it as well—and this also helps maintain *our* enthusiasm!

Self-Mentoring in Special Circumstances

Sometimes we face situations for which solutions aren't obvious. Maybe we have a particularly troublesome student or feel that we're not able to hold students' attention the way we would like. Maybe we don't even know what the specific problem is—things just aren't going well. At times like this, we can use self-mentoring in a more deliberate and systematic way. We can take the role of a *helpful other*, and ask ourselves the same questions we would pose to a colleague who came to us with our problem. "What seems to be the nature of the problem?" "What might be some likely causes of the problem, based on what I know about myself, and the situation?" "What kinds of things might I do to solve the problem?" These questions speak to the *expertise* aspect of mentoring.

Avoid the *Negativity Trap*

Reflect for a moment on our role as a mentor to others. Sharing our expertise is important, but we often help the most by encouraging others and reminding them of their capabilities and positive qualities. Sometimes we can get caught in a *negativity trap* blaming ourselves or blaming our students. When this happens, it's important to remember to serve ourselves as well as we would serve others, tuning into our strengths and positive qualities. Encouragement and acceptance can produce the same payoff for ourselves as they do for others!

Conclusion

Self-mentoring can optimize our enjoyment of teaching and keep us *alive* in the classroom as we mature in our profession. If you're not already doing it, give it a try!

Recommended Readings and References

Angelo, T. A., & Cross, K. P. (1993). *Classroom assessment techniques: A handbook for college teachers* (2nd ed.). San Francisco: Jossey-Bass.

Baiocco, S. A., & DeWaters, J. N. (1998). *Successful college teaching: Problem solving strategies of distinguished professors.* Boston: Allyn & Bacon.

Davis, B. G. (1993). *Tools for teaching.* San Francisco: Jossey-Bass.

Lowman, J. (1984). *Mastering the techniques of teaching.* San Francisco: Jossey-Bass.

Chapter 3

Self-Knowledge of a Job Well Done: Reflections on A Teacher's Self-Appraisal

Stanford C. Ericksen
University of Michigan

Since the time of Socrates, great teachers have held true to their distinctive selves; to *know thyself* continues as a good rule for the rest of us. Institutional awards for good teaching may yield money in the bank and a quick fix to self-esteem, but over the long haul, self-knowledge of a job well done is the more lasting reward for the career teacher. Self-appraisal, however, can drift into self-deception if not guided by a clear conception of what good teachers do and the ideas that influence their thinking and action.

This article is a summary of teaching concepts I've emphasized over the years. I hope it confirms to teachers that they have the ability and standards necessary to examine their own interaction with students.

About good teaching, opinions differ. Two self-serving opinions stay in memory: *My job is to give students the opportunity to observe the scholarly mind at work;* and *My responsibility is to teach the subject matter; if students don't want to learn, that's their problem.* Show-and-tell stories about instructional events and polemics about the art of teaching make easy reading, but college teachers are better served by having access to conceptual information about how to help students learn, remember, and form lasting values.

From the beginning of pedagogical time, teachers have learned about teaching from their own teachers. Plato learned from Socrates and these two demonstrate, well enough, that good teaching is not a new invention. One hundred years of scientific analysis has sharpened our understanding of what does and does not work in the classroom; but dramatic new findings about the interchange among teacher, student, and book are not likely. Over the centuries, good teachers have, in their own way, *discovered* such basic principles as reward works better than punishment, and students learn what they care about and remember what they understand. In comparison, most rules of teaching are secondary.

Books, films, and computers have speeded and expanded access to information but the in-head machinery for processing remains steady from grandparents to children to grandchildren. Biological evolution has not had enough

This article first appeared in the January 1998 APS Observer.

time to change how the brain works. Students learning to navigate cyberspace are perceiving, learning, and remembering in about the same way as did students who survived the saber-tooth tiger curriculum. The task for the teacher, then as now, is to recognize and to direct the use of basic conditions for learning.

The Smooth and the Zig Zag Curves of Learning

The smooth curves carry nomothetic messages about general conditions for learning while the zig zag curves mark the idiosyncratic progress of the individual student. The professional teacher works at the interface between the abstract and the concrete, between general laws of learning and the instructional realities. As the cook in charge of a kitchen, the teacher draws on principles of pedagogical nutrition that must then be modified and adapted to meet the special requirements of the subject matter, the characteristics of the students, and the teacher's own distinctive self.

The pressures of instructional mass-production notwithstanding, the individual teacher and the individual student are still the de facto units of instruction. This educational reality is intrinsic for helping students learn and store information, skills, and values in long-term memory. By voice, print, and good intentions, I have been preaching about this kind of teaching for more than 30 years and my scripture was derived from what the science of psychology has had to say about motivation, learning, memory, and thinking as extended to the classroom.

To admonish and exhort about better teaching barely ripples the course of instructional events and teachers report that books tell me more than I want to know about instruction. The message is clear: teaching is a thoroughly personal engagement and this privacy is respected and, by campus common law, well guarded by fellow teachers. Thus, self-appraisal remains as a voice frequently heard and individual teachers will agree and use material from these guidelines in terms of their own distinctive selves and habits for managing the classroom hour.

Five Guidelines for Self-Appraisal

Course Content

Insofar as the teacher controls course content, the first measure of good teaching is the quality of knowledge students carry away when the course is over. Students are able to adapt to less-then-exciting modes of teaching, but compensatory mechanisms are not available for what should have been taught but was not. They place their trust in a teacher's decisions about course content and the only instructional sin greater than teaching obsolete, irrelevant, or trivial information is to test and grade students about such stuff.

Books and computers are powerful technological aids for the delivery of course content but the classic question remains: What knowledge will be worth a student's knowing five or 10 years hence? Value judgments of this order call for a touch of prophetic vision which is helped along by listening to what discipline colleagues have to say and by reading about intra- and interdisciplinary developments. In one form or another, *relevance* continues to be a legitimate challenge to the substance of a course of study.

The Motivation to Learn

In any year and any language, the phrase, "May I have your attention please?" triggers the start of the learning process. Teaching draws a blank in the absence of student interest and good teachers enhance this interest without even thinking *motivation*. Successful teachers are working demonstrations of a single sweeping principle: enthusiasm for the job at hand. Enthusiasm does more to counter student apathy and indifference than do contrived efforts to attack motivation directly, that is, showmanship, entertainment, or threats of a low grade. If the instructor is indifferent, negative, and simply going though the mechanics of doing a job, students will sense this flat motivational climate and respond in kind.

Enthusiasm is contagious—By precept and example, teachers perform a dual role: presenting information and indicating its worth. Enthusiasm can be wild, charismatic, and spellbinding but it can also be soft, quiet, and low key. The *earthworm professor* is my favorite example: Professor Jones truly enjoyed teaching but was totally oblivious to matters of instructional technique, classroom style, and laws of learning. What he did have was a deep, abiding, and visible enthusiasm for the structure and function of the earthworm and the wonders of its emerging synaptic nervous system. Students soon took unto themselves the motivational intensity for understanding more about this small part of the biological world.

The *earthworm professor* is, for most of us, a more likely model than the spellbinding, charismatic, preacher-teacher in the classroom. Low-key teachers may not win prizes, but their quiet enthusiasm for the interchange with students about a subject they love has a powerful impact on what students learn. Enthusiasm is one of the more significant dimensions of a teacher's distinctive self.

Enthusiasm for intellectual curiosity—Intellectual curiosity is on display when the teacher probes the ambiguities within the discipline and questions out loud one's own understanding. As a matter of fact, students give closer attention to a lecture involving questions and conflicting issues than to a recital of neatly encapsulated facts, rules, and conclusions.

Fear of failure may be a handy tool for prodding students into line but, as a steady diet, negative motivation is educationally weak. To find students working at their cognitive best, look past the grading system and observe the excitement that comes when students sense they understand what they had set out to study. The hour-after-hour fixation of students at their computers confirms, again, the holding and rewarding power of informational curiosity. When it comes to motivation, the *Eureka* experience is hard to beat.

Teaching To Remember

On-the-job training is learning today for use today, but college students learn today for remembering tomorrow and, thus, the essence of teaching is defined: to help students store information for retrieval in later courses and in times and places beyond graduation. This is more easily said than done. One classical view, the *Doctrine of Formal Discipline*, defended the belief that hard mental effort, as in the study of Latin and Mathematics, strengthens the faculties (muscles) of the mind, e.g., reasoning and memory. Today, the instructional line is straightforward and to the point: what students study is what students learn, i.e., what students understand is what they remember.

The motivation to remember—Motivation directs the course of memory. *Will this be on the next test?* A *Yes* immediately directs student attention (motivation) to what information needs to be remembered. On a more lasting level, the college experience creates and shapes attitudes and values as motivational patterns that may last a lifetime. These well-rooted motives have a selective influence on what information will move into long-term memory and in the retrieval of same. The heart, as it were, tells the brain what to learn and to remember.

Teaching to remember means hard work for the student—The *sunburn* theory of instruction says to sit quietly and look interested while the teacher shines the light of knowledge in your face. This is wishful thinking and a reality check will show that to study at the kitchen table is more productive than propped on pillows in bed. A mild degree of muscle tension helps the information go down.

Active participation is intrinsic to learning and students working at a laboratory bench, in a clinical setting, or in a discussion group, generate more learning than passively listening to the talking teacher or gazing at a film. Writing is an established resource for helping students to remember; putting things in black-and-white seems to generate a file copy in the writer's long-term memory. The fact that writing involves the student's own understanding and thinking, and modes of expression may account for the memory benefits of this form of active participation.

For many students *overlearning* is a dreary term, and society does better with *practice makes perfect*. Bicycle riding is overlearned and this skill lasts a lifetime, as does knowing how to add, subtract, and multiply. The principle of overlearning applies across the curricular board—and beyond. *The longer I live, the more convinced I am that (such-and-such) is true.* To rehearse and review a unit of information beyond threshold levels of understanding is to generate a stronger fix in long-term memory. Contemplation may be a quiet form of rehearsal but memories are made stronger by writing 50 repetitions of a correctly spelled word or a rule of behavior—as I recall.

Learning to Manage Concepts

Teaching students how to think is too grand a topic for these few pages but to examine concept learning is more than a substitute. We live in a wordy world and students will be engaged with semantic distinctions for the rest of their lives. Understanding what abstract words do and do not mean taps the peak intellectual strength of students, that is, their ability to manage ideas that go beyond the limitations of time and space. The ability to memorize is a weak second. A teacher can feel that the job is well done when students demonstrate they comprehend the important ideas (concepts) in the course.

Concept learning—The basic task is to recognize the common features in otherwise different instances—to link an array of independent events into a meaningful unit. *Dog* and *cat* are easy concepts but extra study is needed to understand how the principles in the Bill of Rights apply to the religious right, the political left, and to everyone in between.

Using example after example, the teacher places positive (or negative) instances within the frame of reference of the target concept (the negatives help define a conceptual boundary). The concept of *reinforcement*, for example, takes on depth and breath with material from Pavlov, Skinner, and such areas of application as education, business, sports, and family life.

Conceptual learning involves tracing an idea through an array of specific sites, particular issues, or anecdotal events. The aim is to understand how a concept (rule, principle, procedure, generalization, theme) functions as a frame of reference giving meaning to otherwise isolated facts. Conceptual thinking is the foundation process for problem solving and for making decisions on one's own. Memorizing sets of words will not do this.

The maturation of each student's conceptual knowledge continues as he and she study different subjects and live and learn away from the classroom. They find that conceptual understanding can be exciting as it reduces their own uncertainties and offers some degree of unity and continuity in a world of kaleidoscopic events. Above all else in the teacher-student interchange, the moment of instructional truth is, for me, helping a student grasp the meaning of a significant idea. (Would that we had a video of Plato as he walked and talked Great Ideas with his students in the groves of Academe, a Greek farmer.)

Testing and Grading

Faculty standards for A-grade performance should be the preferred institutional measure of educational excellence. These standards, however, are stretched and weakened by grading on the curve. In this system, the grade measures how well students compete against one another rather than against standards of achievement set by the teacher.

Students work hard for grades that serve as a basis for special awards, admission to advanced training, and the entry job. The GPA is one step removed from the essence of education but has become the most visible measure of academic success; it has become a kind of institutional currency in the exchange with society. With such a payoff, it is unfair for a teacher to be casual or careless when assigning the *grade* contribution to this index of achievement.

Evaluation is more instruction-specific than is grading. Students need guideposts to confirm they are moving in the right direction and, for this, evaluation has a stronger impact than does grading. A low grade gives little or no feedback about how to answer the questions and usually comes too late for the student to take corrective action. In contrast, a teacher's evaluative comments written in the margin of a term paper or exam give more specific and constructive information than does the grade on the cover page.

Tests are tools for teaching—Students study for tests and fair play requires that teacher and student be on the same wave length about material to be covered and the mode of testing. Examination time is not the time for tricks, ambiguities or the outmoded game, *I've got a secret, see if you can guess what it is.* Testing, grading, and evaluation are difficult and demanding responsibilities and the self-assessing teacher might benefit more from a workshop on the technical aspects of testing and grading than one on the technical matters of telling things to students.

Tests have various instructional functions. Grade-free diagnostic testing offers an intellectual X-ray showing the strengths and low points in a student's inventory of information. On the other hand, frequent testing for a grade helps both students and teacher hold their focus on course content. Further, multiple entries in a grade book add reliability to the course grade. The final examination measures, ideally, how well students have packaged worthwhile knowledge for storage in long-term memory. Within the context of this column (students remember what they understand), a term paper is better than an essay exam which, in turn, is better than a machine-scorable test.

Conclusion

From the beginning, college teaching has, for me, been a delightful way to earn a living. Few of us are heroes but the self-knowledge that we are helping students prepare for their own future has a sustaining quality that grows stronger through the career years. As a member of the faculty, these years probably include your share of conflicts, frustration, and disappointment. In contrast, the self-examined life of teaching finds, for most, little discontent.

Recommended Readings and References
Bransford, J. D. (1979*). Human cognition.* Belmont, CA: Wadsworth.
Ericksen, S. (1984). *The essence of good teaching: Helping students learn and remember what they learn.* San Francisco: Jossey-Bass.
Nisbett, R. E., Fong, G. T., Lehman, D. R., & Cheng, P. W. (1987). Teaching reasoning. *Science, 238,* 625-631.
Pascarella, E. T., & Terenzini, P. T. (1991). *How college affects students: Findings and insights from twenty years of research.* San Francisco: Jossey-Bass.

Part 2

Course Planning

Chapter 4

How to Improve Your Teaching With the Course Syllabus

Drew C. Appleby
Marion College

D id you ever have a student misunderstand an assignment, express surprise that you had considered attendance important, or want an explanation of how you grade after the final exam has been scored and the semester is over? If, like most teachers, you receive a few such remarks every semester, you already appreciate the need for clarity in your communication with students.

One of the best ways to clarify such communication is through your course syllabus. As a teacher, you have probably distributed thousands of them and no doubt have written a score or more, yet often the syllabus is given little serious attention. But as Rubin (1985) has pointed out, "We keep forgetting that what we know—about our disciplines, about our goals, about our teaching—is not known (or agreed upon) by everyone. We seem to assume that our colleagues and our students will intuitively be able to reconstruct that creature we see in our mind's eye from the few bones we give them in the syllabus" (p. 56). A poorly written and incomplete syllabus can frustrate both students and teachers and disrupt the whole learning process.

One of the easiest ways to improve your teaching is to increase the communication effectiveness of your syllabi. To do this, you need to understand the purposes of a course syllabus and its essential elements.

The Purpose of a Course Syllabus

The course syllabus serves at least seven basic purposes (Rubin, 1985). Some of these directly serve your students and are readily apparent to them. But as you will see, the syllabus should serve some of your needs as well. In summary, a syllabus:

Helps Plan and Clarify Your Course

This article first appeared in the May/June 1994 APS Observer.

The very process of writing a well-constructed syllabus forces you to crystallize, articulate, organize, and communicate your thoughts about a course. This thought and writing produces what Gabbanesch (1992) calls the enriched syllabus, which compels you to publicly reveal your previously well concealed assumptions. In other words, it makes explicit that which was implicit, and it is the implicit that often confuses and frustrates students.

Try inviting a person who has no expertise in your academic area to critique your syllabus. You will be surprised by the number of vagaries and gaps the naive reader will identify. Teachers can easily overlook important matters or be unclear about them in their syllabi, even after they have taught the course for years.

Introduces You to Students

Your syllabus allows you to share your pedagogical philosophy. Students may not perceive it in quite this way, but that is one of the things you achieve through the syllabus. A syllabus tells your students whether you view learning as an active or passive process and whether you emphasize knowledge enhancement, skill building, or a combination of both.

The syllabus reveals how your course is structured (e.g. simple to complex or chronologically) and should include the purpose of the organization. Syllabi tell your students if the parts of the course are mutually exclusive or whether success in its later stages depends upon skills mastered earlier. The syllabus also reveals your teaching style. Are you organized or disorganized, flexible or rigid, rigorous or lax?

The tone of your syllabus can indicate how approachable you are, and students often form an immediate impression of whether they will like you—and your course—from reading the syllabus. Needless to say, it is better if the impression is positive.

Explains Why Students Should Take Your Course

After students read your syllabus, they should know how your course satisfies departmental or institutional requirements, how it fits into their major, or why it is a valuable elective. Is the course a prerequisite for more advanced courses? How would you define the course (e.g. introductory, intermediate, or capstone level)? You may want to indicate who can benefit from the knowledge and skills acquired during this course. Faculty know the answers to these questions—or at least they should—but it is a mistake to assume that students do. If you do not clearly state the purpose and value of your course, your students may believe the main purpose of taking it is simply to fulfill a poorly understood curricular requirement.

Explains the Various Aspects of Your Course

Your syllabus should be explicit about assignments and methods of evaluation. Tell your students how your assignments will enable them to accomplish course objectives. Specify elements such as criteria for excellence in assignments, the number and nature of tests, and the weighting of assignments in determining the final grade.

Do not forget to communicate the level of participation required. Will your students listen passively as you lecture or should they expect to participate in challenging discussions requiring advance preparation? Similarly, will the emphasis be on primary or secondary materials and why? You might also want to explain the difference between primary and secondary sources.

A syllabus should also specify prerequisites, both in terms of courses and prerequisite skills or experiences your students will need to do well. If you expect students to perform certain skills, will you teach these skills during the course or will you assume your students already possess them when they enter the course?

Explains How Students Will Develop by Successfully Completing Your Course

Students should understand what content they will learn, what skills they will develop, and what attitudes, values, and feelings may change as a result of taking the course. Including such information will help you develop some well considered course objectives, if you have not already done so.

Communicates the Course's Nature and Content to Faculty/Administrators

In addition to informing your students, a good syllabus provides a record of your course for colleagues who may teach it later. It can also aid departmental and institutional curriculum planning, and assist outside agencies in assessing your program's goals and effectiveness.

Provides a Documented Record of Your Teaching Career

Your course syllabi are an important teaching legacy. They often provide the only permanent record of your teaching philosophy, commitment to teaching, and pedagogical innovations. If you keep old copies of your course syllabi and read several years' worth at one sitting, you can easily see how you have developed as a teacher. This growth and development is often striking.

When job hunting, syllabi are also integral components of the application portfolio. They can also serve as salary, promotion, and tenure documents that evaluation committee's request when assessing teaching ability. A good syllabus can be as important to you as to your students—unless, of course, you are an independently wealthy tenured professor.

The Essential Components of the Course Syllabus

Once you know the purpose of the syllabus, its basic elements are easily defined. The following may serve as a simple checklist as you review syllabus content.

Basic Identifying Information

Include the name of your institution, the semester, year, course title and identifying code, location and time of class meetings, and the credits earned for successfully completing the course.

Instructor's Personal Information

Include your name and title, office location, office telephone number, office hours, and email address if students can communicate with you via that medium. Some instructors include their home telephone numbers, but may specify restrictions in calls to their homes (e.g., no calls between 10PM and 8AM).

Texts and Other Materials

Specify the titles, authors, and editions of your texts, differentiating between required and recommended status. It is wise to specify locations for obtaining course materials (e.g., bookstore, library, your office, or computer lab), the conditions for obtaining them (e.g. whether they must be purchased, are on two-day reserve, or are cleared for photocopying), and the number of copies available (e.g., for reserved materials).

Course Description

This usually comes directly from your institution's catalog and should include a brief description of the following items: the major topics covered; the knowledge, skills and attitudes acquired; prerequisites; and any special opportunities (e.g., field trips).

Course Objectives

This section is of particular importance because of the current emphasis on the assessment of student learning outcomes. Clearly state your objectives. I recommend Gronland's 1991 publication, *How to Write and Use Instructional Objectives*, if you are unsure of how to write objectives in this manner. Objectives can be cognitive (e.g., understands the nature-nurture controversy), affective (e.g., appreciates the role of psychology in everyday life), or behavioral (e.g., can administer an IQ test). A clear set of instructional objectives provides direction for instructional methods, yields guidelines for testing, and communicates instructional intent to students.

Course Requirements

Explain exactly what a student is expected to do in your course including a clear description of the tests administered, the papers written, and the oral presentations made.

Course Calendar

Your calendar contains the dates of specific lecture topics, reading assignments, exams, and deadlines for papers and other projects. Any changes to your calendar should be supplied to students in writing.

Grading Procedures and Scales

Make explicit your procedures and criteria for evaluating students' performance and assigning grades. Clear policies regarding extra credit, make-up tests, deadlines, and penalties for post-deadline work are necessary. Include an academic honesty policy with definitions of academically dishonest behaviors (e.g., plagiarism and cheating) and sanctions for their occurrence if your school does not emphasis this concept in its literature (i.e. catalog).

Caveat

A syllabus is written contract between you and your students. End each syllabus with a caveat, such as the following, to protect yourself, your department, and your institution if changes in the syllabus must be made once your course is underway: "The above schedule and procedures in this course are subject to change in the event of extenuating circumstances" (Altman, 1989).

It is imperative that all teachers adhere faithfully to the policies and requirements set forth in their syllabi. Do *not* forget the reciprocal nature of this contract. By requiring students to abide by the rules and procedures spelled out in your syllabus, you are also agreeing to do the same. A well written syllabus will make these expectations clear to all concerned. You should plan to discuss the syllabus in detail during the first class meeting. This brings up the need for prompt distribution of syllabi. They should be available on the first day of class, not a week or a month into the semester. After all, if you expect students to meet deadlines for examinations and other course requirements, you should also meet your own teaching deadlines, and distributing the course syllabus during the first class meeting is one such deadline you should not miss.

Conclusion

Good syllabi fulfill specific purposes, possess essential components, and answer crucial questions. However, few syllabi perform all these functions equally well. My advice is this: try to write syllabi that are as brief and focused as possible, but that communicate the nature of your course to students in a clear and understandable manner. The better your students understand the purposes and procedures of your course, the more likely they are to enter enthusiastically into the learning partnership you offer them.

Recommended Readings and References

Altman, H. (1989). Syllabus shares what the teacher wants. *The Teaching Professor, 3*(5), 1-2.

Bloom, B. S., Engleheart, M. D., Furst, E. J., & Krathwohl, D. R. (1956). *Taxonomy of educational objectives: Cognitive domain*. New York: McKay.

Gabennesch, H. (1992). The enriched syllabus: To convey a larger vision. *The National Teaching & Learning Forum, 1*(4), 4-5.

Gronland, N. E. (1991). *How to write and use instructional objectives*. New York: Macmillan.

Lowther, M. A., Starks, J. S., & Martens, G. G. (1989). *Preparing course syllabi for improved communication*. Ann Arbor, MI: The National Center for Research to Improve Postsecondary Teaching and Learning.

Rubin, S. (1985, August 7). Professors, students, and the syllabus. *The Chronicle of Higher Education*, p. 56.

Chapter 5

Finding the Right Introductory Psychology Textbook

Russell A. Dewey
Georgian Southern University

S uppose you were preparing to teach introductory psychology for the first time in many years, or for the first time ever, or that it was just time to change textbooks and start afresh. You might stack all the current year's offerings on your desk, and the desk might break.

Since the early 1970s there have been in excess of 100 introductory psychology textbooks in print at a given time. Realistically, only a small number of those are *major contenders*, but even if you confine your attention to a dozen or so, choosing a text can be a difficult decision. The purpose of this column is to present some criteria and procedures to aid you in choosing the one text that will best serve you and your students.

Difficulty Level

Textbook sales representatives cheerfully parse the field into three mutually exclusive categories: low-level, mid-level, and high-level. This scheme is like the three-part classification pediatric nurses use for newborn babies: easy, medium, or difficult. It probably succeeds about as well in capturing the essential aspects of individuality. For example, a simple text—characterized by short sentence length and simple vocabulary—is not necessarily a clear or an enjoyable text. Sometimes such a "dumbed down" textbook is actually harder to understand—not to mention boring to read—because it is so general and superficial that there is nothing to sink your teeth into. On the other hand, a textbook with some depth can be fun to read, if it captures your interest.

From Your Own Experience, Does the Text *Draw You In*?

The single most important characteristic of a textbook is its flow of ideas. This sounds obvious, but how many of us actually sit down and read a chapter, in silence, in the manner we expect of students? This simple act could prevent a lot of disappointment and disillusionment. The shameful truth is that most of us probably skim a book to decide if we like it. We know what happens when students skim instead of really reading and the same thing can happen to us. Skimming is appropriate during the first pass through a stack of 100 competing textbooks, to rule out which are clearly unsuitable. But when you have

This article first appeared in the March 1995 APS Observer.

narrowed your choice to a few, there is no substitute for a close reading.

Can You Skim?

Perhaps the most revealing experience of all occurs when skimming proves impossible! Sometimes a book is so well-written that you try to skim but you find yourself drawn into the text. That is very good sign! I ran into a report of such an experience in a review by Rogoff and Morelli (1990) of Cole and Cole's *The Development of Children* (1989):

> The book is masterfully written, with a flow among topics that allows the reader to apprehend the points with little effort. The writing is so good that although we tried to skim sections of the book in preparation for this review, we were drawn into reading them through because the material was presented so well.

And there is more!

> One reason for the clarity and effectiveness of the writing is the sensitive use of examples and illustrations, which instruct rather than simply decorate the book. In addition, they convey the reality of children and their lives in a compelling fashion, and draw the reader into ideas that might otherwise be difficult to grasp. (p. 44)

Get me that book!

These passages suggest an alternative to the impractical strategy of giving every book an in depth reading. Instead, when faced with a huge pile of introductory textbooks, skim a few chapters and see what happens. See which ones draw you in. Then read these slowly.

The Prime Directive: Clarity of Explanation

We may also, of course, demand thoroughness of coverage, accuracy, current references, and clarity of explanation. The latter may be the hardest to find, although some people seem to have a gift for clear explanation. This dimension of individual difference between psychologists is apparent in lectures, presentations, and also in textbooks. If a book has nothing else, it must have the ability to explain. The question is: can the author write so students can assimilate something new and unfamiliar without pre-existing expert knowledge?

Don't be fooled by an appealing table of contents or clear-looking chapter outlines. Most tables of contents look sensible and appealing. Editors know that committees or individuals faced with a daunting pile of competing introductory textbooks will eliminate many based on a glance at the table of contents and chapter outlines, so a lot of effort goes into making those sketchy summaries look well organized. The worst book I ever used had beautiful macrostructure. The microstructure was the problem. The book failed at the level of individual sentences and paragraphs. Students often could not *catch* the concepts, so I, the instructor, was left with the job of cleaning up afterwards. By contrast, I have fond memories for the second edition of McConnel's introductory text. While not the best organized book I have ever used, the students loved it. The writing had life and fascination, and explanations were beautifully clear.

Looking back, I could have detected the problems in the *bad* text I once used if I had merely forced myself to read individual paragraphs, with great concentration, at five or 10 different locations in the book. Then I would have realized it was abstract and wordy; its ability to explain was poor.

Compare Test Items, Chapters, and Summaries

There are students whose keen interest motivates deep, independent inquiry beyond what is assigned. They are to be celebrated and encouraged. However, most students more greatly resemble the rat in an operant lab whose responses deteriorate to the absolute minimum needed to obtain the reinforcer— the desired grade in a course. The natural tendency of students to economize effort means that testing procedures are absolutely critical in determining what students will actually do for a course. That means that the test item file which comes with a book can be surprisingly important. If students discover they can answer the test items without reading the text, or by attending only to the chapter summaries, that is exactly what many of them will do.

To get a realistic idea of how students will behave in your course, you must make systematic comparisons between: test items, the body of the chapter, and the chapter summaries. If all the information needed to answer the test items is in the summary, the student (being a rational creature) will confine attention the summaries. If you want students to read the text, a quiz or test must require its reading and comprehension. This makes test construction central, not peripheral, to the quality of a course and the selection of a text.

If the book's test item file does not accomplish this, you may find yourself writing your own questions (which takes a lot of time). Or you may realize you do not have time to rewrite the test item file. Either way, you may end up kicking yourself for not having taken a long, hard look at the test item file while it was still possible to pick a different book.

Though test items may be the most important part of a textbook *package* after the book itself, the typical modern book comes with many other enticements. Ancillaries such as study guides, instructor manuals, video disks, and computer simulations may be seductive, but think twice about whether you will really use them. If you plan on using a study guide or instructor's manual, be aware that these are often written hastily at the last minute by graduate students or instructors whose main qualification is that they teach large classes at a school that is a good "catch" for the publishing company. Top notch instructor's manuals are pleasant exceptions to the rule and are typical of the best, most established textbooks.

Others' Wisdom

Colleagues at your institution who have taught introductory psychology may be in a unique position to recommend textbooks that work well with your type of students. They may have a good *pick* that you were not even considering, or they may know of problems with the text you favor. A good source of recommendations about all aspects of teaching, from text-books to in-class demonstrations and techniques, is the TIPS discussion list (e2pysou@fre.fsu.umd.edu).

Contemporary Psychology is a source for introductory textbook reviews. The table of contents is clearly divided into sections, and every few months there is an *Introductory Psychology* section. Thanks to this clear organization, you can browse through a year's worth of issues and identify introductory psychology textbooks in about 45 seconds. Reviews in *Contemporary Psychology* are generally of high quality, with useful information and strong opinions in the space of two to three pages. Of course, only a fraction of the available textbooks can be reviewed each year. In the first nine months of 1994, the section on *Introductory Psychology* occurred twice and reviewed a total of 10 books.

Teaching of Psychology also features reviews of introductory books, and while it reviews only three or four in a year, the reviews have a unique format. The reviewer gives a detailed description of the whole package (not just the book), and the author gives an inside look at the design philosophy and rationale of the book. Again, the reviews are easily found in the table of contents in a section titled *Book Reviews in Duplicate*.

Textbook salespeople often provide valuable information by indicating consistent top sellers in your area, which of the company's books are doing well, and alleged problems with competitors' books. Salesmen are particularly good at exposing their own book's angle or special features, which they assume is the best way of getting you to adopt it.

In the End, Remember Your Students

What most of this advice has in common is the requirement that we put ourselves in the place of our students. When we evaluate text content to see if it matches our interest, we use our own preferences as a reference point. Taking the point of view of our students is harder, yet that is the most valuable thing we can do. We must try to select a book—whether it is for Introductory Psychology or any other course—that we anticipate will engage student interest, make difficult concepts clear, and motivate serious study. And, the book must leave students satisfied and happy—and maybe even wanting to keep the book and take more psychology courses.

Recommended Readings and References

Cole, M., & Cole, S. (1997). *The development of children* (3rd ed.). New York: W. H. Freeman.

Kasschav, R. A., (1994). Picture perfect? *Teaching of Psychology, 21,* 117-120.

Kintsch, W. (1994). Text comprehension, memory, and learning. *American Psychologist, 49,* 294-303.

Nallan, G. B. (1994). Introductory psychology textbooks: Suitable for one semester, or two? *Contemporary Psychology, 39,* 143-144.

Pittenger, D. J. (1994). Try to re-aim psychology's canon. *Contemporary Psychology, 39,* 499-500.

Rogoff, B., & Morelli, G. A. (1990). An advance in understanding development for students and scholars. *Psychological Science, 1,* 42, 44-45.

Chapter 6

Teaching With Original Sources

Philip Banyard
Andrew Grayson
The Nottingham Trent University–United Kingdom

W hy use key studies in teaching? To us the answer is obvious, but we will make the case because we have often found colleagues do not understand why we should teach from primary research, and some who even oppose it vigorously.

We believe the main reasons for using primary research studies in teaching are:

- It shows students the quality of the basic evidence in psychology.
- It demystifies the subject and shows students they do not always need an interpreter (textbook) to read psychology.
- It presents firsthand accounts of methodology.
- It encourages critical thinking because students have real evidence to evaluate. When they read summaries of research in a text it is often difficult to evaluate the evidence because there is not enough detail. On the other hand, when they read the primary research, they are able to criticize the way it was conducted or the conclusions, and so on.
- It avoids the psychological myths that grow up around some prominent studies. A famous example is the Little Albert study by Watson and Rayner (1920) that is incorrectly reported in many texts.
- Students have to read research papers eventually, so why not start them off straight away in a learning context which helps develop the necessary skills?
- And finally (but perhaps most importantly for teachers) students enjoy them.

All these points make us believe that using primary research is the very best way (if not the only way) to teach introductory courses (defined as the first undergraduate course in a subdiscipline area such as social, developmental, or abnormal). What we don't understand is why some of our colleagues challenge the academic rigor of this approach. Still, we here in the United Kingdom are able to deal with them in the time-honored traditions

This article appears in the September 1999 APS Observer.

of British academia by nodding sagely, murmuring sweetly, stroking our chins, and then ignoring them completely. American teachers spending time over here should bear this technique in mind.

Choosing the Studies

Any psychologists choosing a number of studies for a course will come up with different lists. The issue is not which are the most important, but which studies will bring the most educational value to your course. When choosing a study we can consider a number of questions.

Does It Have *Star Quality*?

The study has to have that something extra, which we call *star quality*. Sometimes studies are referred to as sexy or are said to have charisma. Whatever you call it, the study has to have that indefinable extra edge. Star quality is difficult to define and to predict in a research study. As a teacher, it is difficult to read the study with the eyes of a student and anticipate their response to it.

Some studies in psychology have obvious star quality including the classic studies of social psychology such as Milgram's obedience studies, Zimbardo's prison simulation (Haney, Banks, & Zimbardo, 1973) and Sherif's ethnocentrism studies (1956) with the boys' camps. We would also add, perhaps more controversially, the case studies of Freud. Our favorite is the study of Little Hans which is always engaging for students even though many will dismiss the conclusions out of hand. It is also very funny.

Does It Stimulate Students' Questions?

One of the aims of education is to interest and engage students so that they want to find out more. An example of a study that inevitably provokes questions is the multiple personality study of Thigpen and Cleckley (the Three Faces of Eve). You can't help but think about whether this woman really had a multiple personality, and what this means. What is a single personality? And, what is the difference between having different sides to your personality and having a multiple personality?

Many studies take a lot of time and effort to state the startlingly obvious. For example, some memory studies say it is easier to remember meaningful than meaningless material. If students find this kind of research interesting or provocative we suggest they need urgent medical help. For the majority it is important to choose studies that are provocative and do not produce a "So what?" response.

Does It Stimulate Ideas For Practical Work?

One of the basic features of a scientific subject is that the material generates research questions. Reading primary research can encourage students to design empirical work that addresses their own research questions or tests their own hypotheses. Of course, there are problems with encouraging this. Not the least of these is the controversial ethical nature of many of the most interesting studies in psychology. We are alarmed at the number of students who have acted out assaults or feigned heart attacks in public (after Piliavin, Rodin and Piliavin's subway study, for example), or humiliated people in group pressure studies (after Asch, for example), or offended shoppers with obscene words in perceptual defense studies, or shown their young nephews and nieces violent videos to observe their aggressive response (after Bandura, Ross, & Ross, for example). The list of horrors is endless.

Does It Raise Contemporary Issues?

There is a trend in psychology to quote the most up-to-date study as if this represents the most accurate description of a particular topic. An alternative view says recent studies have not yet been subjected to the same level of scrutiny, replication and verification. We tend to prefer studies that have stood the test of time and still have something to say to people today.

The studies of Milgram (on obedience) and Zimbardo (on the prison simulation) tell us something about our behavior today even though they were conducted a generation ago. We also believe that the work of British psychologist Frederick Bartlett on remembering offers insights that are relevant today and act as a useful balance to the mechanistic mayhem of the information processing approach that still dominates discussions of memory in introductory texts. The famous Bobo doll study by Bandura, Ross, and Ross is still heavily cited and contributes to our discussions of the effects of television on young people. All of these examples are at least 30 years old but still contribute to contemporary debates.

Do The Studies Illustrate A Range Of Psychological Methods?

As well as considering the features of individual studies, we need to look at the whole program to achieve a certain balance. It is important to show students just how wide our sources of evidence are, and also to allow them to weigh the relative merits of one method over another. In memory research, for example, methodologies include people sitting in front of tachistoscopes and computer screens, case studies, and use of neuropsychology techniques. Psychologists use survey methods, physiological measures, observations, field experiments, simulations, detailed textual analysis, and so on. In fact students may come to the conclusion that one of the strengths of psychology lies in the diversity of its methods.

Do The Studies Illustrate A Range Of Psychological Ideas?

The obvious way of thinking about this issue is to carve up psychology into its subdisciplines. An introductory general psychology course might

---

The Banyard & Grayson Top Ten Teaching Studies

◆ Milgram, S. (1963). Behavioral study of obedience. *Journal of Abnormal and Social Psychology, 67*, 371-378.

Simply the best! Though it is also worth encouraging students to search out Milgram's accounts of his other innovative research techniques.

◆ Thigpen, C., & Cleckley, H. (1954). A case of multiple personality. *Journal of Abnormal and Social Psychology, 49*, 135-151.

Very readable and direct account of a therapist's encounter with a rare phenomena.

◆ Bandura, A., Ross, D., & Ross, S. (1961). Transmission of aggression through imitation of aggressive models. *Journal of Abnormal and Social Psychology, 63*, 375-382.

Walk your students through the study as if they are the subjects.

◆ Gardner, R., & Gardner, B. (1969). Teaching sign language to a chimpanzee. *Science, 165*, 664-672.

Everyone wants Washoe as a friend, but did she ever acquire language?

◆ Rosenhan, D. (1973). On being sane in insane places. *Science, 179*, 250-258.

Very readable and provocative account of how people can be depersonalized by giving them a label.

◆ Bartlett, F. C. (1932). Experiments on remembering: The method of serial reproduction. II picture material. In F. C. Bartlett (Ed.), *Remembering: A study in experimental and social psychology* (pp. 177-185). Cambridge: Cambridge University Press.

Work on real life remembering rather than the recall induced by simple laboratory tasks.

◆ Freud, S. (1909). *Analysis of a phobia in a five-year-old boy,* The Pelican Freud Library. (1977). (Vol. 8, pp. 169-306). Harmondsworth: Penguin.

Many would argue that this should be number one in the list, but just as many would argue that it has no place here at all. A fascinating read and bound to raise a chuckle.

◆ Skinner, B. F. (1960). Pigeons in a pelican. *American Psychologist, 15*, 28-37.

An excellent account of Skinner's attempt to interest the Pentagon in missiles flown by pigeons.

◆ Haney, C., Banks, C., & Zimbardo, P. (1973). A study of prisoners and guards in a simulated prison. *Naval Research Reviews, 30*, 4-17.

Perhaps we should all turn our psychology departments into prisons.

◆ Sperry, R. (1968). Hemisphere deconnection and unity in conscious awareness. *American Psychologist, 23*, 723-733.

Raises questions about what we mean by *mind* and what will happen to it if we split our brain in two.

---

cover social, developmental, cognitive and biological psychology, for example. Take a few studies from each of these areas to ensure that students get a feel for the diversity of the discipline. A most effective technique is to choose pairs of studies that deal with a particular psychological idea in radically different ways. This gives students the opportunity to develop grounded arguments concerning the strengths and weaknesses of the competing approaches, and illustrates to them the analytic power of the compare and contrast process. Pairs of studies that we have found especially productive are:

◆ Bartlett, (1932) and Ebbinghaus, (1885) on memory. The former looks at the constructive nature of remembering and the latter describes some of the earliest controlled experiments into recall and recognition.

◆ Koff, (1983) and Bem, (1974). The Koff study uses projective techniques to look at the changes in a young woman's identity as she experiences menarche, and the Bem study takes a psychometric approach to the issue of gender.

◆ Thigpen and Cleckley, (1954) and Sperry, (1968). Thigpen and Cleckley describe the multiple personality study mentioned earlier, and Sperry describes a number of case studies where people had their cerebral cortex surgically cut into two.

◆ Asch (1955) and Sheriff (1956). The Asch study is a controlled laboratory investigation of social compliance and the Sheriff study is a field experiment.

Do The Studies Illuminate the Lives of a Wide Range of People?

A good starting point here is George Miller's argument about giving psychology away made in his 1969 APA Presidential Address. If we are to convince students that psychology is worth giving away then it must demonstrably speak to them as individuals. Everyone who studies psychology should be able to find something in this rich, fascinating and diverse discipline that excites them, intrigues them, and leads to an "I wonder what if...?" kind of response. We choose our key studies to explore issues of human diversity and so deal with the ongoing problem of ethnocentrism in the subject.

Finding Good Original Sources

The most obvious way of finding good sources is to look through books of readings, talk to your colleagues, and ask students what interests them. Strangely enough, we can't seem to remember doing any of this so it is our belief that some studies have just become magically more visible to us in the relief map of psychology. They have touched us in such a way that we felt we had to go to the library to get a copy. Maybe that is the way to select studies, and this approach would fit with our belief that the enthusiasm and interest of the teacher is an important ingredient of any successful lesson.

Tips For Teaching With Original Sources

Introduce Them and Put Them in a Context

In one of our typical *key studies teaching sessions*, we look at two related papers which bear on a particular theme or topic. Before we look at the papers themselves we give a brief introduction that puts the work into an appropriate context. For example, we might contextualize Milgram within the questions raised about human behavior following the horrors of the Second World War. Other studies have a more obviously scientific context that develops out of previous research.

Explore the Relevant Research Questions

Discussion of the papers typically begins with some work on the relevant research questions: what are they and where did they come from?

Decide What You Want Students To Attend To and Learn

Think about what it is you want your students to learn by reading each original source. For us, the class is constructed around the following set of questions for each research paper:

How was the research question examined?
What methods were used and why?
What were the measurement tools?
What participants were used?
◆ What data were collected?
What interpretations were made of the findings?
How did the researchers deal with quality control issues (ethics, validity, reliability and so forth)?
What efforts have been made to replicate the study and to what effect?
Where has this line of research gone since this study was conducted?
How do the interpretations fit into the theoretical background summarized at the outset of the class?

We have found it useful to devote a significant proportion of the time available to discussion of the data from the studies. This normally involves producing an overhead transparency with copies of original tables, and perhaps setting the students to work in small groups on questions that require studying the data fairly closely. In our experience students are not always good at looking at, thinking about, and reasoning with data, so this activity provides them a chance to practice and develop some important skills.

One crucial part of the whole process is that students be required, as much as is possible, to read the original papers. For some sessions it makes sense for the students to have read the papers beforehand, for others it is more appropriate to assign the papers afterwards. For example, you may want to draw out the students' expectations before they read an original source. Milgram's obedience study is a good example. It is best read after you have discussed how we expect people to behave under pressure. On the other hand, if the teacher wants to concentrate on a study's methodological aspects, it is probably more helpful if the students have read it beforehand.

Knowing that Students Are Reading and Learning From Original Sources

Our goal is that students develop critical reading skills. These skills include analysis of the key issues in an original source, evaluation of the evidence, and the development of opinions. To ensure that students are reading original sources, we use examinations that require them to comment on a selection of the studies.

Conclusion

In the end there always seem to be too many studies that cry out to be included in our courses. It is important, though, to be ruthless and restrict their number so that students can consider them in some detail. It is our opinion that one of the most common teaching mistakes is to give students too much information, and in so doing inhibit their understanding and evaluation of any of it. The key studies approach hopefully avoids this problem, and with a careful choice of studies it can excite and motivate your students. Box 1 presents our Top Ten Teaching Studies, though we are sure readers will have their own favorites. The reader may want to try Banyard and Grayson, 1996, which provides readable summaries of 60 key papers in psychology, emphasizing what was done and concluded. It is designed to enable students to tackle the articles in their original form.

Recommended Readings and References

Asch, S. E. (1955). Opinions and social pressure. *Scientific American, 193*, 31-35.

Banyard, P., & Grayson, A. (1996). *Introducing psychological research.* New York: New York University Press.

Bartlett, F. C. (1932). *Remembering.* London: Cambridge University Press.

Bem, S. (1974). The measurement of psychological androgyny. *Journal of Consulting and Clinical Psychology, 42*, 155-162.

Ebbinghaus, H. (1964). *Memory: A contribution to experimental psychology* (rev. ed.). New York: Dover. Original work published in 1885.

Haney, C., Banks, C., & Zimbardo, P. (1973). A study of prisoners and guards in a simulated prison. *Naval Research Reviews, 30*, 4-17.

Hock, R. R. (1999). *Forty studies that changed psychology: Explorations into the history of psychological research* (3rd ed.). Upper Saddle River, NJ: Prentice Hall.

Koff, E. (1983). Through the looking glass of menarche: What the adolescent girl sees. In S. Golub (Ed.), *Menarche* (pp. 77-86). Lexington, MA: D. C. Heath.

Piviavin, I. M., Rodin, J. A., & Piliavin, J. (1969). Good Samaritanism: An underground phenomenon? *Journal of Personality and Social Psychology, 13*, 371-378.

Sheriff, M. (1956). Experiments in group conflict. *Scientific American, 195*, 54-58.

Sperry, R. (1968). Hemisphere deconnection and unity in conscious awareness. *American Psychologist, 23*, 723-733.

Thigpen, C., & Cleckley, H. (1954). A case of multiple personality. *Journal of Abnormal and Social Psychology, 49*, 135-151.

Watson, J., & Rayner, R. (1920). Conditioned emotional responses. *Journal of Experimental Psychology, 63*, 575-582.

Chapter 7

Twenty Tips for Teaching Introductory Psychology

Robert J. Sternberg
Yale University
with the Authors of the *Teaching Introductory Psychology* Project*

No matter how much experience one has teaching introductory psychology, there is always more to learn about teaching this challenging course. One can learn not only from one's own experience, but from the experience of others. Realizing the value of this collective experience I asked a set of individuals who would be particularly knowledgeable about teaching introductory psychology—some authors of major introductory-psychology texts—to collaborate with me in a project to pool our collective experience.

The result was an edited book, *Teaching Introductory Psychology* (Sternberg, 1997b). This article summarizes 20 of the main tips for teaching introductory psychology that emerged from our shared effort.

What You Cover

1) Be selective

There is always one more fact, theory, or experiment you could include in your lecture, but teaching time does not expand to fit additional material. Therefore you must be selective and avoid the temptation to try to include everything. An expert teacher knows not only what to include but what not to include. Leave it to the textbook to include what you do not have time to cover.

2) Emphasize the core

Given that you cannot cover everything, decide carefully in advance what you believe to be the core of psychology. That's one decision where your ex-

---

This article first appeared in the January 1999 APS Observer.

* The chapter authors in the Teaching Introductory Psychology project (Sternberg, 1997b) are Douglas A. Bernstein, Peter Gray, Lester A. Lefton, Margaret W. Matlin, Charles G. Morris, David G. Myers, Rod Plotnik, Robert J. Sternberg, Carole E. Wade, Camille B. Wortman (with collaborator Joshua Smyth), and Philip G. Zimbardo. Commentaries are by Charles L. Brewer

pertise as a teacher is critical. There is always the textbook and, if students wish, upper level courses they can take to learn about what you did not cover.

3) Balance classic and contemporary studies

By teaching students about contemporary theory and research, you show students that psychology is a rapidly evolving science. But psychology is not reinvented in the two to four years that constitute the typical cycle of new editions of textbooks, so it is important to balance new material with the classic studies that constitute our core knowledge about psychology.

How You Cover It

4) Help students organize their knowledge base

Research shows that people develop expertise not only by acquiring knowledge, but by organizing it effectively (e.g., Chi, Glaser, & Farr, 1988). Help students organize their knowledge base by using introductory outlines, integrative summaries, tree diagrams, maps showing interconnections among ideas, or any other useful organizing aids.

5) Take into account students' starting points

Chances are good that you are teaching primarily freshmen and sophomores. Consider where they are in their lives, and that their study skills, knowledge base, and motivation for psychology may all be at relatively modest levels. Teach to where they are, not where you might hope they would be.

6) Be patient

Because of where students are in their lives, you have to be especially patient with them. They often do not have the maturity to respond in the ways you might hope. You also need to be patient with yourself in your attempts to reach them.

7) Teach students to think like psychologists

The facts that constitute an introductory psychology course will change greatly over the years, but the tools for thinking critically and creatively about psychology will not. In a good introductory psychology course, students think to learn as they learn to think. Research shows that students who are taught in a way that emphasizes critical and creative—as well as practical—thinking not only learn to think better, but even learn the facts better (Sternberg, Torff, & Grigorenko, 1998). Students emerge from the course more knowledgeable and critical consumers of psychology with less susceptibility to the inflated and sometimes patently ridiculous claims of pop psychology.

8) Teach to diverse styles of learning and thinking

Not all students learn the same way. Some prefer auditory presentation, others, visual. Some prefer to analyze material, others to go beyond the material, and still others apply it. By teaching the material in a variety of ways, you motivate students as you help them to capitalize on their cognitive strengths and to ameliorate their cognitive weaknesses. Research shows that students learn better when you teach to their diverse styles of learning and thinking (Sternberg, 1994, 1997a, 1997c).

9) Show students how to apply what they learn to their lives

When you hear a lecture that has nothing to do with your life, chances are you tune out. So do students. By relating the material directly to their lives and showing them how they can use it, you increase their attention and improve their learning.

10) Encourage active learning and thinking

Large lecture courses can foment passive learning and thinking, as students sit quietly waiting for instructors to spoon-feed them information. Encourage active learning through in-class demonstrations, oral participation, brief writing exercises, or any other techniques you can formulate.

11) Match assessments to instruction

Encourage critical, creative, and practical thinking not only in the classroom, but in your assessments. Occasionally, teachers foster higher order thinking in the learning process, and then assess students in ways that measure little more than rote recall. Students quickly come to perceive higher order thinking as a useless and even cruel game. Equally bad is to teach for rote and then assess achievement for critical thinking. It is important that your assessments reflect what you value and implement in your teaching.

How You Communicate It

12) Have a clear vision for your course and communicate it to your students

What do you want your students to get out of your course? How do you want it to change their lives? Formulate a clear vision of your course objectives and intended outcomes and then communicate this vision so that students know explicitly both what you hope to accomplish and what you want them to accomplish.

13) Communicate your expectations clearly and early

Students early in their college careers often have only the foggiest idea of what teachers expect. Are they expected to memorize names? How about dates of studies? What level of detail in the book or lectures are they supposed to absorb? If there are essay examinations or papers, how are these products evaluated? Students always appreciate clarity regarding your expectations for them. Try to give a quiz, exam, and/or writing assignment relatively early in the semester so that students have feedback on how they are doing.

14) Teach with passion, energy, and enthusiasm

Nothing is quite so contagious as passion and enthusiasm. If you want your students to be enthusiastic about the subject matter, communicate your own enthusiasm to them. Students will enjoy your course more in all its aspects (Ceci & Williams, 1998).

15) Use lots of relevant concrete examples

Psychology encompasses so many wonderful ideas that it is easy for you to get lost in abstractions, and for students just plain to get lost. Using many relevant concrete examples to illustrate ideas helps students to remain grounded and to follow your lectures.

16) Allow students to ask questions

Allowing students to ask questions means at least two things. First, it means encouraging students not just to answer questions, but to formulate them. Second, it means setting aside the time to allow students to ask questions, even in large classes. Otherwise, the confusions of the moment are more likely to become permanent confusions in their minds.

How You Put It Together

17) Portray psychology as a unified and integrated discipline

Students can complete an introductory psychology course believing that psychology constitutes the 15 to 20 relatively distinct subdisciplines that may happen to correspond to the chapters of their text. Don't let this happen. Show them that different subdisciplines merely represent different pathways toward a common goal: the understanding of the mind and behavior in all its diversity.

18) Show students how psychological ideas evolve

Ideas in psychology evolve, and it is important for students to learn how these ideas evolve. It is for this reason that those early lectures on history are so important—not for students to learn about discarded ideas from the dusty past, but to learn how the ideas of today build on the ideas of the past, as the ideas of the future will build on the ideas of today. Show the connections between past and present ideas not just in one or two early lectures, but throughout the course.

19) Emphasize that psychological thought evolves within a sociocultural context

Psychological thought, no matter how scientific, evolves within a sociocultural context, and you need to encourage students to be both aware of and critical of the assumptions of all traditions and schools of psychological thought. The psychologies of diverse countries, such as Russia, France, Germany, Japan, and the United States, have evolved in quite different ways. Too often, we teach our own psychological tradition as though it were the only one, which of course it's not.

20) Encourage students to be sensitive to issues of human unity and diversity

Humans all have sets of values; they all think; and they all seek self-esteem. But their values, ways of thinking, and means to attain self-esteem differ widely. It is important to emphasize both the unity and diversity that characterizes all human beings.

The teaching tips in this article are all relatively easy to implement and, for the most part, are things you already know how to do. The trick is to remember to do them. All you need do is get started, and there is no time like the present. Try them, and chances are both you and your students will see a difference.

[Preparation of this article was supported in part under the Javits Act Program (grant number R206R50001), as administered by the Office of Educational Research and Improvement, U.S. Department of Education. The article does not necessarily represent the positions or policies of the government, and no official endorsement should be inferred.]

Recommended Readings and References

Benjamin, L. T. Jr., Daniel, R. S., & Brewer, C. L. (Eds.). (1985). *Handbook for teaching introductory psychology*. Hillsdale, NJ: Erlbaum.

Ceci, S. J., & Williams, W. M. (1998). "How'm I doing?": Problems with student ratings of instructors and courses. *Change, 29*(5), 12-23.

Chi, M. T. H., Glaser, R., & Farr, M. (Eds.). (1988). *The nature of expertise*. Hillsdale, NJ: Erlbaum.

Flores, R. L. (1997). Teaching psychology from a cross-cultural perspective. *APS Observer, 10*(6), 20-22.

Galliano, G. (1997). Enhancing student learning through exemplary examples. *APS Observer, 10*(4), 28-30, 37.

McKeachie, W. J. (1994). *Teaching tips: Strategies, research, and theory for college and university teachers* (9th ed.). Lexington, MA: D. C. Heath.

Sternberg, R. J. (1994). A triarchic model for teaching and assessing students in general psychology. *General Psychologist, 30*(2), 42-48.

Sternberg, R. J. (1997a). *Successful intelligence.* New York: Plume.

Sternberg, R. J. (Ed.) (1997b). *Teaching introductory psychology*. Washington, DC: American Psychological Association.

Sternberg, R. J. (1997c). *Thinking styles*. New York: Cambridge University Press.

Sternberg, R. J. (1997d). What does it mean to be smart? *Educational Leadership, 54,* 20-24.

Sternberg, R. J., & Spear-Swerling, L. (1996). *Teaching for thinking*. Washington, DC: American Psychological Association.

Sternberg, R. J., Torff, B., & Grigorenko, E. L. (1998). Teaching triarchically improves student achievement. *Journal of Educational Psychology, 90,* 374-384.

Chapter 8

How to Create a Good Exam

Catherine H. Renner
Michael J. Renner
West Chester University

W hile many students believe that exams solely exist to torture them or give the instructor a day off from teaching, the most obvious purpose is to assess the students' retention and comprehension of the course material. A related purpose is to maintain institutional standards by requiring students to meet some minimum performance standard before giving them credit. These types of performance evaluations provide the basis for assigning grades.

This column will focus on some rules of thumb for creating a good examination, test, quiz, evaluation, or trial-by-fire. We will discuss such topics as the function of exams, how exam creation has changed, planning a good exam, time requirements, specific tips about writing items, and the place of humor in exams.

Functions of Exams

A well-written exam serves several functions that support effective instruction. First, an exam can teach by prompting study and by reminding students what they learned. It can challenge students to use their new-found knowledge in ways that have practical or intellectual value. Second, students' exam performance can provide instructors with diagnostic information about what the student did or did not comprehend. High-quality exams can fulfill these dual goals of instruction and evaluation, but poorly constructed exams may fulfill neither.

How Exam Creation Has Changed

As demands on faculty members have increased (e.g. increased class size, teaching loads, and research expectations), instructors typically have come to rely more on outside sources for exam questions. Instructors may now have a collection of more publisher-supplied ancillary materials than they could possibly use in a single exam. But more work exists than simply

This article first appeared in the July/August 1995 APS Observer.

picking items for your next test.

Types of Exams

Exam questions come in many styles, including multiple-choice, true false, matching, fill-in-the-blank, and various forms of essay questions. Neither of us has much confidence in true-false items: Any item that the proverbial three blind mice could get right half the time isn't likely to make a real contribution to the students' learning experience or your evaluation of it. Matching and fill-in items are fine, but nearly anything that can be tested in these formats can also be assessed via multiple-choice items. For simplicity, we will focus on multiple-choice and essay questions.

Planning a Good Exam

The first principle in writing an exam is to plan ahead. Before you begin, it is important to review your course objectives and identify important concepts, issues, and terms students should have learned. This allows you to match the emphasis in the exam to your ideas about what is most important. A common mistake is to skip the planning process. It's tempting but inadvisable to simply begin writing or selecting questions.

If you want to encourage certain behaviors in your students, the first exam is critical; what students find when they arrive for the first exam can have a major impact on how they approach the rest of the course. Students use the first exam in a course to judge what the instructor really thinks is important for them to learn, and how hard they will need to work. Your first exam should make your expectations clear.

Time Requirements

Even experienced instructors may write what they think is a great exam, only to discover that it is too long or too short. For multiple-choice exams, a conservative estimate is to allow one minute per item. Nearly all students will finish well before this, but it will allow enough time for even the most thorough student. For short essays, five to 10 minutes per question should allow most students (who have some mastery of the material) enough time to prepare and answer. For longer essay items, estimating the time required is more difficult. One useful strategy is to assign point values to questions that are proportional to the amount of time you expect or want or expect students to spend on the question, and then inform the students that you have done this by listing the points assigned to each question.

Writing Good Multiple-Choice Items

It's a painful truth that a test-savvy student can often get a respectable grade on a poorly constructed multiple-choice exam without having learned the course material. It's equally possible that a substandard exam will make a good student look bad. Whether you're writing your own items or choosing them from an item file, a good multiple-choice exam should have several characteristics, which we'll summarize as *Dos* and *Don'ts*.

◆ Do remember that one of your goals is to make the student think. This means using a variety of question types. Minimize use of items requiring simple memorization, and ask yourself for every question: Why is it important that they know this?

◆ Do read the questions through the students' eyes—make sure the answer key is correct and doesn't contradict something you've told them or assigned for reading. Otherwise, students can reasonably argue that the question is unfair or that an incorrect answer is also correct.

◆ Do make sure that each response option is the correct answer approximately as often as each of the others, and that the correct answer is typically the same length as the distractors. Students quickly pick up on extraneous cues that can signal the correct answer.

◆ Do write each stem (the beginning of the question) as a complete question. The student should be able to write the answer to the question without reading the response options.

◆ Do rewrite poor test bank items that can be salvaged if a useful item will result.

◆ Do put items in order of the content in the textbook and your lectures. This provides a context for reading and understanding them. If you use multiple forms of an exam (same questions, different order) this may not be possible.

◆ Don't overuse questions that include "all of the above" or "none of the above" as keys or distractors, or that take the form "which of the following is not…" Students often expend so much effort decoding the syntax of the question that they lose track of the underlying concept.

◆ Don't write questions for which the correct answer is identified in another question. It makes little sense to ask for a definition of a term in one question if the stem of a neighboring question provides the definition.

◆ Don't use incorrect answers that are obvious fillers, or those that are grammatically or logically inconsistent with the stem. Eliminating these is a no-brainer for the student.

◆ Don't take all of your questions from the item file for your textbook, and don't randomly pick items from the test bank. The resulting exam may not cover the concepts you have emphasized and may not fairly represent the material in the textbook.

◆ Don't worry about having five response options for your questions if you normally use four, or vice versa. If the distractors are of high quality it makes little difference.

Writing Essay Items

Essay exams can be fun if the questions are clearly stated and allow the student to stretch their understanding. Essays require students to think about material differently than multiple-choice questions; students must recall information they have learned rather than simply recognize the correct answer. Research indicates that students study more efficiently for essays than for multiple-choice exams.

But writing good essay questions is only half the job. It's important to prepare an answer key before you administer the test that lists what information you expect to see and the points you will assign to it. Decide beforehand whether you will deduct points for digressions, and so inform the students prior to the test. If a student digresses, point this out, and apply your standards consistently.

In creating a good essay question, it is important that the question be specific enough that the prepared student can answer it to your satisfaction. There are key words in essay questions that signal the student how to structure their response. For example, 'compare' asks students to analyze the similarities and differences among concepts, whereas 'contrast' tells students to focus only on differences. 'Define' yields the meaning of a concept, and 'list' will elicit just that, a simple list. 'Discuss,' 'explain,' 'relate,' and 'interpret' all require the student to move beyond the description or definition of concepts to detail cause and effect or present other opposing ideas. Using key words like these in an essay question will signal specific tasks to the student. Reviewing the meaning of these key terms in class before the exam may help the student understand better what type of information a question is requesting.

It is tempting to include broad, all encompassing questions as larger essay questions. However, if an essay question is too broad, the student may resort to the "memory dumping" strategy. This occurs for a number of reasons. First, the question itself may not be specific enough for the student to discriminate relevant from irrelevant information. Second, the student may not know the material well enough to determine what is and isn't relevant, and so writes down everything in hopes that something will count. Your having prepared an answer key before the test will help guide your grading to ferret out the information you seek and thereby discourage "memory dumping" in the long run. A student's answer that incorporates large amounts of material—of which some aspects may only be tangentially relevant—may be well informed and well written, but may still not be a good answer to a particular question. If you assign full credit to this type of answer without informing the student that some aspects were irrelevant, he or she may come away believing that this type of response was what you wanted. Subsequent essay answers will become longer and less focused as the semester progress.

The Use of Humor

Some students believe that humor in an exam helps them by breaking the tension and reminding them that it is not the Spanish Inquisition. For other students, humor in an exam breaks their concentration and distracts them.

Try to structure your exams so that students can choose whether or not to deal with your attempts at comedy. For example, you might offer several essays or problems, one of which is supposed to be funny, and give students a choice of questions so they may choose to avoid the funny one. For multiple-choice questions, you might tell students that option (e), when present, is never correct and may be ignored. Then, when you have inspired pun or loose association to inflict upon your students, place it as option (e). This allows students who are distracted by humor to avoid it and preserves the four choice character of the exam.

Conclusion

Creating a good exam involves a pinch of science and a large scoop of art. If you are willing to combine your expertise in the content of psychology with compassion, alertness, and an ongoing effort to keep your goals for teaching in sight, you can develop the skill of creating challenging, fair, and interesting exams. This makes an exam an important part of the student's learning experience, and can give you feedback for continually improving your teaching.

Recommended Readings and References

Davis, B. G. (1993). *Tools for teaching*. San Francisco: Jossey-Bass.

Gullette, M. M. (Ed.). (1984). *The art and craft of teaching*. Cambridge, MA: Harvard University Press.

McKeachie, W. J. (1994). *Teaching tips: Strategies, research, and theory for college and university teachers* (9th ed.). Lexington, MA: D. C. Heath.

Weinstein, C. E., & Meyer, D. K (1991). Implications of cognitive psychology for testing: Contributions from work in learning strategies. In M. C. Wittrick & E. L. Baker (Eds.), *Testing and cognition* (pp. 40-61). Englewood Cliffs, NJ: Prentice-Hall.

Chapter 9

How to Develop Multiple-Choice Tests

Lee Sechrest
University of Arizona

John F. Kihlstrom
University of California–Berkeley

Richard Bootzin
University of Arizona

S ooner or later, almost everyone who teaches psychology has to develop a multiple-choice test. Many lower-level textbooks come with sets of questions distributed by the publishers, but those items do not cover unique lecture material. Moreover, even the published items ought to be carefully reviewed, for they may not be of uniformly high quality. And, many of them violate what might be considered standard rules for writing good items (Ellsworth, Dunnell, & Duell, 1990). In any case, beyond lower-level courses, teachers are likely to be mostly on their own with respect to developing multiple-choice tests. What is one to do?

Start at the Beginning

Why give a test in the first place? The easy answer is "Well, of course, we want to find out how much students have learned." The difficulty is we can't know how much students have learned without first having a pretest or baseline measure. We can't assume students have started at zero (or at any specific level greater than chance). Houston (1985) gave a set of test items from an introduction to psychology class to a group of 60 diverse persons (aged 16-61) with no formal training in psychology, and this group exceeded chance performance on 76 percent of the items.

Start at the End

The temptation is to propose a *final* exam at the *outset* of the course and to consider this baseline in evaluating performance on subsequent tests, but that's got its own set of problems. So, an alternative answer to the question "Why give a test…?" is that we at least want to know how much the examinees know about psychology. In that case, we could identify some more or less critical knowledge that students ought to have acquired and determine how many actually did acquire that knowledge. That would in-

This article first appeared in the January 1993 APS Observer.

volve the construction of a *criterion-referenced* test. That is, specify a criterion level that represents successful performance.

If you choose this approach, you are not much concerned about differences *among* students above or below the criterion level. For example, if teaching differential equations, you're not much interested in the fact that some inept students were more inept than others or that some students could do the problems faster—but no more correctly—than others. Or, if teaching psychology using the Keller (1968) method, in which all students are expected to reach criterion performance, there would be little interest in differences among students.

Norm-referenced Test

Usually, however, teachers construct exams to distinguish between students with different levels of knowledge—in other words, they create *norm-referenced tests*. They want to order students with respect to their knowledge, and to be able to say—for any level of performance—which students know more. That aim raises issues (i.e., reliability and homogeneity of sets of items) that are not inherent in criterion-referenced measures and that should affect how items are written and scored.

Reliability, in this context, refers to the dependability of conclusions about differences in ability inferred from test scores. Nearly everyone understands that on, let us say, a 60-item test, the difference between 42 correct and 43 correct is trivial. (That is why most instructors like to position the borderlines between letter grades at points at which natural breaks in a distribution of scores occur. This minimizes the number of students whose letter grade is affected by a single answer.)

Half Wrong, Half Right: Uncovering a Difference

In order for test scores to allow some ordering among test takers, items must be constructed to result in a distribution of scores. That is, the variance of the score distribution should be large. The maximum variance for any given item will occur when its difficulty level is .50 (i.e., when half the respondents get it correct and half get it wrong).

In general, differentiation among examinees on a test will be greatest when the difficulty level of the test causes subjects to get about half the items correct. Put another way, neither very difficult nor very easy items assist much in differentiating among examinees.

Ideally, each and every item in a test should *work*, that is, help differentiate maximally among examinees. Teachers may try to vary item difficulty by writing some easy and some difficult items in the mistaken belief that these test results will better represent the knowledge distribution. But reduced variance contributes to reduced differentiation.

Even so, there are good reasons to include some easy and some difficult items. Some teachers reason that including some easy and some difficult items may serve motivational purposes. Easy items may reduce anxiety about the exam and difficult items may reassure the best students that their knowledge is being fairly evaluated. Difficult items may also serve a diagnostic function for the instructor, who may want to know whether a specific construct has been learned by the students who have best mastered the material.

Difficulty Level and Fairness

Items with a difficulty level of .50 are not easy to write, and a test consisting only of such items may be somewhat demoralizing to students expecting to do better than 50 percent correct. Item variance is actually not much reduced unless the difficulty level is fairly extreme, say beyond .80. That is, if the correct/incorrect split on items is not worse than .80/.20 (or .20/80), variance is not much reduced. For the sake of student morale, a test with a mean percentage correct of about 70 may be desirable.

Also, a test should be fair. Students do sometimes complain that a particular item is too detailed, ambiguous, or otherwise inappropriate. From a psychometric point of view there is a clear and objective index of fairness: the item-to-total correlation. An item belongs on a test if the correct response is positively correlated with scores on the remainder of the test. Most test-scoring software has the capacity to calculate these correlations. Of course, with a large N (such as that encountered in most introductory and survey courses) even very small correlations become statistically significant. A reasonable threshold for retaining an item might be that its item-to-total correlation should be at least .20 (for $N=100$, this correlation is significant at $p <.05$); items failing to meet that criterion then would be eliminated from the test (e.g., by scoring the item correct for all responses).

Students immediately grasp the idea behind this practice and appreciate the extra effort entailed in rescoring the test to ensure fairness. And when confronted with the fact that a particular item did in fact discriminate between high and low scorers on the test, their complaints are almost always withdrawn. This assumes, of course, that most of the items on the test are perceived as fair. It is unlikely, but possible, to construct entire tests in which the variability between students is due to irrelevant considerations rather than to knowledge about the course material. In those cases, item-to-total correlations are not helpful.

Sources of Variance

Variance in test scores is determined in complex ways. Preferably, nearly all the variance should be determined by differences in knowledge at the time the test is given. In fact, however, the number and variety of determinants of variance will be large. Scores will vary because, among other reasons, some students: (1) are better and faster readers than others; (2) are test-wise (i.e., have learned heuristics to identify an answer that has a good chance of being right); (3) are smart enough or lucky enough to sit next to a better student from whose paper they may copy; (4) will have been lucky enough to have studied the exact material on which a few items are based; (5) will be relaxed and in a good frame of mind for taking the test, while others are anxious and distracted.

Instructors can fairly easily reduce some of these sources of variance (e.g., cheating, reading ability) but must accept other sources (e.g., luck in what was studied). Instructors should certainly construct items to mini-mize unwanted sources of variance. Correct response choices should, for example, be balanced across the options so that any position bias (e.g., the inclination to choose the last alternative) should not be either an advantage or a disadvantage. Characteristics of response alternatives not reflecting particular content (e.g., length, format) should not be cues to correctness. Extraneous material and difficult vocabulary should be excluded from the stems and distractors of items so that reading ability is minimized as a source of variance.

Research Bias of Item Construction

Advice about how to write multiple-choice items is not scarce. For example, a study of educational psychology textbooks found guidelines offered in 32 of 42 texts, and 12 of the guidelines were given in half or more of the 32 (Ellsworth, Dunnell, & Duell, 1990). Unfortunately, most of the advice is, apparently, just that—advice. Empirical support for many guidelines is lacking (Haladyna & Downing, 1989), but where it does ex-ist, the support is usually thin, being limited to a study or two of dubious generalizability.

A Summary

Nonetheless, a review of empirical support, combined in an informal Bayesian way with expert opinion, reported by Haladyna and Downing (1989), is useful. (For a more general summary of research and expert opinion, see McKeachie, 1986.) We summarize, and edit, to some extent, their recommendations here:

1) Consider using only three instead of the usual four or five options for questions. Item statistics are generally as good with three options as with four or five, and because time per item is reduced, the number of items and content covered can be increased. Very often, it is difficult to come up with three or more good distractors anyway.

2) Balance the key so that the correct answer appears approximately equally often in every position. Students who have a tendency to choose one alternative (e.g., the last one) whenever they are uncertain should be neither more nor less likely to be right across items than would be expected by chance.

3) Do not use all of the above, none of the above, and similar alternatives as possible answers. Such choices generally make items a bit more difficult but are not helpful in other ways, since they introduce additional response biases. Also, do not use " I do not know" as a response option; after all, arguably, in many cases this answer is literally correct.

4) Keep lengths of options fairly consistent within items (e.g., so that the correct response is not notably longer that the distractors), and avoid giving the answer away by grammatical construction of the item. For example:
An episcotister is an
a) instrument   b) computer software   c) theoretical construct

5) Try to use only plausible distractors and avoid distractors that contain clues that might be used by test-wise examinees. Ideally, for classroom tests, distractors should be diagnostic in the sense that incorrect answers should reveal specific deficits in knowledge or lapses in thinking. For example:
A dog hears a tone immediately before a puff of air is presented to the cornea of its eye. The puff of air is the:
   a) conditioned stimulus   b) distal stimulus
   c) unconditioned stimulus   d) generalization stimulus
An implausible distractor should attract very few responses, and thus represents a nonfunctional response option. Distractors including such adverbs as *never* and *always* tend to be avoided by test-wise students, when they are uncertain, and such distractors tend to produce biased patterns of responding that may favor one group of respondents over another. That is, the final score distribution will have an unwanted component of variance that is systematic but unrelated to knowledge of the material.

Distractors
     The purpose of distractors is to reduce the probability that a student can get the correct answer to a question by guessing. For that to happen, distractors must attract a reasonable share of responses. An implausible or nonsense distractor, in effect, changes the difficulty level of an item. For example, in a four-choice item, the chance level of difficulty for the item is

.25. But if one of the distractors is a throwaway, the chance level for the item becomes .33. That does not necessarily hurt either the reliability or the validity of the test, but it does change how you interpret how much students have learned.

Our personal experience suggests that tests should begin with three or four fairly easy items so that anxious students are not *paralyzed* immediately by difficult material. Other than that, ordering test items more or less in the sequence in which the material was presented in books and lectures seems to help students do better (Blach,1989). To the extent that such an order effect is constant across students, it has no effect on variance, and, hence, on differentiating between students. It may, however, put students more at ease, particularly if the test is difficult.

Reduction of Irrelevant Variance

To reduce variance associated with individual differences in test-wiseness, as opposed to competence in the course, we also suggest informing all students at the outset of the exam of useful test-taking strategies. These include: reading the test all the way through before answering any items (because one item may give hints about another); trying to eliminate at least one option as clearly wrong (thereby increasing the likelihood of getting the item right by chance); reasoning to the correct answer (when fact retrieval fails) from some general concept or principle (assuming that the instructor has not nefariously asked a question about an exception that tests the rule); and guessing (when all else fails), because in the absence of explicit memory, implicit memory for studied material is likely to bias responding toward the correct answer. Instructors probably should not offer the disclaimer proposed by the public-radio humorist Michael Feldman: "All questions have been carefully researched, though the answers have not; ambiguous, misleading, and poorly worded questions are par for the course."

True or False?

Very often the idea to be tested by an item may lend itself better to a true-false than a multiple-choice format. For one thing, it may be difficult to come up with three or four good distractors. Besides, if the distractors are poor ones the item may be inadvertently converted to a two-choice item (i.e., the equivalent of a true-false item). For example, the item:

Who first formulated the concept of correlation:
a) Karl Marx   b) Ronald Fisher   c) Francis Galton   d) Sigmund Freud

This question would for informed students be a two-choice item that could be rephrased as "Ronald Fisher first formulated the concept of correlation: true or false?" If the answer is false, then the correct answer to the item must be Galton.

There is nothing wrong with true-false items; in fact, they result in tests with about the same psychometric properties as multiple-choice tests. True-false tests are likely to produce higher overall scores since chance-level performance is .5. What probably is not a good idea is mixing multiple-choice and true-false items in the same section of a test. Mixing item types tends to produce response errors that have nothing to do with what students know. Multiple-choice and true-false items used in the same test probably should be separated into two sections, preferably with answer sheets marked in such a way that the student cannot put a mark in a wrong space.

Objections to Multiple-Choice Tests?

The usual objection to multiple-choice tests is that they reflect only rather low-level memory processes rather than the higher-order concepts deemed "really important." However, there is no reason why multiple-choice tests cannot tap fairly abstract, conceptual knowledge. For example:

The fundamental process in classical conditioning is:
   a) association by contiguity   b) vicarious reinforcement
   c) association by contingency   d) continuous reinforcement

Now consider the following alternative:

In a classical conditioning experiment, a tone CS is paired with an electric shock US. For Group A, the CS precedes the US by 10 seconds. For Group B, the CS and US are presented simultaneously. For Group C, the US precedes the CS by 10 seconds. After 20 conditioning trials, the experimenter measures the magnitudes of the fear CR. The most likely ordering of the CR magnitudes is:
   a) B>C =A   b) B>A>C   c) A>B>C   d) A=C>B

Arguably, a student who gets the alternative item correct has a fairly good conceptual understanding of classical conditioning, at the level appropriate for Introductory Psychology.

If items designed to measure higher-order concepts correlate highly with items depending more clearly on memory (e.g., Ferland, Dorval, and Levasseur, 1987), is that an indictment of multiple-choice tests? Not necessarily, for the results suggest just as strongly that memory functions are related to those involved in higher order cognitive processes. Amazingly, after years of multiple-choice testing, we still do not have a very good notion of just what functions are tapped by such tests. In the meantime, we rely on the widely shared observation that it is unusual to find a student who does well on a multiple-choice test who is at the same time incapable of displaying other forms of comprehension of the course material.

Of course, this is an empirical question begging to be investigated. In general, we encourage teachers to experiment with tests. What exactly *is* the correlation between multiple-choice, short-answer, and essay tests of the same material? Does performance on items drawn from the text correlate with performance on items drawn from lectures? If a test is factor-analyzed, will the resulting structure mirror the organization of the course? When an instructor relocates to another institution, it may be useful for him or her to repeat readings, lectures, and exams from the previous year and to measure differences in student performance. This may yield useful clues about differences in the student populations being served.

Finally, tests are intended to evaluate, and promote, the learning process. Students should be encouraged to do more than score their tests against a key, count up the number correct, and slink away. Rather, they should be encouraged to treat the exam itself as a learning experience—to try to determine mastery of the course material. Instructors should consider preparing detailed feedback on their exams, perhaps short essays indicating what the question was about, why the right answer was right, and the wrong answers wrong. And, of course, similar considerations apply to the instructor. If students consistently do poorly on items testing particular concepts or principles, then the text or lecture material is a candidate for revision.

Recommended Readings and References

Balch, W. R. (1989). Item order affects performance on multiple-choice exams. *Teaching of Psychology, 16*, 75-77.

Ellsworth, R. A., Dunnell, P., & Duell, O. K. (1990). Multiple-choice test items: What are textbook authors telling teachers? *Journal of Educational Research, 83*, 289-293.

Ferland, J. J., Dorval, J., & Levasseur, L. (1987). Measuring higher cognitive levels by multiple-choice questions: A myth? *Medical Education, 21*, 109-113.

Haladyna, T. M., & Downing, S. M. (1989). Validity of a taxonomy of multiple-choice item writing rules. *Applied Measurement in Education, 2*, 51-78.

Houston, J. P. (1985). Untutored lay knowledge of the principles of psychology: Do we know anything they don't? *Psychological Reports, 70*, 567-570.

Keller, F. S. (1968). Good-bye teacher. *Journal of Applied Behavior Analysis, 1*, 79-89.

McKeachie, W. J. (1994). *Teaching tips: Strategies, research, and theory for college and university teachers* (9th ed.). Lexington, MA: D. C. Heath.

Chapter 10

Using Extra Credit

Joseph J. Palladino
University of Southern Indiana

G. William Hill IV
Kennesaw State College

John C. Norcross
University of Scranton

P ractically all faculty members have been approached by students requesting opportunities to earn extra credit. These requests appear to increase in frequency and urgency as the term comes to a close and students realize their potential grade is lower than they would desire.

Suddenly, previously disinterested students come to life, show interest in the course material, and request opportunities to prove to the instructor that their abilities and knowledge are above that currently indicated by their grade. But opinions on granting these requests, as well as the appropriateness of extra credit itself, vary widely among faculty and students.

Attitudes Toward and Advantages of Extra Credit

A survey of faculty members' and students' attitudes toward extra credit found that approximately 75 percent of the faculty respondents in a variety of disciplines did not currently offer extra credit and 21 percent thought it should never be offered (Norcross, Horrocks, & Stevenson, 1989). A follow-up study (Norcross, Dooley, & Stevenson, 1993) found that an instructor's general attitude towards extra credit rather than the circumstances of the individual case (e.g., illness, English as a second language) largely determined whether it was provided.

Norcross et al. (1989) also reported that the faculty members and students see different advantages and disadvantages of extra credit. For example, students are more likely to see extra credit as a second chance while faculty members view it as an opportunity to explore a topic in depth. Both faculty and students agreed, however, that the major disadvantages of extra credit are that it tends to encourage a lax or irresponsible attitude and that it is unfair when offered only to selected students.

Specific Extra Credit Opportunities

Hill, Palladino, and Eison (1993) extended the Norcross, et al. (1989,

This article first appeared in the September 1995 APS Observer.

1993) inquiry by surveying faculty members concerning specific extra credit opportunities rather than attitudes towards extra credit in general.

They compiled a list of 39 actual extra credit opportunities, including participating as a research subject, summarizing an article from a professional journal, attending and summarizing a lecture by a visiting speaker, donating blood, and correctly answering trivia questions unrelated to course content on exams.

Psychology teachers (N=91, all members of the APA Division on Teaching of Psychology) rated each of the extra credit opportunities on the following: likelihood they would use the extra credit opportunity, educational value, and equality of access for all students.

In general, items with high ratings for educational value tended to be the ones that faculty would be likely to use. The top two in terms of educational value were participating as a research subject and writing a research paper.

This study also revealed a relatively high rate of use of extra credit by psychology teachers (82 percent used it to some extent), which probably reflects the common practice of offering extra credit for participating in faculty and upper-level student research.

When and When Not to Use Extra Credit

Two significant issues concerning extra credit can be identified: educational (pedagogical) value and equal access to extra credit (ethical).

Let's use donating blood as an example. Almost all would agree that donating blood is an admirable and socially desirable deed. However, its relationship to the typical goals of a college class is unclear and somewhat questionable. In *The Ethics of Teaching: A Casebook* (1993) Patricia Keith-Spiegel and her colleagues write, "Professors must justify why extra (as in 'outside') credit is appropriate, and assignments should be pedagogically sound. 'Good deeds,' while having a laudable place in one's personal moral philosophy, are not proper assignments for academic credit unless they are related directly to course content" (p. 45).

Moreover, such an extra-credit opportunity is not accessible to all students. Some students are unable to donate blood, and thus unable to avail themselves of this opportunity for medical reasons (e.g., anemia, hemophilia, hepatitis), religious prohibitions, or psychological reasons (e.g., fear of blood or needles).

Ethical guidelines require us to offer alternative ways for students to earn credit that are equal to that offered for research participation, if for some reason the student cannot morally or ethically participate. A similar approach should be followed for extra credit.

A Pedagogically Sound and Ethical Extra Credit Assignment

Among the multitude of extra credit possibilities, a few merit special consideration by those who want to offer extra credit. For example, faculty members often do not assign all of the chapters in an introductory text because there is not enough time to cover them. Thus, some material will not be presented in class nor included in exams.

Extra credit could be awarded for correctly answering multiple-choice questions that cover the unassigned material. In some cases the points are earned only if the student's score is well beyond chance-level responding. Compared to many extra credit opportunities, this one appears to be pedagogically sound, is accessible to all students, and can be implemented by simply adding items to an exam.

Guidelines for Using Extra Credit

Should one desire to start a verbal brawl in a university faculty club, the desirability of extra credit is appropriate incendiary material. Whatever position one holds on the matter, the research (Hill et al., 1993; Norcross et al., 1993) indicates that many psychology faculty are currently using extra credit as a component of their grading and will continue to offer it in the future.

Therefore, we would like to offer several guidelines to consider when offering and implementing extra credit:

◆ Make extra credit available to all students in the class, build it into the course structure, and describe it in the syllabus. These practices mute criticism that extra credit is selectively and covertly provided to a few, possibly undeserving, students. At the same time, this avoids access problems due to time constraints when extra credit is offered late in the semester and enables faculty members to build it into their overall grading scheme.

◆ Select extra credit opportunities that are pedagogically sound and clearly connected to the course content. It is difficult to justify the use of extraneous or frivolous extra credit opportunities like giving blood or adopting a pet to either your students or your colleagues.

◆ Provide several choices of extra credit opportunities. These choices should be roughly equivalent in effort required, time commitment, and pedagogical value. This equity allows students to choose which opportunities they complete. In addition, this procedure corresponds to our ethical guidelines for alternatives to research participation.

◆ Explain to your students (and yourself) why you are offering extra credit. Is it for pedagogically sound reasons? Is it intended to enhance the students' educational experience or is it simply *makeup* work to improve their grade? Well considered and rational reasons for offering this opportunity will blunt colleagues' questions about whether you

are contributing to low standards and grade inflation with such practices.

◆ Address how much extra credit is appropriate. This is a difficult matter
to resolve, but one general rule of thumb is that the points available
from extra credit should be no more than 5 percent (some faculty argue
for up to 10 percent) of the total possible number of points for the
course. This restriction may help address the concern that extra credit
encourages a lax or irresponsible attitude among students.

◆ Examine carefully your choices of extra credit assignments. If your
extra credit opportunities are pedagogically sound, should they be included as required assignments? Are you potentially devaluing an assignment in the eyes of your students by relegating it to extra credit?
This may be particularly problematic if, for example, writing assignments are designated as extra credit.

◆ Reflect seriously on the purposes of your grading. Your grading rationale will in turn influence your decisions concerning extra credit. If
grades are a reward for hard work, for example, then it seems fair to
offer students additional chances to work hard to master the material
and boost their grades. Alternatively, if grades are quantitative esti-
mates of subject mastery, then allowing students to improve their grade
through extra credit may decrease the validity of the estimate.

Conclusion

The use of extra credit as a pedagogical tool is a controversial but common practice.

Careful consideration of the points presented above and the guidelines
we have suggested should help you to clarify your position on the issue,
and to improve both your theoretical basis for and the practical implementation of, extra credit opportunities if you choose to provide them.

Recommended Readings and References

Hill, G. W. IV., Palladino, J. J., & Eison, J. A. (1993). Blood, sweat, and trivia:
Faculty ratings of extra-credit opportunities. *Teaching of Psychology, 20,* 209-
213.

Keith-Spiegel, P., Wittig, A. F, Perkins, D. V., Balogh, D. W., & Whitely, B. E., Jr.
(1993). *The ethics of teaching: A casebook.* Muncie, IN: Ball State University.

Norcross, J. C., Dooley, H. S., & Stevenson, J. F. (1993). Faculty use and justifica-
tion of extra credit: No middle ground? *Teaching of Psychology, 20,* 240-242.

Norcross, J. C., Horrocks, L. J., & Stevenson, J. F. (1989). Of barfights and gad-
flies: Attitudes and practices concerning extra credit in college courses. *Teaching of Psychology, 16,* 199-203.

Chapter 11

Teaching Tips Review
*Science Teaching Reconsidered: A Handbook**

Baron Perlman, Lee I. McCann, and Susan H. McFadden
University of Wisconsin–Oshkosh

I f you choose to read only one book (other than this one) this year related to your teaching, consider *Science Teaching Reconsidered: A Handbook*, a practical handbook that emphasizes ways to enhance students' learning of science. It presents a multitude of successful teaching practices, encouraging the reader to integrate creativity, imagination and innovation, with sound planning, practice and decision making about one's teaching. It is the best practical guide to teaching science the reviewers have ever read.

Handbook Highlights

The opening chapter on *How Teachers Teach: General Principles* emphasizes the often forgotten notion that our teaching is not successful unless someone else has learned. Students in science should not merely learn content; they also should participate in the process of moving from their initial state of knowledge and understanding to the instructor's desired level. This chapter presents data supporting the conclusion that many students leave undergraduate science majors, not because of their complexities, but because of poor teaching. These are the types of problems for which this book attempts to provide solutions.

This first chapter also presents the fundamental question for teachers of science: "Is the primary goal of my course for each student to gain specific information, or for each student to master how to organize and apply new information independently to new situations" (p. 3)?

The answer to this question depends on the course being taught, stu-

This article first appeared in the May/June 1997 APS Observer.

* Committee on Undergraduate Science Education. (1997). *Science Teaching Reconsidered: A Handbook*. National Academy Press, 2101 Constitution Avenue, N.W., Lock Box 285, Washington, DC 20055, (800) 624-6242. Available on-line at http://www.nap.edu. The project was approved by the Governing Board of the National Research Council, whose members are drawn from the councils of the National Academy of Sciences, the National Academy of Engineering, and the Institute of Medicine.

dents' science backgrounds, and the instructor's values and goals. The issue is described as one of balance, how much specific content information is emphasized as compared to critical thinking, and the process of doing science. Because science curricula are vertically structured, a base of factual knowledge is imperative before students take more advanced courses. On the other hand, when we teach courses in general education to the nonmajor we may want to place additional emphasis on ". . . the essence of what science is and the nature of the scientific enterprise" (p. 4). In either case, as we organize our courses, this book encourages us to keep both goals in mind.

Once we have reached a decision on the primary goal(s) of our courses we must organize them. Three fundamental guidelines recommended for course design are being aware of the students' prior knowledge and taking it into account, identifying the major and minor concepts and the connections between different concepts, and relating new information to a context the student understands.

Finally, we are urged to integrate active learning into our science courses whenever possible. The research on the learning of science concludes that "students learn best if they are engaged in active learning, if they are forced to deal with observations and concepts before terms and facts" (p. 4).

The handbook tells the teacher how to support such active learning, within the financial and time constraints of a *real* course.

Lean on Learning

In Chapter 2 and subsequent chapters, the handbook provides specific suggestions and examples of how to increase student learning in our science courses. Briefly, one wants to teach scientific ways of thinking, actively involve students in their own learning, help students to develop a conceptual framework, as well as develop problem-solving skills, promote students' discussion and group activities, help students experience science in varied, interesting, and enjoyable ways, and assess student understanding at *frequent* intervals throughout the learning process.

These chapters offer practical advice about lecturing, asking effective questions, teaching the large class, using demonstrations, and conducting discussions.

Unlike many books on pedagogy, the focus on science in this book provides an opportunity to specifically address laboratory teaching and students' work in the lab. The suggestions for developing a successful laboratory experience for students are especially helpful. The commitment of instructor time and energy required to do this is substantial. "Are you prepared to go through all of this and still get mediocre student evaluations" (p. 19)? is a sobering yet highly realistic question.

Teaching and Learning

Chapter 3 links teaching with learning, acknowledging the failure we all feel when some students do not learn basic concepts of science. The section in this chapter on *Scientific Research as a Teaching and Learning Model* answers the question of how we can "make better use of traditional formats to help [our] students gain knowledge and *understanding*" (p. 23). The advice given includes ways to engage students, establish a context for scientific exploration, propose explanations, and assign student reading and writing for understanding. For example, the *Pair Problem Solving Technique* in which "one student of the pair attempts to solve a problem while the other listens and tries to clarify what is being said" (p. 24), helps students learn to apply difficult concepts, and become aware of their thought processes and errors in reasoning. After reading this chapter, you will never teach your courses the same way again.

Chapter 4 discusses the problems preexisting misconceptions about science cause for students who are trying to understand science, and for teachers who are trying to teach it. The suggestions given will help you to identify the types of misconceptions your students have about psychology or scientific methodology in general, and to begin to correct them.

Evaluating Teaching and Learning

Chapter 5 looks at the evaluation of teaching and learning. Frequent feedback on what your students are learning is encouraged to allow you to know if your teaching is meeting the goals you have set, and to allow you an opportunity to revise your approach to improve teaching *during* the semester. Determining what students know in order to assign them grades is only one small part of this more complete assessment. A more thorough approach to assessment will enable you to teach so fewer students are lost to the discipline, or to the specific content of your course(s).

The same emphasis on student learning appears in chapters on tests and grading, and choosing and using instructional resources, from texts to the Internet. We are urged to know our students, in order to help raise their confidence about studying science, lower their mathematics anxiety, counteract their own and society's inaccurate ideas and attitudes, and better prepare them to know what science is. The appendices provide a helpful list of organizations offering a wide array of information as well as names of journals that address science education.

The Handbook is concise, clear, insightful, and incredibly helpful and stimulating. We recommend it highly.

Part 3

Using Technology

Chapter 12

Teaching With Overheads: Low Tech, High Impact

Neil Lutsky
Carleton College

D o you covet your neighbor's multimedia classroom presentation but lack the expertise to prepare your own? Is your administration unlikely to provide that state-of-the-art LCD (light crystal display) system that every other teaching psychologist seems to be using to project dynamic 3-D animation from their fancy laptop computer? Well, stop fretting!

In all likelihood, you already possess a powerfully effective technology: the lowly and commonplace overhead projector. While you may suffer anxiety attacks whenever your lecture depends on the performance of a machine that requires a cable, you can still aspire to be the perfect teacher— informative, stimulating, witty, and captivating!

Ready-Made vs. Do-It-Yourself

What can a simple overhead projector do? Most obviously, it can project transparencies from sets accompanying basic textbooks. Some textbook publishers even make overheads available for downloading from the world-wide web and these professionally prepared transparencies are worth using. Colorful and informative, they help students better understand important material. But textbook overheads often only repeat figures from the book, and may not address what an instructor wants to cover in a particular class.

The alternative this column promotes is a highly accessible, do-it-yourself approach to transparency construction and use. Any instructor can create compelling and helpful overheads using two or three common machines: a computer, a photocopier, and a transparency maker (which could be a dedicated machine, photocopier, or laser printer). Of course, access to a digital camera, slide and image scanner, multimedia stimuli, multimedia editing and presentation programs, and an LCD panel would be helpful,

---

This article first appeared in the May/June 1997 APS Observer.

but none of these resources is necessary to produce the highly effective teaching overheads described below.

Three Reasons to Use Overheads

Why might instructors want to invest even the modest amount of time required to prepare tailored overheads? What might overheads contribute to a classroom presentation?

Here are three reasons to add overheads to your teaching.

Attention

Effective teaching depends, fundamentally, on capturing and channeling students' attention. Overheads can help accomplish that throughout the class period. The moment the instructor puts a transparency on the projector, almost invariably students attend to the overhead and the instructor. Their attention will be brief if the overhead is unreadable or packed too densely with material. Student attention will be more intense if the overhead is engaging. The mere act of placing or changing an overhead on a projector usually interrupts the talk of a teacher, and that alone alerts students and prepares them to be influenced by the contents of an overhead. And you won't lose your students in the dark. Most conventional overhead projectors and some LCD systems for computer and video do not require dimming lights to achieve a visible display. Present a new overhead every five minutes or so and observe the positive effect on students' attention.

Effective Communication

The words, pictures, and graphics constituting overheads can help teachers communicate more effectively. First, overheads accommodate diverse student learning styles, because pictures and graphics may better convey a concept, finding, or model than an *equivalent* verbal description and because individuals can process words on a screen at their own pace. Second, overheads facilitate and almost demand clarity of expression. Words and other stimuli on an overhead make explicit the overall purpose, the structure of an argument, the definition of a concept, the description of a phenomenon, or the procedures and findings of a study.

Overhead presentations that demonstrate phenomena (see "Illustrative Uses" below) represent a particularly effective means to describe psychological effects and to convince students that those effects in fact occur. Moreover, teachers who use overheads model a means of public communication that students themselves are likely to employ in later professional roles.

Active Learning

Overheads can easily elicit active intellectual involvement in course material. Overheads may explicitly pose questions to students or present stimuli that questions address. For example, an overhead could describe the procedures of a study and students could be asked to predict the study's results. Or an overhead could help demonstrate a phenomenon, which students could then explain. Overheads could present a quotation from a reading or other source, or a newspaper headline or photo, and students could explain the events or ideas depicted. Such stimuli also serve as a common focus for a teacher and students and may help both become less self-conscious and more involved in shared problem-solving.

Finally, preparing overheads may promote a teacher's active learning when they require that teacher to identify overarching topical themes, to define terms precisely, to operationalize research procedures for a demonstration, to represent concepts and conceptual relationships visually, or to accomplish any of the other intellectual tasks necessary for overhead preparation.

Preparing Overheads

It is easy and enjoyable to prepare overheads. Simply invest a few minutes of your time and follow these simple tips. Start saving raw materials. Cartoons, quotations, newspaper headlines and articles, pictures, caricatures, results sections from noteworthy articles, the detritus of everyday life—ticket stubs, fortune cookie messages, children's drawings—all may serve as elements in overhead preparation. Anything that can be photocopied can be resized by a copier and then cut and pasted on an overhead master.

Harness Computing Power

Any word-processing program will allow you to type and print out items such as overhead labels, important terms and their definitions, outlines of a lecture or section of a talk, demonstration stimuli, and other verbal content. Use a presentation package to prepare professional looking slides, a graphic package to portray important research findings, an outlining program to construct a flow chart representing steps in a procedure or conceptual model, a painting program to create or manipulate images or models, an equation typesetting program for quantitative material, or a computerized snapshot program to capture instruction windows on your computer screen. (Those snapshots turn your overhead machine into a virtual computer and prove especially useful when teaching students about hardware and software use.)

Make the Overhead Readable

Use large type (i.e., 1/4-inch in height at a minimum; fonts of 24 to 48 points) and a readable font (e.g., the sans serif Helvetica or Swiss fonts). Remember that FEWER WORDS = BIGGER TYPE. The more concise your wording, the larger the type size you can use. Similarly, cartoons with short, direct captions (or none at all) will work much better than those with long captions, no matter how humorous the lengthy captions might seem. And don't forget to give viewers ample time to scan each overhead. For additional reinforcement of these points, see Estes (1993).

Keep it Simple

Do not represent more than a single concept on each overhead. Keep overheads visually simple with ample white space around the focal pictorial or verbal elements. Busy and complicated overheads can overwhelm viewers. It is best to use layered or consecutive overheads to present more complicated or structured content.

Add Some Color

Color may be original to an overhead source (and captured by a color photocopier) or added to a black and white overhead by attaching transparent colored plastic wrapping paper or commercially available color adhesives to the underside of a transparency.

Direct Viewers' Attention

Highlight or organize material using a pointer placed on an overhead or an overhead pen with colored washable inks. Keep in mind that viewers will naturally gravitate toward the upper left segment of an overhead; orient diagrams in light of that and don't place your focal element in the dead center of the overhead plane. Use overhead masks (see the following tip).

Create Suspense

Use opaque masks to progressively and selectively unveil the content of an overhead to induce audience anticipation and control attention. Trimmed manila file folders can serve as effective masks, and their translucency permits you to see the entire transparency even though viewers cannot.

Illustrative Uses

One of the pleasures of working with overheads is that their production and use offers a rich venue for teacher creativity. What follows briefly identifies common applications of this basic technology.

Create Dynamic Demonstrations

Overheads can contribute to compelling demonstrations of basic psychological phenomena (so much so that introductory texts often provide transparencies specifically for demonstration purposes). For example, it is simple to overlay duplicate overheads of an image designed to illustrate the relationship of perceived size and distance and then to move the top overhead to demonstrate the difference or equality of actual image sizes.

Even illusions of visual motion can be created on an overhead. Cowan (1974) describes how the phi phenomenon, for example, can be demonstrated by moving a vertical window back and forth to expose light coming from two small holes in a manila folder or other mask sitting on the projector. And Reed and Pusateri (1996) review uses of overheads and masks to simulate a tachistoscope or memory drum, or to present stimuli for reaction time and other cognitive studies.

Apply Psychology Broadly

Overheads can help convince students that psychological principles and findings have larger applicability in the *real* world. Newspaper stories, quotations from literature, cartoons, and even letters in advice columns can all be used as grist for a budding psychologist's intellectual mill. Ask students to apply a theory or finding to the events described or to contrast what a particular psychological perspective might suggest to the account or response given in the overhead stimulus. Often we share personal or other stories with students to serve this same purpose. Why not enrich that story telling with an overhead of materials associated with the events described?

Enhance Lecture Organization and Appeal

Teaching remains an activity in which we primarily talk to and with our students, but overheads can enhance that interaction. Use overheads to organize a talk by presenting an agenda, guiding questions, or basic themes and points at the beginning of a class session. Return to those overheads at the end of the class for review purposes and to show students what they have learned over the class period. Use overheads to highlight important names and terms (and their correct spellings), definitions and formulae, major theoretical claims, and empirical findings, and elements of structured argument.

Let Overheads Help Create a Positive Classroom Climate

Cartoons, in particular, may enliven a talk and add those dashes of humor that may not come naturally to your speaking style. Remember, although students may not always recognize what it takes to prepare a class presentation, they will notice and appreciate the concrete visual evidence your overheads provide of your investment in teaching.

Promote Focused Discussions

Orient discussions around readings and course content by posing questions about important text quotations or findings presented on an overhead. Compile lists of student ideas, responses, and questions on a blank overhead. Ask students to work in small groups to create their own overheads, which could then be shared with the class as a whole. For example, groups could sketch out a model of a psychological process, generate a research proposal to investigate some issue, identify and clarify confusing concepts or topics, or summarize the central points of an argument or claim. The entire class could then compare and contrast, critique, and address the materials presented by these groups.

So stop using the overhead projector as a coat rack! Flip that switch (but bring an extra bulb) and use the projector to inform your audience, energize your talk, demonstrate your claims, set a positive tone in class, compensate for some of your shortcomings as a teacher, and, most of all, aid your students' learning of psychology.

Recommended Readings and References

Cowan, T. M. (1974). Creating illusions of movement by an overhead projector. *Teaching of Psychology, 1*, 80-82.

Davis, B. G. (1993). *Tools for Teaching*, San Francisco: Jossey-Bass.

Estes, W. K. (1993). How to present visual information: What will we see in Chicago? *APS Observer, 6*(2), 6-9.

Gribas, C., Sykes, L., & Dorochoff, N. (1996). Creating overheads with computers. *College Teaching, 44*, 66-68.

Head, J. T. (1992). New directions in presentation graphics: Impact on teaching and learning. *New Directions for Teaching and Learning, 51*, 17-31.

Reed, S. K., & Pusateri, T. P. (1996). *Instructor's manual for Reed's Cognition: Theory and applications* (4th ed.). Pacific Grove, CA: Brooks/Cole.

Chapter 13

Thirteen Ideas to Help Computerize Your Course

James V. Ralston
Sprint PCS

Barney Beins
Ithaca College

Whether you're a computer neophyte or guru, you will find here ideas for some useful high-tech supplements to traditional education methods, and we hope to persuade you to explore further the many facets of computer-aided instruction.

Below is a brief description of 13 applications of computers to facilitate teaching of psychology. In 13 easy steps you can wean yourself from the shame of teaching without computers or update your computer utilization. While some steps sound complicated, most are rather simple, especially since more sophisticated equipment and software are becoming increasingly available and at decreasing prices.

Keep in mind, too, that as a member of an educational institution you, your students, or your department often will qualify for substantial discounts on software and equipment. For example, very sophisticated computer programs with retail prices in the hundreds or even thousands of dollars are sometimes available in "student versions," allowing students to learn on software that, while often not a full-featured version, is sufficient to enhance student training significantly.

Thirteen Steps to Computerization

1) Teach your students how to use computers

Of course, it's not the job of most psychologists to teach computer courses, but there are very good reasons to teach general and specific computing skills within psychology courses. Let's face it—not all your psychology majors are going to carve out a career in brain chemistry or group dynamics. Those who acquire sophisticated computer skills will be more competitive for jobs in the real world. Those who pursue careers in psychology will benefit particularly from detailed understanding of computers and their operation as well as computer programming at a system level through higher-level languages.

This article first appeared in the November 1996 APS Observer.

2) Digitize your textual materials

Recording your course materials on electronic media probably has the greatest cost-benefit ratio of any effort to add to or enhance the computerization of your teaching. Once in computer memory, materials can be modified easily for use in a wide variety of applications. For example, you can write examinations with a word processor and easily produce alternate forms of an exam.

3) Put your gradebook into an electronic gradebook or spreadsheet

Although useful gradebook programs are available, we've found that general-purpose spreadsheets are fine, and, in some ways, preferable to specialized gradebook software. Any decent spreadsheet has the capacity and flexibility to handle even the most unusual grading scheme, and the results can be easily exported to other applications, such as word-processors. For the less adventuresome, specialized gradebooks are still a large improvement over paper-based records. In either case, electronic gradebooks and spreadsheets save you from repetitive calculations and are much more malleable than more traditional gradebooks. You can almost completely automate the testing process if your institution has an optical scanning system that can produce ASCII text (i.e., plain alphanumeric characters devoid of special codes for features such as bold, italic, indent, tab). Have the ASCII file emailed to you. You can then import the file into your gradebook/spreadsheet file. This is very useful for large survey-type courses.

4) Digitize your analog materials

With the advent of computerized delivery systems such as the Internet, now is a great time to start digitizing your overhead transparencies, sound clips, and video clips. It only takes about a minute to convert an image to electronic form, and digitized materials are easy to incorporate into documents or computerized presentations, using presentation software (see the next item in this list).

5) Present traditional lecture materials

Several varieties of presentation software can help you organize and display notes and graphics on a projector screen. This is a great application of your newly digitized materials; and easily created animation can help engage students' interest. Computer-aided presentations help give a professional touch to your lectures. In order to show a computer display to a large class, you will need to connect your classroom computer to a projection system. This is accomplished with a projection plate that is placed over a high-intensity overhead projector.

6) Teach statistics

Want a novel way to show students how to calculate a standard deviation? Want an in-class method to empirically estimate the distance between the fovea and one's visual blind spot? There is nothing like a projected spreadsheet or statistical program to eliminate chalkboard calculations. Menu-driven statistics programs are also much easier for students to use than more traditional command-line systems, allowing students more time to appreciate the concepts underlying statistics (or, so we hope).

7) Simulate psychological processes or phenomena

Why just talk about neural networks or conditioning? Instead, show your students the real thing, or at least show them a reasonable approximation. There may be nothing so useful as a hands-on exercise in which students train a *virtual rat*, or process an image with a visual neural network. Some programs even allow students to generate hypothetical experimental designs and corresponding, stochastic data sets—allowing students to focus more on the analysis and interpretation of data than on the execution of experiments.

8) Use multimedia as tutorials

There are some multimedia (i.e., two or more types of media, such as text and pictures) titles that provide short sound clips and video clips as well as animations, and text, often in an interactive environment. These are distributed on diskettes, CD-ROM, the Internet, and laser disk.

Lecturing about psychopathology? Why not show a video clip of Charles Manson and let students work their way through a binary decision tree to arrive at a DSM-IV diagnosis? Multimedia is a great supplement to in-class content that may help clarify difficult concepts.

9) Conduct experiments or demonstrations

Experimental control programs generally present pictures, sounds, or video clips to subjects and allow the collection of various types of responses from subjects. There are even control files for the general-purpose experimental control programs or special-purpose programs that are preconfigured to conduct classic psychology experiments.

10) Use the Internet as a resource

Here is just a sampling of teaching-related Internet-based information.

Online card catalogs show the holdings of the Library of Congress and various university's libraries. Ever-evolving conversations about the teaching of psychology are available for participation by subscribing to a listserve.

Online tutorials are available for a variety of software. Remote participation in experiments is possible through several departmental web pages.

UseNet newsgroups provide innumerable opportunities to engage you in conversation in your special interest areas, provided that your computer server provides news feeds from UseNet. Want to get in on some continually evolving conversations about Jungian analysis? Then, subscribe to the appropriate UseNet newsgroup and read on! Several departmental web pages are viewable through a web browser program (e.g., Mosaic, Netscape). Dozens of such departmental pages are accessible through the APS web site at http://www.psychologicalscience.org.

11) Use the Internet as a delivery mechanism

The web can deliver anything that is in digital form, from pictures to experimental programs to administrative materials. Remember the course materials you just digitized? You can provide access to them through the web. If you want to put your materials on the web, it is primarily a matter of formatting the layout of your documents by embedding HTML (HyperText Markup Language) tags in an ASCII file. This task has been made trivial with the advent of WYSIWYG (What You See Is What You Get) web authoring programs, which require no knowledge of HTML. Once the files have been created, they need to be placed on a networked computer with web server software. Web-based materials provide the basis for an aesthetically appealing, paperless system that is accessible virtually anytime and anywhere.

12) Use the Internet as a communication device

You can make yourself more accessible to your students. Electronic mail, listserves, and UseNet newsgroups help break down barriers to communication between faculty and students, providing a nearly foolproof conduit between the two. It provides for *24-hour* office hours, so that students can get information from (e.g., class notes, reading assignments, data) and post information (e.g., completed quizzes or exams, reports, summaries of literature) to a centralized information center.

Electronic services can also help break down barriers between students. For example, they can share information among themselves, such as notes, data sets, or other collaborative works-in-progress. These email based services have already been successfully utilized in courses that ask students to offer observations or reactions on even the most sensitive topics. It is often argued that some students who are reticent to speak in a classroom are more likely to express themselves in these electronic forums.

13) Create new resources

In addition to the wealth of materials that reside in publishing houses or on the net, you can always make a significant contribution by adding your own content. At the least, adding content could mean that you could use a graphics program to illustrate some principle or concept, such as classical conditioning. Or, if you are a little more enterprising, you might write a program to emulate your favorite psychological process or phenomenon. Want to illustrate the effect of presbycusis on speech perception? Use a sound processing program to filter a digitized speech sample. It is also relatively easy to learn to use multimedia authoring software (i.e., programs for creating multimedia documents), so that you can quickly produce multimedia presentations on any topic.

These are just a few suggestions for computerizing your curriculum. If you want to follow-up, we strongly suggest that you contact your local academic computing center. Staff there should have display models of hardware and software or at least some helpful advice. If you lack an Internet connection, contact local, regional, or national Internet service providers and ask for their services and rates.

Recommended Readings and References

Kehoe, B. P. (1993). *Zen and the art of the Internet: A beginner's guide*. Englewood Cliffs, NJ: Prentice-Hall.

Kelley-Milbum, D., & Milbum, M. A. (1995). CYBERPSYCH: Resources for psychologists on the Internet. *Psychological Science, 6*, 203-211.

Issue 2 of Volume *25* of *Behavior Research Methods, Instruments & Computers* (1993) contains several articles on computer technology for psychological instruction and science.

The journal *Teaching of Psychology* publishes regular articles on computer use in teaching.

Part 4

In-Class Skills

Chapter 14

Developing Effective Lectures

Todd Zakrajsek
Southern Oregon University–Ashland

Lectures were once useful; but now when all can read, and books are so numerous, lectures are unnecessary.

—Samuel Johnson, 1799

Although I have a great deal of respect for Samuel Johnson, he missed the boat on this one. Lectures developed as a way to convey a large amount of information to a large group of people in a short period of time. They are still the most frequently used method for instruction in the college classroom, and this distinction is likely to continue. Lectures also happen to receive more abuse than any other method of teaching. Given the popularity of this approach to teaching and its important place in education, I propose that we take a break from bashing the college lecture and devote our attention to improving lectures through research, training, and shared knowledge.

In graduate school I took a one-credit hour course pertaining to teaching, and neither in that course nor at the teaching conferences I have attended over the years, do I recall a single session devoted to this topic. Here is an approach to teaching that we all use to some degree, and yet few of us have had any formal training, and whenever we talk about it all we hear is that it is an ineffective way to teach. I agree with Kaufman (1977) that "it seems obvious that at the very least something should be done to decrease the percentage of poor lecturers" (p. 188).

I have put together a few ideas designed to help us all lecture more effectively. These ideas have been generated from sources listed at the end of this article, comments from friends and mentors, and a few things that I have found to work well over the years.

Types of Lectures

An effective lecture results from an interaction of such variables as the nature of the material to be presented, your personality, and how you present

---

This article first appeared in the March 1998 APS Observer.

the material. There are many types of lectures, and it is important to try them all, seeing which ones best fit both your style and your goals for a specific class period or an entire course. One type may work best for you on a regular basis, but for a given block of material, or to provide variety, try some flexibility in your lecturing.

◆ Highly formal lectures are presentations to groups with no active audience participation.
◆ Informal lectures are based more on the personality of the presenter, are less structured, and allow for limited audience interaction.
◆ Provocative lectures are designed to challenge students' opinions and knowledge base, calling for an integration of information and perhaps a change in perspective.
◆ Lecture-demonstrations are used to show how something works.
◆ Discussion lectures present a topic and then make the students the primary participants, with the lecturer as a moderator.

When Lectures Work Well

In discussing the use of lectures with colleagues or in writing a teaching portfolio, faculty do not have to apologize for using the lecture method. Although well-controlled research is sparse, general findings suggest that the lecture method works well in the following circumstances (Prichard & Sawyer, 1994) to:

◆ Teach factual or perceptual information;
   Give students a variety of viewpoints that are not summarized in print;
   Stimulate and motivate students to do individual research in an area;
   Provide a summary of the background and history of the development of a subject matter;
   Explain vocabulary, definitions, and basic facts;
   Model the thinking process;
   Present an ordered and logical approach to an area of study; and
   Teach large numbers of students economically.

The key point is that to work well in these situations, the lecture must be of high quality. Developing and delivering a good lecture can be one of the most time consuming teaching methods around. Excellent lecturers—the ones who leave you in awe following their presentation—spend a lot of time in preparation.

   Information must be summarized from a variety of sources.
   Facts are checked and integrated into a coherent structure.
   Lectures may be videotaped and evaluated for effectiveness.
   Ineffective material is removed from the lecture and replaced.
   Material is continuously updated.

Organizing a Lecture — Be Prepared

It is a rare person who can enter the class as the period begins, deliver an effective lecture without preparation, and then walk out the door. Lecturing is not an easy way to teach. It takes careful planning and continuous refining. A high school speech teacher once told our class to "tell the audience what you will tell them, then tell them, then tell them what you told them." Start with some form of advanced organizer to let the students know what will be covered. Many textbooks provide an outline at the beginning of each chapter for this same reason. Write an outline on the board before class, or give the students a handout containing key points to be covered that day. A caution: if your outline contains more points than you will cover that day let the students know at the beginning of the class where you will stop. They often experience stress if there are points that you don't cover that day.

Consider what you will take into the class in the form of notes. I would suggest writing down as little information as you can. If you write down everything, you may end up reading to the group. Also, include notes to yourself. Many of my lecture notes look like screenplays with instructions—such as write this on the board, tell 'puppy story' here, ask students how many have had this happen to them, slow down for this next point—scattered throughout.

Starting the Lecture

The most common error is including too much information. Once students feel lost, they will probably remain lost for the rest of the lecture. Lowman (1995) indicates that most students can comprehend only about three to five points in a one hour lecture and four to five points in a one and one-half hour lecture. Davis (1993) provides several suggestions for helping the student understand your basic points.

- Use memorable examples (Galliano, 1997).
- Liberally use metaphors, analogies, anecdotes, and vivid images.
- Call attention to the most important points.
- Move from the simple to the complex, the familiar to the unfamiliar (Nairne, 1997).
- Begin with general statements followed by specific examples.
- Create a sense of order for the listener. Explain what you will cover, develop the ideas, then summarize.

Delivering the Lecture

Aside from the actual time and energy put into lecture content, the way in which the information is presented is very important. Students will not learn from a lecture if they are daydreaming, and one of the most common criticisms of lectures is that they are boring.

Yet they need not be. We have all heard lectures that were so exciting that it was disappointing to have them end. There are several things you can do to make your lectures more interesting, and to improve future lectures.

Choose the Right Style

Choose the lecture style best suited to your personality, the material, and your goals for the presentation.

Organize the material

Lectures should not wander from topic to topic. Present the information in a way that allows the student to follow a logical sequence of material.

Be Enthusiastic

You cannot expect the audience to be interested in the material if you are not.

Use Humor

You need not be a stand-up comedian to be a good presenter, but most good presenters know the value of humor. Students can often repeat a joke heard only one time, and material that is fun is often easier to remember. Use personal anecdotes and stories. I often tell students about events in my life that illustrate a psychological point. This provides a concrete example and demonstrates that I believe in what I am presenting. Humor, jokes, and stories are very effective, but should always pertain to the topic.

Make a Good Presentation

You may have to videotape yourself to improve in this area. Watch for distracting mannerisms such as: moving too much or not enough, awkward hand or eye movements, speaking in a monotone or, overuse of certain words or vocalizations (short silence is better than the often inserted um, ah, OK, or you know). Do not read from your notes. This style is painful for anyone to sit through. Read about the lecture method; there are some good resources. If you lecture often, you are doing a great deal of public speaking. Get a book or two on public speaking and learn from the experts, or even take a course on the subject.

Observe a Good Lecturer

There are many people giving lectures these days (although few admit they use this technique). Ask to sit in on other faculty members' classes. You can learn a great deal about what works and what doesn't by doing this. If you are interested in sitting in on a colleague's class, be certain to explain that you simply want to see how others lecture. Give them an easy out if they feel uncomfortable with your request, and plenty of lead time. Ask them to pretend you are not there, so that you don't disrupt the class. Ask them if they are willing to come to your class and give you some feedback about your lecturing.

If You Don't Know, Say So

When I first started teaching, I was so afraid of being asked a question that I couldn't answer that I would unintentionally respond to questions as though they were accusations. Then, one day when I couldn't answer a question, I simply said, "that is a really good question, I don't know what the answer is, but I will look it up and have an answer during the next class session." Many students later commented that they appreciated a teacher who was willing to admit when he or she didn't know something. Now I give one extra credit point for anyone who can stump me on a question (directly related to the lecture topic) and then bring the answer to the next class.

Watch the Audience

Students often tell me that one thing they really like is that I stop periodically and say "this last block of material didn't make any sense to you did it?" I then pause, and if they agree, we switch to a discussion format until they understand. There are many ways to determine whether students understand what you are presenting: rate of note taking, body posture, clarifying points with one another, and nodding.

Periodically Check for Understanding

Lectures can be passive for the students, so stop occasionally and make certain that they are understanding what you are presenting. There are several ways to accomplish this: periodically ask someone to summarize the last major point; collect notes and see what is being written; form small groups toward the end of the hour to discuss material presented during the lecture; have students list one item they liked best and one they had the most trouble understanding; and/or ask them to write down one thing that would have helped them to understand the material better. Keep in mind that reading the responses to some of these questions requires skin of considerable thickness.

Don't Lecture all the Time

The lecture is a great way to convey a lot of material, but it should not be used all of the time. Break up lectures with demonstrations, question and answer periods, audiovisual presentations, and computer work. Treat a class session as though you were a researcher collecting data, and have the students provide data. For example, have one-half of the students complete difficult anagrams, followed by moderately difficult anagrams. Have the other half complete easy anagrams and then moderately difficult anagrams. Ask how each subsample did on the moderate anagrams and tie to a lecture on learned helplessness.

Critically Evaluate your Lectures

Make notes to yourself immediately after class about what worked and what didn't. (Tim Sawyer, my undergraduate advisor, actually gives himself a grade after every lecture.) I have always updated my notes to provide the best possible content but it was only recently that I thought to work on how I deliver the material and to improve that aspect of the lecture.

Ending the Lecture

A good ending is very important.

◆ Summarize. Help the class see the importance of what you were presenting and why it was worth their time to attend.

◆ Finish with a logical and solid ending. Do not weaken your entire presentation by trying to add "just one more idea" before you end the lecture period.

◆ Invite questions and spontaneous discussion. Try to leave a few minutes for this. Try to assess students' understanding of the material. This is often a good way to end a class period.

McKeachie (1994) wrote that "effective lecturers combine the talents of scholar, writer, producer, comedian, showman, and teacher in ways that contribute to student learning" (p. 53). This is not an easy task, and if you really want to be a good lecturer, it is a task that requires constant work. The good news is that help does exist, but not enough. As I proposed at the beginning of this column, we must stop bashing the lecture method and work harder to improve it as a teaching method. There are many outstanding lecturers out there, and I for one would like to hear what they have to say.

Recommended Readings and References

Davis, B. G. (1993). *Tools for teaching.* San Francisco, CA: Jossey-Bass.

Galliano, G. (1997). Exemplary examples for teaching and learning. *APS Observer, 10*(4), 28-30, 37.

Grasha, A. F. (1996). *Teaching with style.* Pittsburgh, PA: Alliance.

Lowman, J. (1995). *Mastering the techniques of teaching* (2nd ed.). San Francisco: Jossey-Bass.

Kaufmann, W. (1977). *The future of the humanities.* New York: Reader's Digest Press.

McKeachie, W. J. (1994). *Teaching tips: Strategies, research, and theory for college and university teachers* (9th ed.). Lexington, MA: D. C. Heath.

Nairne, J. (1997). Bringing relevance into the classroom: Lead with the function of behavior. *APS Observer, 10*(5), 26-27, 42.

Prichard, K. W., & Sawyer, R. M. (1994). *Handbook of college teaching.* Westport, CT: Greenwood Press.

Chapter 15

Enhancing Student Learning Through Exemplary Examples

Grace Galliano
Kennesaw State University

I hear and I forget. I see and I remember. I do and I understand.
—ancient Chinese proverb

I rely on this old Chinese proverb daily to guide my teaching, and I keep it posted on the wall next to my desk as a constant reminder of the lesson contained in it. In the ideal psychology classroom, students would come to understand phenomena—such as classical conditioning—by actually undergoing classical conditioning, or *diffusion of responsibility* by playing a role in a pretend scenario designed to demonstrate this social phenomenon.

But the real classroom is not ideal. Large classes often involve hearing lectures punctuated by an occasional demonstration. Even the *doing* that occurs within the laboratory is limited by time, equipment, and the nature of the concepts with which we deal. Yet the dedicated instructor's ultimate goal continues to be learner understanding.

Given the limitations mentioned above, we often find that an effective method for making our lectures more meaningful is the use of examples. Examples can improve both teaching and learning, in classes large and small, while requiring little preparation or class time, and no equipment.

In preparing this column, I examined relevant research on cognitive processes and an array of sources in educational psychology. Then came the fun part: I interviewed about a dozen colleagues from several disciplines and a dozen students about the use of examples in teaching and learning. Without exception, my interviewees looked off into the distance, and began their fourth or fifth sentence with the words, "For example, when ..." This was usually followed by a little giggle when they realized how easily they fell into illustrating or emphasizing some point by using an example. Most agreed that using examples was among the most powerful, frequent, and useful instructional and learning strategies, improving teaching by the

This article first appeared in the July/August 1997 APS Observer.

use of metaphors, analogies, and models. But few had ever stopped to think about the nature of examples. What makes one more helpful than another? Exactly how do examples facilitate mastery and understanding? What are the qualities of both good and bad examples? What about the difficulties of coming up with good examples?

Why Should You Use Examples?

To Form Connections to Existing Knowledge

Let's begin by updating the concept of the student as an *empty slate* upon which we *write* psychological knowledge. Cognitive psychology has made it clear that a *Velcro patch* may be a more appropriate metaphor: Some things will stick to the learner and others will not. To have a concept stick, it must be connected to something the learner already knows. Cognitivists call this encoding.

The degree to which something is meaningful or understood is related to the number of connections or associations formed between a new idea and others already in the learner's long-term memory. Students refer to the process of creating such connections as studying; psychologists call it elaboration. Ideally, examples are strong connecting agents.

To Actively Organize Understanding

A second reason to use examples is that learners are not passive recipients, but rather are active organizers of their own understanding. Learners organize information and construct a meaning for information that makes sense to them, regardless of how chaotic or superficial that organization may seem to the instructor. Poor students who appear to organize virtually nothing may lack the relevant background knowledge to which to attach new concepts. Thus, little understanding results.

An example is a good one if it acts as a catalyst to facilitate the process of connecting new information to the knowledge the learner brings to that lecture or activity. An example is also a good one if it matches a student's learning style. Thus, a good example for students who learn best when material is related to their everyday lives connects a new idea or concept to their real world. Using more than one example is better to the extent that it increases the chances that the concept will be made meaningful to more students.

To Construct Knowledge

A third lesson from cognitive psychology that supports the use of examples is that knowledge must be built up by each learner. It cannot be transmitted on a "conveyor belt" of words. Meaningfulness or understanding is a subjective construction based on the individual's experience. In attempting to teach our students about human language, for example, we might tell them that unlike naturally occurring animal communication, human language is characterized by *displacement* and *productivity*. While most students can repeat this back to us (and we can reinforce this repetition), it is only through examples that these concepts take on any meaning or adhesiveness. So, we can easily convey the psycholinguistic concept of displacement, since we all have had direct experience with lies and lying. Students can quickly grasp how displacement is related to the uniquely human ability to lie, because one can demonstrate how language allows us to communicate about events that are displaced (i.e., removed from the speaker and listener in time and/or place). This permits communicating about plausible (or even implausible) things that did not (or could not) have happened (i.e., lying).

Or, try this example to teach the linguistic concept of productivity. Have a student open a textbook to a page at random and read a randomly selected sentence. Then ask what the probability is that any two people (now or in the future) will produce exactly that sentence.

Since the probability is virtually zero, it brings home the message that human language allows and encourages unique productions. Examples facilitate an understanding of abstract concepts such as displacement and productivity.

Practical Tips—The Basics

The More Vivid the Example, the Better

The teacher wants the example to create a powerful image in the learner's mind. At the very least, a vivid example can move the learner from merely hearing to seeing.

Connect examples to the student's everyday experience, not the teacher's. My first years of teaching social psychology were filled with great examples based on my decades of riding the New York subway and walking urban streets. These colorful images went over like the proverbial lead balloon with my thoroughly suburban/rural students who move through the world encased in cars, actively avoiding activities that require any lengthy walking in public.

Apply the KISS Principle: Keep It Simple, Stupid

Complex examples are full of irrelevant features that interfere with students grasping the key components of the example. William James tells of the teacher who used an example to teach the passive voice. The teacher explained that a murderer says, "I am killing you," an example of the active voice. The victim says, "I was killed," and that's the passive voice. The child asked how someone who was dead could speak. The impatient teacher responded that the statement was made just before the victim died. Later, when asked to explain the passive voice, the child described it as "the voice that you speak with when you ain't quite dead." Simple examples decrease the frequency with which that voice is heard in our classes.

Make Abstract Ideas Concrete by Using Several Examples

Move from theoretical to real-life examples, and from simpler examples to more complex ones. Be sure the examples differ in significant ways. One of my more successful uses of examples (as measured by exam scores) was in a lecture on learning principles such as positive and negative reinforcement, and stimulus control. I illustrated each concept with examples involving a rat in a Skinner Box, a young child, and finally a college student.

Point out how essential features of the concept are contained in the example. Evolutionary principles suggest that organisms evolve physical features that improve their performance in competition with others, thus increasing the likelihood of survival and reproduction. Sociobiology applies these principles to behavior (e.g., cooperation, competition, male promiscuity, and female selectivity). Can the same principles be applied to complex organizations such as corporations or government agencies? Have students identify the similar and distinctive features of these entities. What is it about organizations that allows them to compete successfully with others and survive?

The Advanced Course

Ask learners to generate new examples of a recently presented concept. Pairing students to collaborate on this activity facilitates interaction and active learning, even in a large lecture section. They can write their examples on index cards to be collected and read to the class. Warning: an instructor may need a strong constitution to survive students' constructions of this new knowledge, but discussing why an example is inadequate often improves understanding of the concept (and is good training for the type of exam questions described below).

Offer novel examples or scenarios in the stem of a multiple-choice exam question. Then ask what principle or concept is illustrated. On essay questions, ask for a *new* example of some concept introduced during class. If students are told to expect that such questions will occur, they might spend time trying to identify or create novel examples, and understand the material better in the process.

Use advance organizers. When I first read about the concept of *advance organizers*, I connected it to the more familiar concept of analogy. An advance organizer or analogy is an initial statement that provides a structure for new information and relates it to what the student already knows. For example, (ooops!), the body's immune system is often compared to a nation's military defense forces. Each component of the immune system deals with enemies in specialized ways much as a navy, an air force, or a land army would. Can the students carry the analogy further and account for immune system equivalents of elements such as routine patrols, double agents?

Consider cartoons as examples. Humor often results from an understanding of the principle referred to in a cartoon. For example, (ooops, again!) a recent *New Yorker* cartoon showed a defendant testifying in court. The caption read, "I picked up the gun and loaded it. I pointed it at him. And then suddenly shots rang out." The cartoon provided a lively image with which to begin a discussion of attribution processes. Another of my colleagues assigns students to bring in cartoons illustrating concepts discussed in class.

Become a CaGEE. Become a conscientious Collector and Generator of Excellent Examples. Look everywhere for them, and they will come. Examine relevant texts, ask colleagues about how they present concepts, and begin labeling your everyday experiences. Evaluate the examples you come up with by asking students (either post-lecture, post-exam, or post-course) about whether particular examples worked or not.

Glory in the superb example. Share it with others. For example, (ahhhhh!) in a research methods course, I struggled to make the concepts of within-group and between-group variation understandable. Finally, it came to me. I returned to the next class with three very different muffin pans, each filled with muffins. Students could compare variations among the muffins within each pan with the overall differences between pans. This example has been used by almost all of my colleagues and has been presented at numerous teaching conferences.

Caveats

There is an ongoing controversy about whether it is useful to compare and contrast examples and non-examples of concepts. Some researchers conclude that non-examples of a concept allow the learner to identify the important features of a concept. Others believe that because of the fuzzy boundaries of many psychological concepts, non-examples merely cloud the issue for many learners.

Beware of examples that may be offensive to or exclude certain groups. For example, (there it is again) my undergraduate education was peppered with sports-related lecture examples, particularly in the sciences. References to *punting*, (or was it *bunting?*), setups, or quarterbacking, might as well have been in another language for all the clarity they provided to this nonathletic person.

Beware of examples that become shaggy-dog stories, so that their connection to the concept is crushed under personal idiosyncrasies and irrelevant details. This is often what students mean when they complain about instructors "going off on a tangent."

Beware of violating personal privacy for the sake of a vivid image. A colleague recounted how he had used an unusual interpersonal interaction to illustrate a psychological principle. The person in the example was easily identifiable and my colleague was embarrassed when students recognized the person in the example.

While as teachers we are truly fascinating beings to our students, and examples from our personal lives are inevitably quite scintillating, beware of talking too much about yourself. Also, while our children are really animated psychology textbooks who live out virtually every known developmental concept, their Wunderkind qualities may wear thin with our students as the semester winds down.

It's Simple...

William James wrote that good teaching was really very, very simple. All that the instructor had to do was to

> ...simply work your pupil into such a state of interest in what you are going to teach ... that every other object of attention is banished from [the] mind; then reveal it ... so impressively that he [or she] will remember the occasion to his [or her] dying day; and finally, fill [the student] with devouring curiosity to know what the next steps in connection with the subject will be. (1958, p. 25)

Good examples can help us complete this simple assignment.

Recommended Readings and References

Ausubel, D. P. (1963*). The psychology of meaningful verbal learning.* New York: Grune & Stratton.

Corkill, A. J. (1992). Advance organizers: Facilitators of recall. *Educational Psychology Review, 4*, 33-67.

Eggan, P., & Kauchak, D. (1994). *Educational psychology: Classroom connections* (2nd ed.). New York: Macmillan.

James, W. (1958). *Talks to teachers on psychology.* New York: W. W. Norton. Original publication, 1899.

McKeachie, W. J. (1994). *Teaching tips: Strategies, research and theory for college and university teachers* (9th ed.). Lexington, MA: D. C. Heath.

Petty, O. & Jansson, L. C. (1987). Sequencing examples and non-examples to facilitate concept attainment. *Journal for Research in Mathematics Education, 18*, 112-25.

Tennyson, R. D., & Park, O. (1980). The teaching of concepts: A review of the instructional design literature. *Review of Educational Research, 50*, 55-70.

Zook, R. (1991). Effects of analogical processes on learning and misrepresentation. *Educational Psychology Review, 3*, 41-72.

Chapter 16

The Function of Behavior

James S. Nairne
Purdue University

A s instructors of introductory psychology, we try hard to bring relevance into the classroom. We want the course material to be di-
gestible and meaningful, but our best efforts can be met by blank
stares, or, at worst, empty chairs. Are your students mystified by the topics
in the introductory course? Do they fail to understand why coverage of
learning is filled with drooling dogs and key-pecking pigeons? Are they
turned off by topics such as attribution theory, the availability heuristic, or
synaptic transmission? Do they wonder why there is a section on biology?

Part of the problem may be our ingrained tendency, as instructors, to
do things backwards in the classroom. We typically present an abstract
topic, such as classical conditioning or attribution theory, and delay treatment of its relevance, function, and purpose until deep into the discussion.
Rather than leading with the function, as we should, we lead with the topic
itself (e.g., classical conditioning) and expect the student to assume that
it's important. Such an organizational scheme is fraught with difficulties—
not just pedagogical ones, but philosophical ones as well.

Stop Teaching Like a Structuralist

To place the argument in historical context, consider what James
Rowland Angell said about the proper way to treat mental processes in his
American Psychological Association presidential address in 1906:

> It makes a great difference whether one is directing attention pri-
> marily to the discovery of the way in which a mental process oper-
> ates, and the conditions under which it appears, or whether one is
> engaged simply in teasing apart the fibers of its tissue. The latter
> occupation is useful and for certain purposes essential, but it often
> stops short of that which is as a life phenomenon the most essen-
> tial (pp. 64-65).

Angell's comments in this case were directed at the structuralists who
proposed that the topics of psychology were best attacked by breaking them

This article first appeared in the September 1997 APS Observer.

into fundamental elements—much like how a chemist analyzes a chemical compound. Along with fellow functionalists like William James, Angell was convinced that this approach was fundamentally misguided. It is not possible to understand a psychological process, he argued, without focusing first on the function that the process serves for the organism—that is, its adaptive value. To use an analogy that William James made famous, you cannot expect someone to understand a house by picking apart its bricks and mortar. You need a clear idea of what the structure is for—what function the house is designed to serve—before things like bricks and mortar will begin to make sense. They are understandable only in terms of the role they play in some larger picture.

Sounds fairly noncontroversial, doesn't it? I suspect that most modern psychologists would agree with Angell and James, and, the field continues to embrace many of the basic tenets of the functionalists approach. Yet for some reason when we get into the classroom we continue to present psychology as if we were all structuralists rather than functionalists. We force-feed our students lots of facts about a topic—we break it down into bits—and we relegate function to a secondary role.

Introductory Textbooks Are Part of the Problem

If you need convincing, open virtually any introductory text and examine the chapter outlines. You will find that the subject-matter in each of the chapters is broken down into a series of elements; in the case of learning it's a set of procedures called classical conditioning, operant conditioning, and observational learning. These elements are then broken down further in subtopics—acquisition, extinction, generalization, and so on.

You will find nothing in the organizational structure of most learning chapters to indicate anything about function or purpose—there will be little, if anything, in the organization to indicate why these topics are important, or even relevant to the study of learning. Only deep in most chapters, if at all, will you find any reference to relevance or function, usually in sections called "Applications."

Is it any wonder students rarely have any idea why we cover the topics we do? We have engaged the students in "teasing apart the fibers" of learning rather than directing their attention to the function and purpose of these processes in everyday life. I am convinced that relegating function to a secondary role is a recipe for disaster in the classroom. Not only is it a poor pedagogical technique, producing bored and mystified students, but it fails to build on one of the most important lessons of 20th century psychology: You cannot understand a psychological process without first considering its proper context.

The Prescription: Frame Your Lectures Around Adaptive Problems

What is the secret to putting function first in the classroom? Rather than leading with the facts and methods specific to various topics (e.g., classical and operant conditioning), try framing your lecture around a relatively simple set of real-world adaptive problems. Then, the solutions inherent in a particular psychological process (e.g., conditioning) can be illustrated in relation to that real-world problem (or other problems) under consideration.

For example, one of the most important things that we learn about in our environment is that certain events are reliable predictors of other specific events. For example, it's useful to know that if we're walking along a mountain trail and hear a sudden rattling sound nearby, we could encounter a dangerous snake on our path. Classical conditioning is a set of procedures that tells us how people learn about signals in their environment. It's not merely a procedure for getting a dog to drool in response to a ringing bell; it's a preparation for studying how expectancies are acquired—how we learn that certain events predict the occurrence of other events. By leading with the adaptive problem—learning about signals—the student is prepared to understand and appreciate classical conditioning for what it really is: a set of procedures that help psychologists learn about the signaling properties of events.

With operant conditioning, a similar logic applies. Humans and other animals need to learn about the consequences of their behavior. Children need to learn that if they flick the tail of a cat once too often, they might receive an unwelcome surprise; the family dog will learn that if he hangs around the dinner table, an occasional scrap of pork chop might come his way. This is not rocket science. Students immediately recognize that learning about the consequences of behavior is important, and operant conditioning makes sense as a tool for helping them understand how we solve this important adaptive problem.

Finally, for observational learning, again there is obvious adaptive value in learning by observing others. Think about what the world would be like if we could only learn through direct trial and error. We might learn to avoid eating certain foods, for example, but only after eating them and getting sick. Our children could learn not to play in the street, but only if they successfully leap out of oncoming traffic in time. Observational learning (e.g., modeling) thus becomes a relevant and meaningful topic to the student.

Notice that we don't have to change the topics that are covered. Traditional *learning* material is simply reframed to emphasize function first. Classical, operant, and observational learning are presented as solutions to everyday adaptive problems.

The Advantages of Adaptive Problem-Solving

I am convinced that framing your lectures around practical problems offers a number of advantages:

◆ The subject-matter of psychology becomes more relevant. You are giving students a reason why they should care about a procedure such as classical conditioning, and they are likely to pay more attention and learn more, as a result.

◆ The resulting discussion naturally promotes critical thinking. When you lead with an adaptive problem, the student is forced to figure out why the process or procedure being discussed actually helps resolve the problem. How exactly do the principles of classical conditioning help us learn about the signaling properties of events? What is it about the procedures of operant conditioning that tells us how we learn about the consequences of behavior? You don't need any special trick to get the students to think critically—it falls directly out of the organizational structure.

◆ This organizational structure also makes it easier to remember what the chapter is about. It's easier to remember that we talked about signals and consequences than to remember abstract terms such as classical and operant conditioning. Giving the student four or five adaptive problems provides a nice rubric for chapter organization and helps to classify and categorize the details of the lectures.

◆ I believe that psychology as a whole gains cohesion when the material is presented with a functional theme. People don't act haphazardly; they think, act, and feel for reasons. We're always trying to resolve some on-line problem—even if it's something as simple as crossing the street without being hit by a car. Many of our behaviors are best understood as adaptive reactions to the problems we face.

◆ Finally, when we stress the idea that our behaviors reflect the problems we face, it is easier to get students to appreciate the importance of individual differences. People from different cultures or socioeconomic classes, for example, are faced with unique sets of problems to solve, and many of the individual differences that we see reflect this fact. A discussion of individual differences and cultural diversity flows naturally from the problem-solving approach.

Apply Adaptive Problem-solving Widely

We've only considered the topic of learning, but this same approach can be used to present most other topic areas in the introductory course, or other courses.

Biological Processes

When you're talking about biological processes you can introduce the mechanics of neural transmission by highlighting the problem of internal communication. If you're driving and a small child runs into your path, that message needs to get from the environment to your brain and down to the muscles controlling your arms and legs.

Sensation and Perception

Similarly, when teaching sensation and perception, it is clear that we need a way to translate environmental messages, which come in the form of electromagnetic or physical energy, into the electrochemical language of the nervous system. We need some internal translator to change what are quite different external messages into a common internal code. The principles of transduction help us solve this very important adaptive problem.

Further, once the message reaches the brain, we need to maintain stability in the image interpretation. As you watch someone move across a room, the two-dimensional retinal array changes dramatically, but we still see the same person, who remains constant in appearance, shape, and size. How? Well, the answer lies in a discussion of organizational principles in perception. Again, the idea is to introduce the topic as a kind of solution to an easy to understand adaptive problem.

Social Psychology

As a final example, consider attribution theory. I suggest that once again you lead with a concrete adaptive problem. Suppose you're walking down the street, and you see a sloppily-dressed man weaving towards you. Do you help him? Do you avoid him or hide from him? In cases like this, we need to interpret the behavior of others—to assign causes to behaviors so we can react appropriately. Attribution theory and social schema are then solutions to an important and easy to understand adaptive problem.

Put Function First

I encourage you to try the adaptive problem solving approach in your lectures. I've found that it works extremely well. Putting function first provides a nice counterbalance to textbooks, which always seem to do it backwards. This is one way to get our students to be enthusiastic about the subject matter. Lead with the function of the topic and your students will thank you as a result.

Recommended Readings and References

Angell, J. R. (1907). The province of functional psychology. *Psychological Review, 14,* 61-91.

Nairne, J. S. (1997). *Psychology: The adaptive mind.* Pacific Grove, CA: Brooks/ Cole.

Chapter 17

Class Discussions: Promoting Participation and Preventing Problems

Thomas J. Kramer
James H. Korn
St. Louis University

"I tried to have a discussion today, but hardly anybody said anything. You'd think a class of 95 students really would get into arguing about Jung's theory of the collective unconscious."

We suspect that many class discussions use the following format. The instructor lectures, pauses, then asks the class, "what do you think about X?" Most students either try to look busy, continue to read the newspaper, or wait for this irritation to pass so they can continue to take notes. The only advice we have for instructors using this approach is, don't bother.

Goals of Class Discussions

A discussion is an exchange of ideas where all members of the group have an opportunity to participate and are expected to do so to some degree. Discussions are the best way to accomplish at least three important objectives: (1) to integrate course content with personal experience, (2) to explore the basis for feelings and opinions of one's self and others, and (3) problem solving. Class discussion is a good way to accomplish other important educational objectives, such as developing critical thinking skills and learning to appreciate the ideas of others.

Guidebooks that provide tips for beginning teachers always include chapters on managing discussions, with advice on how to handle problems such as students who talk too much or not at all. These books emphasize the importance of preparing for discussions, with the preparation usually recommended for teachers rather than the students. Our purpose in this column is to suggest techniques that can be used to help students become good participants in class discussions, and perhaps prevent problems from arising later in the semester.

Practical Problems

Large Classes and the Limits of Time and Space

In theory, size is no limit for small group discussions. Any class can be

This article first appeared in the September 1996 APS Observer.

divided into subgroups. The logistical limits are set primarily by space and time. There should be sufficient space to minimize noise and cross-talk between groups, and time may be needed for reports from each group to the whole class. The sheer size of a class may put realistic constraints on small group discussion: try to imagine forming 100 small groups in a class of 600.

The limits of space and time lead us to conclude that discussions, as we have defined them, are not practical in classes larger than 100. You can have question and answer sessions, develop a dialogue with a few favorite students, and use writing or other individual active learning exercises, but these are not discussions. In large classes students can be asked to pair up or to form buzz groups, but there is no control over the content of the conversations and it would be difficult to do more than sample the results of these discussions.

Discussion Group Size

We think that discussions are most effective in groups of four to nine, and suggest breaking larger classes down into multiple small groups. As the size of the whole group increases beyond 10 it becomes more difficult for all to be heard and easier for students to fall into passivity while the teacher assumes a more dominant role.

Forming the Discussion Group

How do you form the groups? If you let students choose their own groups, those who know each other will stay together, which may lead to a situation where one or two strangers in the group are ignored. Counting off is a better method of assignment to groups, e.g., start in the front row and count off by five's. We favor changing the composition of the groups during the semester so that students encounter different learning styles.

The Fish-Bowl Technique

It is impossible to avoid passivity when classes have more than 25 students, but using the fishbowl technique allows the instructor to involve all students in discussions sometime during the semester. Select six to eight students to form an inner-circle for the discussion. The remaining students are observers and are responsible for taking notes on the content of the discussion and forming questions or comments of their own. When the inner circle discussion has been completed, time should be allowed for other students to comment or ask questions. If time permits, a new inner circle can be formed. Space is not a problem with the fish bowl, but class size again presents limits. In larger classes there will be fewer opportunities for participation, and shy students will be even more reluctant to become the focus of attention.

Quiet or Shy Students

Even in small groups, some students are quiet. When we use learning logs, these students often describe their anxiety about revealing their ideas. Stating that all students are expected to participate in a discussion is likely to heighten that anxiety.

We have these suggestions concerning shy students. First, the course description should make it clear that discussion is expected, and this should be emphasized in the first meeting of the class. Second, help should be available for shy students, from either the instructor or a counseling center. We strongly prefer helping students learn to participate, rather than helping them avoid taking part. Third, be accepting of degrees of participation. Students who have the courage to confront their shyness need time to develop, and all of us have bad hair days, when things are going terribly, and we need to be QUIET.

Promoting Participation

There are three things an instructor can do to promote full participation in class discussions, which means active listening as well as talking, and to prevent the most common discussion problems: establish clear ground rules, clarify instructor and student roles, and provide training.

Establishing Ground Rules

We define a discussion as an exchange of ideas where all members of the group have an opportunity to participate and are expected to do so to some degree. It is difficult for students to participate, however, if the instructor is doing almost all of the talking. Most instructors dominate the conversation even though they may not intend to do so. Brown and Atkins (1988) determined that instructors talk as much as 86 percent of the time during discussions. Establishing ground rules will help to ensure more balanced participation.

When a group agrees publicly on how to carry out its work, the purpose is not to stifle behavior but to reduce ambiguity, promote participation, and maintain order. Ground rules can be set either by asking students to participate in developing them, or suggesting a list that is open to modification. Asking the class to generate their own rules increases commitment, but when the course is just starting it seems reasonable to suggest guidelines with input from the class, and be open to revision after a few discussions have taken place.

We assume that we want people to be open to sharing their views, that we want as diverse a set of views as possible, that participation is to be maximized, and that agreement is not a necessary outcome. Given these assumptions we offer the following guidelines that apply to both the instructor and the students (adapted from Schwartz, 1994):

◆ The discussion always starts with a question that all members understand.
◆ Some level of participation is expected of everyone, but members may participate at different rates or levels.

◆   Domination of the conversation by one or two people is unacceptable.

◆   Let people finish their thought: do not interrupt.

◆   Listen: concentrate on what others are saying rather than on formulating a response.

Use the techniques of paraphrasing and summarizing to increase understanding.

Ask for and give the basis for opinions or observations.

Divergent views are encouraged: assume that everyone may have a piece of the truth.

Debating the goodness, badness, right or wrong of a position is discouraged.

Be specific: use examples whenever possible.

Keep the discussion focused on the question at hand.

Share: rotate roles and responsibilities for discussion management within the group.

Post your ground rules during class discussions.

Clarify Roles

The instructor can fill one of three roles: leader, facilitator, or observer. For a successful discussion it is critical for the instructor to understand her or his role and to clarify it for the class. At the same time, students should understand that they are expected to participate at an appropriate level, listen with an open mind, show respect for the views of others, and follow the ground rules established for the class.

The instructor as leader is an active participant, who contributes ideas when they seem relevant, but focuses on asking questions rather than giving answers. Given the ground rules above, the instructor needs to move toward being an equal partner in the discussion and avoid dominance. Instructor dominance can be reduced by having an observer monitor the time they speak, until it is reduced to 50 percent or less. The instructor also can boomerang questions back to the class so that students will provide answers.

As facilitator, the instructor does not participate in the discussion itself, but helps to manage it. This includes keeping the conversation on track, helping to even out the amount of participation by individuals, paraphrasing and summarizing, and encouraging students to respond to one another.

The instructor must become an observer when the class is divided into small groups. In this format, one student in each group is assigned the facilitator role. This student helps to manage the conversation in the small group just as the instructor might do, including holding the group accountable for following the ground rules. Another student has the responsibility of summarizing and reporting out to the larger group on the main points brought out in the discussion. As observer, the instructor clarifies the discussion questions in the beginning, monitors the process and progress of each group, manages the reporting out, summarizes points across the groups, and draws out the implications of the discussion.

Involving students in the facilitation and management of discussions provides them with an opportunity to learn valuable communication skills, to begin to see the process that occurs in a group interaction, and to assume more responsibility for their own learning, and prepares students to operate more effectively in groups outside the classroom.

Provide Training

Active participation in a discussion includes speaking at appropriate times and listening carefully to understand what others are saying. Most students and teachers have had no formal training in these skills, so we suggest that this be provided either by the instructor or a colleague with more experience in this area. We suggest devoting class time to the introduction, demonstration, and practice of most or all of the following:

◆ Participation
◆ Paraphrasing and summarizing
◆ Listening
◆ Acceptance of divergent views
◆ Keeping on track
◆ Dealing with domination
◆ Interruptions
◆ Handling conflict
◆ Enforcing the ground rules
◆ Facilitation

How much time should be devoted to training? You may have a lot of material to cover, but consider your objectives. If you want to accomplish those objectives for which discussion is best suited, then it is worth the time. We happen to disagree on how this should be done. Kramer believes that two hours of training is time well spent. Learning these skills requires many examples and a reasonable amount of practice.

Korn thinks that in 45 minutes, an instructor can explain the reasons for discussions, what makes a good discussion, present the ground rules, and find a few volunteers who will model what has been learned. Feedback after later discussions will provide the advanced training. If even 45 minutes seems like too much, then discussions may not be that important for you and you shouldn't mess up your lectures with all that noise from students.

Regardless of how much time one allocates to training in the beginning of a course, discussion skills require reinforcement. After each of the first two sessions, review the discussion process: how students feel about it and how it might be improved. Then make appropriate adjustments in the discussion format.

It is impossible to guarantee the success of all class discussions, but we think this method is more likely to work if you know what your objectives are and establish ground rules for your class. Clarify your role as leader, facilitator, or observer, and then help students understand what is expected of them by providing training in discussion techniques. Finally, evaluate both the discussion process (e.g., the extent to which the rules were followed) and the outcomes. One final bit of advice is to be patient and trust the process.

Recommended Readings and References

Brown, G., & Atkins, M. (1988). *Effective teaching in higher education*. London: Methuen.

Davis, B. J. (1993). *Tools for teaching*. San Francisco: Jossey-Bass.

Doyl, M., & Straus, D. (1983). *How to make meetings work*. New York: Jove.

Schwartz, R. M. (1994). *The skilled facilitator*. San Francisco: Jossey-Bass.

Chapter 18

Tell and Show:
The Merits of
Classroom Demonstrations

Douglas A. Bernstein
University of Illinois at Urbana-Champaign

After years of watching undergraduates nod off during what I thought were well-organized and fascinating lectures on research methods in psychology, I had no choice but to become a psychic. Expanding on an idea suggested by Morris (1981), I now casually mention my psychic ability on the first day of each semester, claiming that it emerged in the aftermath of a car accident that had left me in a coma for several days.

Students are invariably enthralled; they can tell this is going to be a really good course! After lamenting that there will be no time in the course to explore parapsychology, I offer to demonstrate my powers of psi by trying to predict the future or read someone's mind. A few simple but very impressive tricks—described in magic books, textbook instructor's manuals, and other sources—are more than enough to convince students that I am indeed capable of precognition and telepathy.

Their astonishment is short-lived, because I immediately debunk the tricks (without revealing the methods of trickery) and assign as homework the task of explaining how I might have accomplished *psychic* feats. The next class session is inevitably a lively one in which students propose a number of explanatory hypotheses and suggest research designs capable of eliminating incorrect alternatives. Reading the assigned chapter on research design makes the students' task easier, and they seem a lot more interested in that chapter than their counterparts in my pre-psychic days.

Using *psychic* demonstrations to teach research design takes a bit longer than presenting a lecture on that topic; indeed, by their very nature, most classroom demonstrations take time away from lecturing. However, I think there are at least three reasons why this may not be such a bad idea.

Three Reasons to Use Classroom Demonstrations

1)   Because demonstrations are distinctive and offer a change of pace, they tend to attract students' attention. This is good, because there is evidence that most students remain focused on our lectures mainly during the first ten minutes of class (Stockin, 1994). The attention-getting value of dem-

This article first appeared in the July/August 1994 APS Observer.

onstrations is especially high when all students can actively participate in them rather than passively observe them. So though you can demonstrate compliance with authority by asking one student to, say, whistle a tune, the others might not be as attentive as they would if you asked the entire class to hop on one foot or to give the instructor a standing ovation. (This particular demonstration has the added advantage of making it impossible for any student to claim immunity to social demand characteristics.)

2)   Even if you never did a single demonstration in the classroom, chances are you will never have enough class time to cover everything in your lecture notes, let alone in the textbook. OK, you could if you talked as fast as that guy in the old Federal Express commercials, but could your students process the information?

Speaking of which, just because we find time to lecture on something does not guarantee that our students will encode, store, and be able to retrieve the material. Thus, even if demonstrations do not themselves teach more than lectures (see McKeachie, 1990 and Muir & Webster, 1994, for data on the relative value of demonstrations vs. lectures for teaching complex vs. simple material), they can certainly illustrate concepts found in the textbook and thus make it easier and more enjoyable to learn by reading the text. In fact, my 30 years of teaching have left me convinced that the best use of class time is not so much to teach things as to do things—tell stories, give examples, present new concepts, and of course offer demonstrations—in ways that motivate the students to read the book, ask important questions, and learn for themselves. The resulting student interest, attention, and participation help them in learning concepts and principles, and they may learn better.

3)   Classroom demonstrations, like other breaks from the straight lecture mode, can provide highlights that make teaching more enjoyable for you as well as the students. Having highlights to look forward to each day is important because teaching courses again and again can easily become boring. When teachers are bored, their students know it (Appleby, 1990) and they become bored, too. And passive. And maybe even a little hostile, especially when filling out class evaluation forms.

It is no wonder that some faculty come to feel that teaching is not much fun, or at least not as much fun as it used to be. Demonstrating course content in ways that generate student involvement, responsiveness, and enjoyment can help maintain your enthusiasm in the classroom year after year.

Demonstrations in Context

I am not by any means arguing that faculty should stop lecturing. I am only suggesting that virtually any lecture can be enhanced by weaving into it demonstrations of varying length and complexity. At one end of the continuum are demonstrations—such as two-point threshold measurements—that require interrupting the lecture, distributing equipment, data sheets, instructions, and other materials, and 15-30 minutes of class time to complete. As already noted, I think exercises like these have a valuable place in the classroom now and then.

At the other extreme are quick demonstrations easily integrated into a lecture so smoothly as to hardly disrupt its flow. When lecturing on size constancy, for example, you can quickly and memorably illustrate Emmert's Law (Perceived Size = Retinal Image Size x Perceived Distance) by having the class look at a camera as you fire its flash unit. The resulting after-image (whose size is fixed) will appear larger when the students look at a distant wall than when they hold their palms in front of their eyes. Similarly, it seems a shame to lecture about progressive relaxation training methods without having the students put down their pens, close their eyes, and listen for just a minute or two to live or taped relaxation instructions.

How do you decide whether, and where, to include more demonstrations in your courses? One way is to ask yourself whether there are lectures that you do not look forward to because they feel stale to you and/or don't seem to interest your students. If there are, there are probably demonstrations that could break up and enliven the presentation. If you choose to add new demonstrations, do keep in mind two important guidelines that many experienced teachers have had to learn the hard way.

Two Important Guidelines For Demonstrations

It is rarely a good idea to try a new demonstration for the first time in front of your class. Practice ahead of time on friends, family, colleagues, or even alone, to be sure that you are clear on all the instructions and procedures, and above all, so the demonstration will actually work correctly.

The importance of rehearsal is well illustrated by the experience of a colleague who shall remain nameless except for his initials, Lou Penner. To demonstrate one of the practical applications of operant conditioning principles, Lou arranged for a local police officer to put a police dog through its paces on the stage of Lou's large classroom. The officer and dog were stationed at one side of the stage and a student volunteer, wearing a protective cuff, stood at the other. At the "attack" command, the animal sprinted for the student and, at the "halt" command, immediately attempted to stop. A rehearsal would have revealed that the stopping distance for a large dog hurtling across a highly polished wood stage is a lot longer than one might think. Contrary to plan, the dog actually reached the student, who was a bit shaken (though unhurt) by the experience. Not all demonstrations can go so dramatically wrong, but a dry run can reduce the chances of losing class time and confusing your students.

It is vital that every demonstration is clearly linked in the students' minds to the principles or concepts it is designed to illustrate. This is an especially important concern when a demonstration is so funny, game-like, or absorbing as to stand alone as a pleasant diversion from the *regular* course material.

Consider the rumor chain, for example, in which a story is passed from one student to another until its content is markedly altered. This exercise can nicely illustrate phenomena such as leveling and sharpening, distinctiveness, constructive memory, or the influence of gender and ethnic stereotypes on recall. However, if the students are not prepared to listen for and take note of changes in the story, and if afterward there is no opportunity for them to identify the principles illustrated by those changes, the time spent on the demonstration, though enjoyable, may have been wasted.

Conclusion

The potential benefits of classroom demonstrations far outweigh their perils. As a means of holding students' attention, motivating them to read and ask questions, and making teaching more enjoyable, demonstrations are hard to beat. And new ones are so easy to find.

Information about effective demonstrations on virtually any topic in psychology is readily available from the instructor's manuals that accompany most textbooks, from specialized handbooks (e.g., Benjamin, Daniel, & Brewer, 1985; Makosky, et al., 1990) from journals such as *Teaching of Psychology*, and via electronic mail networks.

Give some of these sources a try. I know that you will like the results of enlarging your repertoire of demonstrations, and that your students will too. Trust me, I'm psychic.

Recommended Readings and References

Appleby, D. C. (1990). Faculty and student perceptions of irritating behaviors in the college classroom. *Journal of Staff Program and Organization Development, 1,* 41-46.

Benjamin, L. T., Daniel, R. S., & Brewer, C. L. (Eds.). (1985). *Handbook for teaching introductory psychology.* Hillsdale, NJ: LEA.

Makosky, V. P., Selice, S., Sileo, C. C., & Whittemore, L. G. (Eds.). (1990). *Activities handbook for the teaching of psychology*: Vol. 3. Washington, DC: American Psychological Association.

McKeachie, W. J. (1990). Research on college teaching: The historical background. *Journal of Educational Psychology, 82,* 189-200.

Morris S. (1981). Believing in ESP: Effects of dehoaxing. In K. Frazier (Ed.), *Paranonnal borderlands of science* (pp. 32-45). Buffalo, NY: Prometheus.

Muir, J. J., & Webster, D. (1994, March). *Teaching physiological psychology: Effectiveness of demonstrations of physiological measures.* Paper presented at the annual meeting of the Southeastern Psychological Association, New Orleans. Paper available at Dept. of Psychology, Landrum Box 8041, Georgia Southern Univ., Statesboro, GA 30460.

Stockin, B. C. (1994, February). *Sustained attention in the college classroom: The vigilance decrement, its consequences and control.* Paper presented to Phi Kappa Phi faculty, Westmont College, Santa Barbara, CA. Paper available at Dept. of Psychology, Westmont College, 955 LaPaz Rd., Santa Barbara, CA 93108.

Chapter 19

Those Who Can Do: Implementing Active Learning

Marianne Miserandino
Beaver College

Learning is not a spectator sport

—Chickering & Gamson, 1987, p. 7

In the book *Hard Times*, Charles Dickens describes teacher Thomas Gradgrind insisting on teaching facts: "Now, what I want is facts. Teach these boys and girls nothing but facts. Facts alone are wanted in life." Dickens then describes Mr. Gradgrind's pupils as ". . . little vessels then and there arranged in order, ready to have imperial gallons of facts poured into them until they were full to the brim." This image of empty vessels ready to be filled, while certainly a caricature, too often becomes the default model for teaching. We know from cognitive psychology that learning is active and dynamic and we need to involve students through active learning.

Active learning provides students with a hands-on and minds-on experience, stimulating learning through increased cognitive demands. We know that people do not receive knowledge passively; knowledge is discovered and constructed through engagement. By becoming actively involved with knowledge, students form structures of thought that organize experience and direct future acquisition of knowledge. Active learning is therefore a better way of learning. Students are challenged not merely to know and to comprehend, but to apply, analyze, synthesize, and evaluate. In addition, to better learning, increased retention, and critical thinking, active learning impacts on students' personal growth by developing skills and allowing students to explore their own attitudes and values.

The term active learning is often used interchangeably with experiential learning, but the concepts are not quite the same. Active learning refers to learning activities that take from a few minutes to an entire class period. Internships, apprenticeships, laboratories, field work, volunteer work, teaching and research assistantships—which are ongoing beyond the typical class period—are forms of experiential learning.

This article first appeared in the September 1998 APS Observer.

Why You Should Add Active Learning To Your Classes

First, there are phenomena in psychology that only can be learned through doing; these include perceptual illusions, the application of mnemonics, and various group processes. Second, some course goals (e.g., using a scientific attitude in everyday life, understanding the relevance of psychology to current events, employing problem-solving strategies and critical thinking) only can be achieved through active learning. Similarly, human relations and communication skills, and cultural breadth through exposure to others' viewpoints cannot be learned through lecture alone. Virtually any class in which skills must be taught demands active learning. Third, it is my experience that the sheer joy of learning and the motivation to continue learning beyond the classroom are best developed through active strategies. Finally, active learning is fun for both instructor and students.

If It's So Great, Why Aren't You Already Using Active Learning?

Be honest. Do any of the following sound familiar?

My lectures are already prepared —don't make me revise them.

Less can go wrong with a lecture.

Lecturing fits my style.

I can cover more material if I don't stop talking.

I never learned to teach using active learning.

My colleagues, department chair, or the dean wouldn't like me to use active learning.

Demonstrations and activities will make my colleagues jealous.

The biggest obstacle to using active learning is habit and comfort with the way we teach. Active learning demands changing our role of *sage on stage* to *guide on the side*. Admittedly this reduces our control of the classroom, but it fosters students' autonomy and independence and returns the job of learning to them.

Where Do I Start?

Instructors must consider what kind of knowledge is worth having and what activities will facilitate the acquisition of such knowledge. To increase the effectiveness of activities and demonstrations you should:

Provide a background and rationale for the activity.

What will students be doing?

How does it fit the goals of the course?

What kind of participation is expected?

Will it be graded? If not, how will it be evaluated?

Motivate students by creating an atmosphere of challenge and foster in them a tolerance of ambiguity.

Be sensitive to privacy and do not ask students to disclose personal information.

Be aware of students' individual differences (e.g., shyness, personal history, gender).

Examples of Active Learning Techniques

The following techniques are grouped by ease of implementation, the amount of advanced preparation necessary, class time needed, and instructor effort.

Very Easy To Implement

Note-taking—Taking notes, generally regarded as passive, need not be if students receive feedback on them. For example, students may include questions or comments to instructors in their notes which can be used to start a discussion, as a basis of a dialogue with the instructor, or merely to facilitate learning. Writing a one-minute summary of a lecture's key points forces students to process the material in a richer way than merely taking notes.

Use of questions—Instead of just using rhetorical questions, be more active in using such questions. Start with a general, open-ended question to the class, and follow-up a student's answer with a more specific question, directed to the class. In this way, the one student is less likely to feel on the spot and others will feel engaged. Alternatively, have students discuss their views in trios for five minutes and then have a show of hands indicating students' positions. In this way students are exposed to a range of views in a non-evaluative format. Both techniques work best with questions that ask students to weigh arguments and make choices rather than just give information.

Interactive lectures—Students come to class with a degree of familiarity and much misinformation. An interactive lecture piques their curiosity and reveals what students know or don't know about the topic. Start by asking the class to brainstorm everything they know about a new topic, and record their responses on the blackboard or an overhead. Remember that the rules of brainstorming require that all contributions be acknowledged in a non-evaluative way. With the class's input, order contributions into a coherent, rational pattern. It is important that instructors have a clear idea of what should be revealed, but remain flexible enough to depart from their own preconceived ideas. The final creation should reflect the contributions of both class and instructor.

Easy To Implement

Case studies—If you remember Phineas Gage, who had a tamping rod puncture his skull, then you know how vividly theories can be illustrated through case studies. Similar case studies exist for many topics in neuroscience, cognition, child development, psychopathology, and personality. Human-interest stories in the newspaper are another good source and current news events are an especially good source for topics in social psychology. Students can analyze the case using theories presented in class in pairs, small groups, or as a class.

Problem solving lecture—The problem solving lecture begins with a problem, question, paradox, case study, or puzzle to hook students' interest. Solving the problem may require a proof, an experiment, a theory, or an historical narrative. As students listen to the lecture they formulate their own ideas of how the problem could be solved. Ideally, the solution would be revealed utilizing the techniques of the interactive lecture described above, with 10 or fewer minutes left in the class period to heighten suspense and interest.

Writing—Writing assignments ranging from in-class paragraphs to extensive research papers are excellent for fostering active learning (see Nodine, 1990). Writing requires that students analyze, develop, and shape their ideas and presentation. To be most effective, students need feedback from peers or the instructor, and depending on the nature of the assignment, it need not be graded.

Moderately Easy To Implement

Demonstrations and exercises—The best source for demonstrations and exercises specific to your class is usually the instructor's manual for your textbook. Be careful, as not all demonstrations involve active learning. For example, demonstrating discriminative learning by showing a rat in an operant chamber is technically active learning only for the rat. Resources for demonstrations and exercises include teaching journals, newsletters, and books.

Whole class debates—The physical layout of a large lecture hall can facilitate a debate. Students can sit on a side of the room to indicate their position, or the instructor can arbitrarily assign one side to a position. If the room has three sections, those undecided, or those supporting a third position, can sit in the middle. The instructor acts as a moderator calling for statements from each side supporting its position and allowing time for rebuttals. Two or three volunteers from each side can summarize their position and present a conclusion.

More Effort Required To Implement

Group Activities—Large classes, especially, will benefit from group exercises, projects, or discussions that provide a chance for collaborative learning and teamwork. Some schools have recitation sections concurrent with lecture sections for discussion, or demonstrations that would be impossible in the large section. Others require laboratories that serve a similar purpose and give students a chance to do research (Benjamin, 1991). Debates work particularly well as a small group activity.

Role-playing—Have students act out roles to problem solve or explore some issue. Students can work in small groups to develop their scenario and have representatives present it to the class. Famous personality theorists, DSM IV diagnoses, neurological disorders, ingratiating techniques, defense mechanisms, types of love, and conflict resolution techniques can all be effectively demonstrated. As a final step, have the rest of the class identify the concept the actors are illustrating.

Advanced

Simulation games—Simulation games are extended role-plays that may take one to three hours. These are most successful when students are prepared ahead of time and have the chance to fully discuss and process the experience afterwards. These can range from the relatively simple Lost on the Moon task illustrating group processes, to the more involved Barnga or BaFa BaFa for illustrating intercultural communication and culture shock. The most elaborate, but extremely effective simulations, may involve the hiring of a consultant and a weekend afternoon.

Computers—Most instructors are familiar with software packages that run demonstrations or collect data from students to illustrate psychological principles. But with the advent of cyberspace, the possibilities for active learning and interactive classes are limitless. Computer bulletin boards, electronic mail, and the World Wide Web are effective ways to involve students in their learning.

Conclusion

Learning is not a spectator sport. To keep your students from becoming intellectual couch potatoes, get them off the bench and into the game. They will enjoy the class more, and learn and remember more. What more could a coach want?

Recommended Readings and References

Benjamin, L. T. (1991). Personalization and active learning in the large introductory psychology class. *Teaching of Psychology, 18,* 68-74.

Chickering, A. W., & Gamson, Z. F. (1987). Seven principles for good practice. *American Association of Higher Education Bulletin, 39,* 3-7.

Frederick, P. J. (1987). Student involvement: Active learning in large classes. In M. G. Weimer (Ed.), *Teaching large classes well* (pp. 45-56). San Francisco: Jossey-Bass.

Mathie, V. A. (1993). Promoting active learning in psychology courses. In T. V. McGovern (Ed.), *Handbook for enhancing undergraduate education in psychology* (pp. 183-214). Washington, DC: American Psychological Association.

Nodine, B. F. (Ed.). (1990). Psychologists teach writing [Special issue]. *Teaching of Psychology, 17.*

APA's *Activities Handbooks* (Vol. *1-3*)

Benjamin, L. T., & Lowman, K. D. (Eds.). (1981). *Activities handbook for the teaching of psychology:* Vol. *1.* Washington, DC: American Psychological Association.

Makosky, V. P., Whittemore, L. G., & Rogers, A. M. (Eds.). (1987). *Activities handbook for the teaching of psychology*: *Vol. 2*. Washington, DC: American Psychological Association.

Makosky, V. P., Sileo, C. C., Whittemore, L. G., & Skutley, M. L. (Eds.). (1990). *Activities handbook for the teaching of psychology*: Vol. *3*. Washington, DC: American Psychological Association.

Handbooks of Demonstrations and Activities (Vol. *1-3*)

Ware, M. E., & Johnson, D. E. (Eds.). (1996). *The handbook of demonstrations and activities in the teaching of psychology:* Vol. *1*. Introductory statistics, research methods, and history. Mahwah, NJ: Erlbaum.

Ware, M. E., & Johnson, D. E. (Eds.). (1996). *The handbook of demonstrations and activities in the teaching of psychology:* Vol. *2*. Physiological-comparative, perception, learning, cognitive, and developmental. Mahwah, NJ: Erlbaum.

Ware, M. E., & Johnson, D. E. (Eds.). (1996). *The handbook of demonstrations and activities in the teaching of psychology:* Vol. *3*. Personality, abnormal, clinical-counseling, and social. Mahwah, NJ: Erlbaum.

Chapter 20

Teaching Large Classes

James L. Hilton
University of Michigan

A s a sophomore at the University of Texas in the late 1970s I took two classes that, for better or worse, changed my life. The first was a course in U.S. history taught by a professor who, as the semester progressed, I began to refer to as the *Monotone Man*. The second was an introductory course in Social Psychology taught by Rick Archer. Both classes were taught in large lecture formats, had similar exams, were pitched to similar audiences, and relied upon discussion sections to augment the lectures. But that is where the similarity ended.

About the only thing I remember from the history class is one lecture in which *Monotone Man* raised the possibility that the Salem witch trials were due to a community wide hallucination caused by a rare bread mold that has a chemical structure similar to LSD. That's it. Nothing about the American Revolution, the Continental Congress, the War of 1812, or anything else that might have happened in the early years of the nation. It is all gone, lost in a sleepy fog.

In contrast, I remember most of the social psychology course. I remember both its content and its form. I remember that we covered interesting topics. I remember I came to class early and left late. I remember lively discussion. I remember wanting to teach that course.

Today, I find myself confronting the same challenges that these two very different instructors faced 20 years ago. Now it is my turn to stare at the sometimes eager, but often blank, faces of my students and struggle to figure out how to make it work. Since joining the faculty in 1985, I have taught approximately 10,000 students in classes ranging in size from 15 to 1,200. What I've learned over the last decade is that it is harder than I thought and harder than most of my students think as well. Teaching, especially teaching large classes, requires practice, reflection, and perspiration. What follows are lessons I have learned. Some can be found in the literature, others come from my colleagues, and still others from my own experiences in the classroom. None of them will work for everyone. My advice is to take what fits and ignore the rest.

This article first appeared in the March 1999 APS Observer.

Don't Be Apologetic About Teaching a Large Course

Too often we reflexively accept the assertion that big classes are bad classes. I think this is problematic for several reasons. First, the very definition of a *large class* is ambiguous. At my institution, *large classes* routinely enroll 350+ students. Where I went to graduate school, on the other hand, *large classes* enrolled 50 students. With such wide variation, blanket condemnations are risky. Second, although large courses, however they are defined, may not be ideal for many learning situations (McKeachie, 1994), they do have their place and their strengths. For example, large classes are a wonderful arena for engaging student interest. When I teach introductory psychology, a large part of my motivation is the opportunity to evangelize the field. I know that I hook or lose hundreds of students in that course. Similarly, large classes provide an excellent forum for highlighting the big questions that confront a field. They lend themselves to the task of identifying intellectual forests. If you play to the strengths of large classes, there is no reason to be apologetic.

There's a pragmatic reason for avoiding apologia as well. If you begin your course by apologizing for its size, you risk triggering an unfortunate self-fulfilling prophecy. Convey to your students that the class is anything less than ideal at the beginning of the term and they are likely to treat it as such for the rest of the term.

Recognize the Importance of Organization

When Johnny Carson was the host of the *Tonight Show*, everything about the show looked spontaneous. Sparkling dialogue, zany antics, and corny skits all looked as if they were happening for the very first time. In fact, it was all heavily choreographed. Nothing was left to chance. Someone close to the show once went so far as to note that the show was as spontaneous as a shuttle launch. So too with large classes. Large classes live and die by the organization you bring to them for several reasons.

First, organization will calm your class down. One of the two big enemies in teaching a large course is student anxiety. (The other, paradoxically enough, is student apathy.) Students, especially beginning students, are almost always anxious about what will happen in the course and what is expected from them. The more you organize the course, the calmer they become.

Second, organization is an excellent tonic for stage fright. I still write out every lecture I give. I hardly ever give that exact lecture, but I find it comforting to know that if I suddenly go brain dead, I have a beginning, middle, and ending to give to the class.

Third, the bureaucracy that comes with a large course makes it difficult to correct mistakes. In a small class, it's relatively easy to correct something during the next meeting. You can keep track of who has the new and correct information. But in a large class, that's much more difficult. Announce the wrong time for an exam and you will find yourself correcting the announcement to your grave.

Fourth, unlike small seminars where you may be able to allow your students' questions and interests to direct the class, students expect large classes to be meticulously organized. I often think that the difference between the organizational needs of small and large classes is analogous to the difference between an informal brown-bag and a formal colloquium. In the brown-bag, part of the point is to get the audience to help you figure out what's going on. It's a talk that's given while you are still in discovery mode and the audience is part of that process. But a colloquium is an entirely different kind of animal. Colloquia are about presenting your ideas. The last thing you want to do as the speaker is to look like you are just now discovering your points. If you do, the audience will see you as ill prepared, simpleminded, and rude. So will your students—with a vengeance. In my experience, the sin that students are least likely to forgive is the sin of disorganization. They expect their classes to run on time and for the instructor to know what the main point is of every class meeting.

Embrace the Idea That it Takes a Village to Build a Course

As researchers and scholars we tend to think of ideas in a proprietary fashion. We worry about getting credit for our own work and giving sufficient credit for the work of others. That's fine and appropriate in that part of our lives. But teaching is all about the free exchange of ideas. As such, it should be a communal task. Feel free to rely upon the kindness of your colleagues and mentors when you approach the task of teaching a large class for the first time. In all probability, someone in your department has already taught the course. Get their materials. Ask for their notes. Pick their brains to find out what worked and what didn't work. They know what your students are going to be like and what they will expect. Building a course for the first time is a daunting task. Don't make it harder by ignoring your closest and most well informed sources.

Dare to Experiment

I once tried to demonstrate the self-reference memory effect in a large social psychology class. I read a list of words to the class and varied what they were supposed to do with the list. One third of the class was supposed to decide if each word was positive or negative. Another third was supposed to decide if the words were nouns or verbs. The final third was supposed to decide if the words described themselves. What should have happened was that the students in the last group should have had the best memory for the words on the list. They didn't. The show of hands made it clear that they all remembered about the same number of words. The class went wild. They loved it! One reason they loved it, of course, was that I was wrong. Youth always appreciates the opportunity to see the mistakes of their elders. But the larger reason why they loved it was that they knew I was trying. When I first started teaching, I was leery of trying demonstrations and experiments in my class. I was too concerned about what would happen when they didn't work. What I've learned since then, is that students will forgive almost anything if they think that you are trying. So now I use lots of demonstrations and take lots of chances. I try to anticipate where they may go awry, but I don't fear them any more.

Don't Be Afraid to Personalize the Course

By the end of any given semester, my introductory psychology students know a lot about my life. They know I have a wife and two kids. They know I have a moronic Labrador Retriever named Kate. They know that cognitive dissonance is the reason I became a social psychologist. Why do I tell them so much about my life? I do it because I want to find as many ways to connect with them as possible. I want to avoid the chasm of impersonal indifference. I want my students to think of me as a fellow human, not as some remote automaton. I want them to know that the things that we cover in the class affect me as well as them. I do it because it helps them remember. When I cover Piagetian conservation in my introductory course, for example, I show about 10 minutes worth of home movies in which my kids attempt the conservation task. Years later, this is the lecture students tell me they remember the best.

It is, of course, a fine line between personalizing your lectures and wallowing in narcissism. One way to make sure that you do not dwell on your personal life at the expense of pedagogy is to ask whether your anecdote makes a point. If it doesn't, or if it requires a big stretch to see the point, then it is probably a mistake. But if it makes a point and provides a connection, it is well worth it.

Recognize the Importance of First Impressions

The first meeting of any class is critical. The first class is where you set the tone and students form their impressions. I firmly believe that I win my class or lose them in the first 15 minutes and 50 years of person perception research supports that belief (e.g., Asch, 1946). The bad news is that this puts a lot of pressure on the first day of class. The good news is that, if that day goes well, you can bank some idiosyncrasy points for later on.

What this means pragmatically is that you cannot afford many mistakes on the first day. The easiest way to avoid mistakes is to be compulsive about the first lecture when you tell students about the course goals and overview, and what you expect from them and what they can expert from you. This compulsivity should start well before classes begin. I have a colleague who had grand plans for using digital images in his class. He found lots of material on the web and was excited about the possibility of enlivening his lectures with some of it. The problem was, he waited until the day before his first lecture to connect his computer to the projector in the lecture hall. Guess what? It didn't work and there was not enough time to get the connectors that would make it work before classes began. All of his digital dreams went up in smoke.

To minimize these kinds of disasters, check out the room well in advance. What kind of equipment is in it? Will you need a microphone? Can you walk up the aisles while giving your lectures? If you plan to show videos or use the computer for data projection, how does it look? Similarly, on the first day of class double-check everything. Are the slides in order? Do you have extra copies of the syllabus? It is never possible to guarantee that everything will go as planned, but it is possible to minimize the chances of failure. If the first class meeting is handled well, the first *real* lecture is a piece of cake.

Show That You Care

Student evaluations reveal that students want instructors who care about their progress and environments where that concern can come through (Wulff, Nyquist, & Abbott, 1987). Obviously, large classes are not ideal in this respect. There are, however, a number of things that you can do that will help. Hold extra office hours. Give students your email address. Collect midterm evaluations. Do anything that shows the students that you care. I have a colleague who teaches a class of 160. On the first day he takes pictures of them in small groups and writes their names on the back. By the third week of class, he has all of their names and faces memorized. His students know absolutely that he cares.

Realize That You Cannot Be Too Obvious

One way to think about the difference between small and large classes is to think about the difference between movie acting, where the close-up can catch the slightest nuance of behavior, and the stage, where every act must be exaggerated. The dynamics of a large class make it hard for students to ask questions and easy for them to get lost. What this means is that if you are going to err, err on the side of being too obvious, not too subtle. Tell students what the *take away* points are. Provide outlines. Do everything you can to make sure your message is heard and understood.

One useful tool along these lines is simply to ask students what they heard at various points during the term. After making an important point or complicated argument, ask the students to write a one-paragraph summary and invite them to share those summaries with you after class. As you read through the summaries, you will quickly learn whether your students heard what you thought you said and you will be able to calibrate your future classes accordingly.

Find Ways to Keep Engaged for the Long Haul

If the most salient challenge facing the new teacher is stage fright, I think the biggest challenge facing the experienced teacher is complacency. To fight it, I constantly look for ways to mix my courses up. I change books, alter the exam format, or add a web site all in the service of avoiding boredom. Over the last five years, for example, I've invested a lot of time learning how to incorporate multimedia in my classes. Part of the reason I invested the time is that I think multimedia has the potential to make abstract concepts more concrete and accessible for my students. But another reason I invested the time was that it made me see my courses in a different light. Courses that I had begun to find painful through sheer repetition again became new and exciting.

Keep in Mind That It's All New to Them

This is an obvious fact, but one that I constantly forget. No matter how many times you have used a demonstration, made a certain point, or told a particular anecdote, remember that it's new to them every time. You don't need to change your story just because you told the same story last year.
Finally, remember that if you're happy, they're probably happy.

One year after taking *Monotone man's* class I found myself sitting in an auditorium waiting to take an exam in yet another lecture course. As I sat there, I overheard two women in front of me discussing a history professor who was, in their words, "The best teacher they had ever had." Full of curiosity, I asked them who the professor was. Imagine my surprise when they named Monotone himself. When we then compared notes we discovered that we had all been in the same class but clearly we had very different experiences. Keep in mind, your mileage may vary.

Recommended Readings and References

Asch, S. E. (1946). Forming impressions on personality. *Journal of Abnormal and Social Psychology, 41*, 258-290.

Erickson, B. L., & Strommer, D. W. (1991). *Teaching college freshmen.* San Francisco: Jossey-Bass.

McKeachie, W. J. (1994). *Teaching tips: Strategies, research, and theory for college and university teachers* (9th ed.). Lexington, MA. D. C. Heath.

Weimer, M. G. (Ed.). (1987). *Teaching large classes well.* New Directions for Teaching and Learning, *32* (Winter), San Francisco: Jossey-Bass.

Wulff, D. H., Nyquist, J. D., & Abbott, R. D. (1987). Students' perceptions of large classes. In M. G. Weimer (Ed.), Teaching large classes well (pp. 17-30). *New Directions for Teaching and Learning, 32,* (Winter), San Francisco: Jossey-Bass.

Chapter 21

On Critical Thinking

Jane S. Halonen
James Madison University

Several years ago some teaching colleagues were talking about the real value of teaching psychology students to think critically. After some heated discussion, the last word was had by a colleague from North Carolina. "The real value of being a good critical thinker in psychology is so you won't be a jerk," he said with a smile. That observation remains one of my favorites in justifying why teaching critical thinking skills should be an important goal in psychology. However, I believe it captures only a fraction of the real value of teaching students to think critically about behavior.

What Is Critical Thinking?

Although there is little agreement about what it means to think critically in psychology, I like the following broad definition: *the propensity and skills to engage in activity with reflective skepticism focused on deciding what to believe or do.*

Students often arrive at their first introductory course with what they believe is a thorough grasp on how life works. After all, they have been alive for at least 18 years, have witnessed their fair shares of crisis, joy, and tragedy, and have successfully navigated their way into your classroom. These students have had a lot of time to develop their own personal theories about how the world works and most are quite satisfied with the results. They often pride themselves on how good they are with people as well as how astute they are in understanding and explaining the motives of others.

And they think they know what psychology is. Many are surprised and sometimes disappointed to discover that psychology is a science, and the rigor of psychological research is a shock. The breadth and depth of psychology feel daunting. Regardless of their sophistication in the discipline, students often are armed with a single strategy to survive the experience: Memorize the book and hope it works out on the exam. In many cases, this strategy will serve them well.

This article first appeared in the July/August 1996 APS Observer.

Unfortunately, student exposure to critical thinking skill development may be more accidental than planned on the part of most teachers. Collaborating in my department and with other colleagues over the years has persuaded me that we need to approach critical thinking skills in a purposeful, systematic, and developmental manner from the introductory course through the capstone experience. I propose that we need to teach critical thinking skills in three domains of psychology: practical (the *jerk avoidance* function), theoretical (developing scientific explanations for behavior), and methodological (testing scientific ideas). I will explore each of these areas and then offer some general suggestions about how psychology teachers can improve their purposeful pursuit of critical thinking objectives.

Practical Domain

Practical critical thinking is often expressed as a long-term, implicit goal of teachers of psychology, even though they may not spend much precious academic time teaching how to transfer critical thinking skills to make students wise consumers, more careful judges of character, or more cautious interpreters of behavior. Accurate appraisal of behavior is essential, yet few teachers invest time in helping students understand how vulnerable their own interpretations are to error.

Encourage practice in accurate description and interpretation of behavior by presenting students with ambiguous behavior samples. Ask them to distinguish what they observe (What is the *behavior*?) from the inferences they draw from the behavior (What is the *meaning* of the behavior?). I have found that cartoons, such as Simon Bond's *Unspeakable Acts*, can be a good resource for refining observation skills. Students quickly recognize that crisp behavioral descriptions are typically consistent from observer to observer, but inferences vary wildly. They recognize that their interpretations are highly personal and sometimes biased by their own values and preferences. As a result of experiencing such strong individual differences in interpretation, students may learn to be appropriately less confident of their immediate conclusions, more tolerant of ambiguity, and more likely to propose alternative explanations. As they acquire a good understanding of scientific procedures, effective control techniques, and legitimate forms of evidence, they may be less likely to fall victim to the multitude of off-base claims about behavior that confront us all. (How many Elvis sightings can be valid in one year?)

Theoretical Domain

Theoretical critical thinking involves helping the student develop an appreciation for scientific explanations of behavior. This means learning not just the content of psychology, but how and why psychology is organized into concepts, principles, laws, and theories. Developing theoretical skills begins in the introductory course where the primary critical thinking objective is *understanding and applying concepts* appropriately. For example, when you introduce students to the principles of reinforcement, you can ask them to find examples of the principles in the news or to make up stories that illustrate the principles.

Midlevel courses in the major require more sophistication, moving students beyond application of concepts and principles to *learning and applying theories*. For instance, you can provide a rich case study in Abnormal Psychology and ask students to make sense of the case from different perspectives, emphasizing theoretical flexibility or accurate use of existing and accepted frameworks in psychology to explain patterns of behavior.

In advanced courses we can justifiably ask students to *evaluate theory*, selecting the most useful or rejecting the least helpful. For example, students can contrast different models to explain drug addiction in Physiological Psychology. By examining the strengths and weaknesses of existing frameworks, they can select which theories serve best as they learn to justify their criticisms based on evidence and reason.

Capstone, honors, and graduate courses go beyond theory evaluation to encourage students to *create theory*. Students select a complex question about behavior (for example, identifying mechanisms that underlie autism or language acquisition) and develop their own theory-based explanations for the behavior. This challenge requires them to synthesize and integrate existing theory as well as devise new insights into the behavior.

Methodological Domain

Most departments offer many opportunities for students to develop their methodological critical thinking abilities by applying different research methods in psychology. Beginning students must first learn what the scientific method entails. The next step is to apply their understanding of scientific method by identifying design elements in existing research. For example, any detailed description of an experimental design can help students practice distinguishing the independent from the dependent variable and identifying how researchers controlled for alternative explanations.

The next methodological critical thinking goals include evaluating the quality of existing research design and challenging the conclusions of research findings. Students may need to feel empowered by the teacher to overcome the reverence they sometimes demonstrate for anything in print, including their textbooks. Asking students to do a critical analysis on a fairly sophisticated design may simply be too big a leap for them to make. They are likely to fare better if given examples of bad design so they can build their critical abilities and confidence in order to tackle more sophisticated designs. (Examples of bad design can be found in *The Critical Thinking Companion for Introductory*

Psychology (Halonen, 1995) or they can be easily constructed with a little time and imagination.)

Students will develop and execute their own research designs in their capstone methodology courses. Asking students to conduct their own independent research, whether a comprehensive survey on parental attitudes, a naturalistic study of museum patrons' behavior, or a well-designed experiment on paired associate learning, prompts students to integrate their critical thinking skills and gives them practice with conventional writing forms in psychology. In evaluating their work I have found it helpful to ask the students to identify the strengths and weaknesses of their own work as an additional opportunity to think critically before giving them my feedback.

Additional Suggestions

Adopting explicit critical thinking objectives, regardless of the domain of critical thinking, may entail some strategy changes on the part of the teacher. What are some ideas?

Introduce Psychology as an Open-ended, Growing Enterprise

Students often think that their entry into the discipline represents an endpoint where everything good and true has already been discovered. That conclusion encourages passivity rather than criticality. Point out that research is psychology's way of growing and developing. Each new discovery in psychology represents a potentially elegant act of critical thinking. A lot of room for discovery remains. New ideas will be developed, and old conceptions discarded.

Require Student Performance that Goes Beyond Memorization

Group work, essays, debates, themes, letters to famous psychologists, journals, current event examples—all of these and more can be used as a means of developing the higher skills involved in critical thinking in psychology. Find faulty cause-effect conclusions in the tabloids (e.g., "Eating broccoli increases your IQ!") and have students design studies to verify or discredit the headline. Ask students to identify what kinds of evidence would warrant belief in commercial claims. Although it is difficult, even well-designed objective test items can capture critical thinking skills so that students are challenged beyond mere repetition and recall.

Clarify Your Expectations about Performance with Explicit, Public Criteria

Devising clear performance criteria for psychology projects will enhance student success. Students often complain that they don't understand "what you want" when you assign work. Performance criteria specify the standards that you will use to evaluate their work. For example, performance criteria for the observation exercise described earlier might include the following: *the student describes behavior accurately; offers inference that is reasonable for the context; and identifies personal factors that might influence inference.* Performance criteria facilitate giving detailed feedback easily and can also promote student self-assessment.

Label Good Examples of Critical Thinking When These Occur Spontaneously

Students may not recognize when they are thinking critically. When you identify examples of good thinking or exploit examples that could be improved, it enhances students' ability to understand. One of my students made this vivid for me when I commented on the good connection she had made between a course concept and an insight from her literature class, "*That* is what you mean by critical thinking?" Thereafter I have been careful to label a good critical thinking insight.

Endorse a Questioning Attitude

Students often assume that if they have questions about their reading, then they are somehow being dishonorable, rude, or stupid. Having discussions early in the course about the role of good questions in enhancing the quality of the subject and expanding the sharpness of the mind may set a more critical stage on which students can play. Model critical thinking from some insights you have had about behavior or from some research you have conducted in the past. Congratulate students who offer good examples of the principles under study. Thank students who ask concept-related questions and describe why you think their questions are good. Leave time and space for more. Your own excitement about critical thinking can be a great incentive for students to seek that excitement.

Brace Yourself

When you include more opportunity for student critical thinking in class, there is more opportunity for the class to go astray. Stepping away from the podium and engaging the students to perform what they know necessitates some loss of control, or at least some enhanced risk. However, the advantage is that no class will ever feel completely predictable, and this can be a source of stimulation for students and the professor as well.

Recommended Readings and References

Halonen, J. S. (1995). *The critical thinking companion for introductory psychology.* New York: Worth.

Halpern, D. F. (1989). *Thought and knowledge: An introduction to critical thinking* (2nd ed.). Hillsdale, NJ: Erlbaum.

Mayer, R., & Goodchild, F. (1990). *The critical thinker: Thinking and learning strategies for psychology students.* Dubuque, IA: Brown & Benchmark.

Meyers, C. (1986). *Teaching students to think critically.* San Francisco: Jossey-Bass.

Smith, R. A. (1995). *Challenging your preconceptions.* Pacific Grove, CA: Brooks/Cole.

Part 5

Themes Across Psychology

Chapter 22

History Belongs in Every Course

Michael Wertheimer
University of Colorado–Boulder

"Those who know only their own generation remain children forever." A version of this saying, attributed to Cicero more than two millennia ago, is prominently inscribed in stone on the west portico of the central library of the University of Colorado-Boulder. It captures the wise insight that to develop humility, reduce gullibility, and enhance intellectual maturity—in short, to "grow up"—people need to know about their history.

Applying this observation to the teaching of psychology might generate the following prescription: *All teachers of all courses in psychology should develop, and emphasize, an historical perspective on the topic of the course to improve both their students' understanding of the subject and their students' maturity and wisdom.*

In brief, students are much better prepared if they are exposed to material on the history of the subject. The remainder of this column will discuss why teaching history is desirable and provide suggestions on how to include it in our classes.

Why Include History in Psychology Teaching?

It Presents the Development of Ideas and How Science Works
Every academic field and subfield has a developmental trajectory. Points of view evolve and change; significant discoveries yield new understanding and leave their impact upon later work. The unfolding of thoughts in an area can be fascinating intellectual fare, as one realizes how later workers build on, and extend, the work of their predecessors—or distort or oversimplify earlier approaches so that theories and approaches that once worked reasonably well now come crashing down.

Psychologists are not immune to Cicero's proscription of *eternal childhood*, but the easy cure for this form of "infantilism" is the prescription for a healthy historical perspective in teaching. Not every contemporary theorist or computer modeler is aware that if a "new" theory or model looks

---

This article first appeared in the March 1997 APS Observer.

promising today, somebody else probably had the same basic idea previously. And if a brilliant and unassailable contemporary theory reveals a flaw, chances are that its flaw—or at least some aspect of it—was identified long ago.

Discovering that one is not necessarily the innovator of an idea may be a blow to one's perceived creativity, but such disappointments do not necessarily stem from a lack of historical knowledge—because most specialists are the first to admit that the sheer volume of contemporary scientific information prevents even the most studious scientist from keeping abreast of all contemporary theories and approaches. But the study of disciplinary history helps demonstrate to the student the relative impermanence of accepted wisdom of the day and instills a healthy caution in accepting current theories and ideas.

Fifty years ago, nobody could talk responsibly about learning, for instance, without copious references to rats running in mazes and 30 years ago the Skinner box was all the rage. The field of verbal learning used to mean endless variations on the memorizing of nonsense syllables, but now psycholinguists are talking about schemas, scripts, and frames. Projective tests like the Rorschach were vying with dream analysis as the royal road to understanding the most significant depths of the human psyche in the middle of this century, until massive empirical studies questioned their validity. The group mind that was the theoretical panacea for social psychologists less than a century ago was discarded in favor of balance theories, cognitive dissonance, and many other taken-for-granted explain-it-all theories that in turn are being replaced today. The resourceful instructor can readily identify historical examples that can help students realize that today's "answers" to current questions often are not likely to be the ultimate answers.

The Intended Outcome of a Liberal Education Is Wisdom

Including history in your classes will provide your students with a broader perspective, and an understanding that today's taken-for-granted orientations, methods, problems, and theories are as time- and place-bound as their predecessors. Your class will make a more significant contribution to students' liberal arts education and help them realize that what they are learning in your course relates to the rest of their education. For example, learning how John Locke's primary qualities fit in with the notions of Newtonian physics, how associationism relates to the idea of elements in chemistry, or how Gestalt concepts are related to field theory in biology and in modern physics all help make the student's entire curriculum more meaningful and integrated.

Different disciplines use similar epistemological approaches to related problems. And their varying perspectives on the same kinds of problems can be enlightening. Your students' education is enhanced if they develop such historical perspectives.

How to Teach History in Your Courses

The *how* may be a bit of a puzzler for today's teachers of psychology—especially those who never had a course on the history of psychology, even as undergraduates. And unfortunately, in this time of fragmentation and hyper-specialization in the field, fewer and fewer new psychologists have studied the history of the discipline. Yet to be able to compete for teaching jobs in an ever tighter academic market, a healthy dose of historical sophistication could actually make them more marketable, and more successful once they get the job.

Use Historical Examples Throughout the Course

Psychology teachers who have some respect for the history of the discipline typically include historical themes briefly at the beginning of a course. While better than no historical content at all, this approach is not enough. Include historical themes in your course in every lecture, and in every unit.

Frequent historical references repeated throughout the course can help ensure that a responsible perspective is never lost. Don't limit your examples to studies published only during the last 10 years, and show how thoughtful the approaches to a problem were when it was first addressed. Such discussions should include reference to the way a question was phrased and how that changed over the years. Your classes should also include discussions of how knowledge about an area improved or at least changed. Help your students understand how the field got to be where it happens to be right now.

Use Your Library

It might take a bit of searching to find appropriate historical material for some psychology courses, but once you have the information it can be used for years. Most texts focus on the here-and-now, and strive to be as up-to-date as possible. But visits to the library (if your text contains little about history), and focused queries to your reference librarian (they're specially trained to help with such things), can turn up books and articles on the history of almost any subfield as well as on the history of the entire discipline itself, such as several of the items listed under further helpful readings below. The list also includes some reference books that you're likely to find useful, such as Viney and Wertheimer, 1979, and Watson, 1998.

Develop a Few Excellent Sources of Historical Examples

Where can you find appropriate historical material? As a start, refer to the books listed below. In addition, most general texts on the history of psychology contain narratives about numerous subfields. *The Journal of the History of the Behavioral Sciences* is a rich resource. The newsletter of APS's Division 26 (History of Psychology) is a remarkably varied and rich storehouse of articles relevant to many different fields. That division has just launched a new journal titled *History of Psychology*.

Some slide series have pictures of famous psychologists of the past, shots of historic labs, charts from influential studies, and photos of the title pages of classic works, and several suppliers have huge inventories of films and videos. It may take some digging, but the historical material relevant to your course can be found.

Don't forget your library's journals. Many college and university libraries now have volumes of journals that go back at least 50 years. Students can be fascinated by reading selected older articles, both to see how far we have come and to gain respect for the scholarship of the past. Good ideas are not a monopoly of today's prominent psychologists; many wise scholars long ago had insights that are still highly enlightening, even about issues that are currently in the limelight.

Use Sketches of People and Contributions

One way to make history come alive, of course, is to present sketches of the contributions—and lives—of some of the major figures in the field you are teaching. APA and Lawrence Erlbaum Associates, Inc., have jointly published several volumes of *Portraits of Pioneers in Psychology* (Kimble, Boneau, & Wertheimer, 1996; Kimble, Wertheimer, & White, 1991; Kimble and Wertheimer, 1998).

Most of the chapters in these books are lively, often irreverent, accounts by experts in the pioneers' fields, sometimes with the author impersonating the pioneer. The biographies include not only the typical general psychologists of the past, but figures relevant to specialized courses. For example:

◆ *Cognitive Psychology*: Mary W. Calkins, John Dewey, Karl Duncker, Hermann Ebbinghaus, Laurens P. Hickok, Wolfgang Kohler, Jean Piaget, William Stern, Benton J. Underwood, Max Wertheimer, Wilhelm Wundt

◆ *Learning*: Edwin R. Guthrie, D.O. Hebb, Clark L. Hull, Walter S. Hunter, Karl S. Lashley, Ivan P. Pavlov, Ivan M. Sechenov, B.F. Skinner, Edward L. Thorndike, Edward C. Tolman, John B. Watson

Biological Psychology: Barbara Burkes, Charles Darwin, Leon Festinger, Clarence Graham, D.O. Hebb, David Krech, Karl S. Lashley, Myrtle McGraw, Henry Nissen, Paul H. Schiller, Robert C. Tryon, Robert Yerkes

Sensation and Perception: Karl Dunker, Gustav T. Fechner, Leon Festinger, James J. Gibson, Clarence Graham, Wolfgang Kohler, Jean Piaget, Joseph B. Rhine, Max Wertheimer, Wilhelm Wundt

Individual Differences: Floyd H. Allport, Alfred Binet, Edgar A. Doll, Leta Hollingworth, William Stern, L.L. Thurstone, Robert C. Tryon

Personality: Mary W. Calkins, Milton Erickson, Sigmund Freud, Carl Jung, Kurt Lewin, Carl Rogers, Silvan S. Tomkins

Applied Psychology: Lillian Gilbreth, Harry Hollingworth, Ethel Puffer, Joseph Jastrow, B.F. Skinner, L.L. Thurstone

Behavioral Genetics: William E. Blatz, Barbara Burks, Francis Galton, Robert C. Tryon

Clinical Psychology: Dorothea Dix, Edgar A. Doll, Milton Erickson, Sigmund Freud, Leta Hollingworth, Carl Jung, Carl Rogers, Harry S. Sullivan, Silvan S. Tomkins, Lightner Witmer

Animal Behavior: Charles Darwin, D.O. Hebb, Z.Y. Kuo, Henry Nissen, Ivan P. Pavlov, Paul H. Schiller, John B. Watson, Robert Yerkes

Social Psychology: Floyd H. Allport, Dorothea Dix, Leon Festinger, David Krech, Kurt Lewin, Stanley Milgram

Impersonate the Famous

An approach that can work well and be enjoyable for you—and keep you on your toes—is to begin most class sessions by impersonating a famous deceased figure from the past, using a first person format in a five to 10 minute lecture to talk about some early ideas on the subjects of the days lecture. Summarizing what that person's main contribution was and then inviting the students to ask questions of the *visitor* work well.

It is not as difficult as one might think to provide "answers" that could plausibly have been generated by the one being impersonated. And, at any rate, you are apt to know more about that than your students, and you can always plead "I don't know" to any question. Besides, you can preface the whole practice by warning your class that if the questions are too difficult, the person you've resurrected might just fade back in to the shadows of the past. You might ask your TA to impersonate a favorite pioneer. Or, if class size permits, require each student to do at least one such impersonation.

Test on History

Use exam questions that reflect the historical perspective you have been trying to convey. You might even make these questions easier than routine factual content questions, to reward students for learning something about context and becoming liberally educated!

An example of an objective question for a course in cognitive psychology might be: Place the following models of cognitive processes in the brain in historical order by circling the number 1 in front of the earliest, the 2 in front of the next, the 3 in front of the next and the 4 in front of the most recent:

1 2 3 4   electronic computers
1 2 3 4   neural grooves
1 2 3 4   telephone switchboards
1 2 3 4   vacuum tubes

A short-answer essay question for a course on perception might ask for a comparison of the use of Ohm's law in audition and in vision, while a longer essay question for a course on neuropsychology might ask students to comment on the advantages of modern brain activity imaging techniques over the classic extirpation and microelectrode recording methods. In any course, you could ask students to indicate what we now know (e.g., about color vision, schizophrenia, neurochemistry, personality traits) that was not known, say 50 years ago. The possibilities are almost endless.

Conclusion

Elements of past scientific approaches, and their sociocultural context, survive within contemporary psychology. At what point in teaching about the field is it appropriate to insert the historical background on these past approaches? At any time, anywhere, and everywhere that you can squeeze it in. Why? So your students get an education rather than just learn to memorize a list of facts that will change over time, and to instill in them a sense of humility, a well-developed intellectual maturity, and an immunization against gullibility.

Help your students become intellectually sophisticated, and prudent and productive members of our scientific community and society. Part of this goal is achieved by training students to have a healthy skepticism about what they are learning and helping them understand why the current discipline of psychology happens to be the way it is. How can you do this? It will take a bit of ingenuity, especially in those fields that are exploding so fast that they are almost ahistorical. But this endeavor will enrich your students' intellectual experience and your own.

Recommended Readings and References

Kimble, G. A., Boneau, C. A., & Wertheimer, M. (Eds.). (1996). *Portraits of pioneers in psychology, Vol. 2.* Washington, DC: American Psychological Association, and Mahwah, NJ: Erlbaum.

Kimble, G. A., & Wertheimer, M. (Eds.). (1998). *Portraits of pioneers in psychology*, Vol. *3*. Washington, DC: American Psychological Association, and Mahwah, NJ: Erlbaum.

Kimble, G. A., Wertheimer, M., & White, C. A. (Eds.). (1991). *Portraits of pioneers on psychology.* Washington, DC: American Psychological Association, and Hillsdale, NJ: Erlbaum.

Murphy, G., & Kovach, J. (1972). *Historical introduction to modern psychology* (3rd ed.). New York: Harcourt Brace Jovanovich.

Postman, L. (Ed.). (1962). *Psychology in the making: Histories of selected research problems.* New York: Knopf.

Viney, W. (1998). *A history of psychology: Ideas and context* (rev. ed.). Boston, MA: Allyn & Bacon.

Viney, W., & Wertheimer, M. L. (Eds.). (1979). *History of psychology: A guide to information sources.* Detroit, MI: Gale.

Watson, R. I. (1978). *The history of psychology and the behavioral sciences: A bibliographic guide.* New York: Springer.

Chapter 23

Tomorrow and Tomorrow and Tomorrow: Teaching The Future of Psychology

Barry D. Smith
University of Maryland

For I dipped into the future, far as human eye could see,
Saw the vision of the world, and all the wonder that would be,
Yet I doubt not through the ages one increasing purpose runs,
And the thoughts of men are widened with the process of the suns.
—Alfred Lord Tennyson

T ennyson's poetic observations are particularly apropos as we rapidly approach a 21st century that promises a bright future for our young science of psychology. Students need and want to know just what the next century of psychology is likely to bring, and their curiosity about the future provides a powerful pedagogical tool.

Most of us teach primarily about past and present developments in psychology, which is certainly consistent with what most textbooks offer our students. Moreover, what we might consider recent developments can seem like ancient history to a freshman born c.1980. My own consciousness about this issue was raised several years ago during my lecture on learning processes in an introductory psychology course. I was deeply immersed in the historically important work of Pavlov, Thorndike, Hull, and Skinner when an excellent student, who always sat in the front row, began to snore loudly. The resulting laughter awakened the now red-faced student, and he apologized, but I vowed to find more interesting ways of teaching about great theories and bodies of research.

Teach the Future to Capture the Past

I soon discovered that one solution to this problem—particularly salient as the Millennium approaches—is to use student interest in the future to teach about the past and present (Smith, 1998). We might call this approach *scientific futurism*—using scientific principles and knowledge to predict future progress. For example, I can talk about the likely future developments in neural networking and neurophysiology as a basis for learning and cognition. Then I can show how the major learning theories have contributed to the exciting future of this field.

This article first appeared in the May/June 1999 APS Observer.

I've found that frequent reference to likely developments down the road makes a number of contributions to the teaching-learning process:

◆ It increases the perceived relevance of much of the course content. Whether a student is 18 or 30, her career—the reason she's in college—is ahead of her. In fact, it is primarily in the 21st century, and looking ahead in psychology is therefore far more salient for most students than looking back.

◆ It changes the teaching-learning process from passive to active because students are forced to use historical information to predict and assess future developments.

◆ It increases student interest in the overall topic. Discussions tend to be much more dynamic, and students participate more energetically as they try to gaze into the scientific crystal ball and predict the future from the past.

◆ It focuses attention on the historical or current subject matter at hand. My experience is that students listen more carefully and effectively to a lecture on Freud or Festinger when they know that these historical theorists will be important in a discussion of future prospects.

◆ It provides a useful frame of reference, an organizing schema for learning about research and theory. A lecture on the neural mechanisms of vision is far more interesting to many students when their frame of reference is the attempt to treat blindness by using a video camera to send visual signals directly to electrodes implanted in the occipital cortex, bypassing the eyes (work that actually began in the 1970s).

◆ It helps to teach critical thinking. For example, what are the most likely future treatments for major depression? Students must use available information on causes of the disorder and effectiveness of current biological and psychological treatments to think critically about developments in the 21st century.

◆ It helps to teach ethical principles. For example, as we learn more about the causes of anxiety disorders, we may well be able to develop new therapies that are far more effective than current ones but expensive to administer. Students might be asked to consider any ethical issues such developments would raise. They might discuss the issue of accessibility to underserved populations and the need for psychologists to be involved in making effective new therapies widely available.

Scientific Futurism that Works

Over the past several years, I've tried a number of approaches to future-oriented teaching, particularly in large introductory psychology courses with discussion sections. I certainly don't use this future-oriented pedagogy for all topics or in all class sessions, but I'll outline here some of the approaches that seem to work. Of course, not all these strategies work for all students.

The Scientific Crystal Ball

In this classroom exercise, I (or my TAs) raise specific questions about likely future developments. We point out that, like clairvoyants, students are being asked to predict the future. However, the crystal ball they use must be a scientific one: They must defend their speculations on the basis of what they have learned (or can learn) about existing research and theory (Smith, Levine, & Wilken, 1998).

As an example, I might ask students to look ahead to possible 21st century treatments for schizophrenia. A student might respond that genetic engineers will insert genes to prevent the disorder or that new drugs will permanently alter brain dopamine receptors or production. I will then ask him to defend those predictions by talking about prior and current theory and research that led to his hypotheses.

Future Applications

Another pedagogical strategy is to ask students to speculate about future applications of current or developing knowledge in psychology. The general approach here is to point out that psychologists have developed a considerable body of knowledge in the area of ____, then ask how that information might be applied to the solution of practical human problems.

One example comes from developmental psychology. Despite the rapid graying of the population, most 18-year-olds have little active interest in the aging process (after all, they'll never be that old!). To enhance their interest, I may ask them to determine the principal cognitive problem in aging and then indicate how it might be addressed in the future by applying and expanding upon what we already know about cognition and memory.

The student must first know from the text and lecture that a reduction in short-term memory ability is the most common cognitive problem. In order to address this problem, she must also know about principles that have been derived from cognitive theory and research and can be applied to the augmentation of memory. She might then suggest that older people be taught to pay close attention to new material they are learning, engage in distributed practice, elaborative rehearsal, and deep processing, and use chunking, imagery, and context cues to maximal advantage. She might even suggest that later-generation acetylcholine-enhancing drugs, representing improvements on such current drugs as physostigmine and tacrine, may eventually be used to improve memory.

Thinking Critically about the Future

Another teaching technique, and one I find especially useful, is to present exercises in which students think critically about future developments in specific areas. In this case, I provide a summary of relevant background information that they have read or heard about in the course, drawing on a variety of related material and providing some integration. The student is then asked to complete the critical thinking exercise. He first formulates one or more specific hypotheses about future developments, then responds to a series of critical thinking questions: (a) What are my hypotheses or predictions? (b) What evidence supports my predictions? (c) Are there alternative interpretations of that evidence? (d) Is additional evidence needed? (e) How good is my prediction likely to be?

Students usually find this exercise interesting, and the need to review relevant material reinforces what they are learning about the literature from reading and lecture. The added bonus is that they are practicing critical thinking, which I teach from day one of the course.

An example of this exercise is to ask how television programming should or might be changed in the future, given the evidence that violent programs increase violence in society. These days I usually pair this with the related question of changes in and control of Internet offerings. And I point out that children spend an average of 15,000 hours watching TV (and increasing amounts of time on the Internet), as compared with 11,000 hours in the classroom, and see five violent acts every hour. To think critically about future developments, students must know about the relevance of Bandura's observational learning theory. They must also be aware of research documenting the role of TV in societal violence and of evidence concerning the effects of other such exposures as violence in the home, neighborhood, and school.

Future Interventions

Many psychologists deal at various levels with the development of more effective methods for changing the behavior of the individual criminal, patient, client, or employee. In the context of a discussion of treatment for psychological disorders or of behaviorism or even neuroscience, I might ask students to predict future developments in intervention. Will we find ways to better modify and control behavior and what might those be?

As an example, I might ask about future possibilities for dealing with the behavior of a patient who is subject to unpredictable rage attacks. The student may speculate that we will implant electrodes in the amygdala (which has already been done) or perhaps perform psychosurgery to create a tiny lesion. I will then ask her to summarize existing research from the text or lecture that led her to those conclusions. In this case—and in any discussion of behavior control—I also address the ethical issues that this possibility raises.

Interviews with Experts

Students can be assigned to assess likely future developments by interviewing an expert, usually a professor in the department, about the future of his field. To prepare for the interview, students must learn as much as possible about the expert's field from the text and outside readings and also learn something about the cognitive science literature that deals with how experts think.

An example here might be the future of psychotherapy. Given the managed care pressures to reduce the cost of therapy, will we see greater use of brief therapy, of drugs, of psychosurgery? If so, how will these changes affect the probability of successful treatment and perhaps even the mental health of the population at large?

Reviewing Articles about the Future

A number of psychologists have written articles in which they project some areas of the field into the future. Included are such figures as David McClelland, Roger Sperry, Eleanor Gibson, David Buss, and M. Brewster Smith. I ask students to read one or more of these or similar articles, summarize them, indicate the extent to which they agree with the author and why, and use the article as a jumping off point to go beyond what the author says. They must cite relevant literature from the course to support their points and speculations. I have used this as a writing assignment in both introductory and more advanced courses. However, it is probably better handled by students in the higher level courses.

Discussion Groups

Teams of three to five students within a discussion section or a relatively small course can be assigned to consider the future of each of several areas within a given field of psychology. The groups then present their conclusions to the entire class, citing theory and research to back up their predictions. In studying social psychology, for example, one group might discuss future developments in attitude change, another social influence, and still others could tackle social perception, interpersonal attraction, and prosocial behavior.

More Windows on the Future

I've given a number of examples of topics that lend themselves to the use of scientific futurism as a teaching technique, but there are obviously many more. Here are a few additional examples:

The role of genetics in normal and abnormal behavior

Approaches to increasing the rate and amount of learning

Neural networks as a basis for learning, memory, and cognition

The development of expert and robotic systems capable of learning and even thinking (already claimed for some systems)

◆ Brain grafts to treat neuropsychological disorders

Increasing longevity by inserting genes that re-extend the telomeres on chromosomes, thereby causing cell division to continue beyond the Hayflick limit

Neurological measures of IQ potential

Using implanted electrodes and precise psychosurgical techniques, such as cingulectomy and subcaudate tractotomy, to treat intractable schizophrenia, depression, and anxiety disorders.

Ethical Issues in Scientific Futurism

In using scientific futurism to teach various topics in psychology, it is important to address actual or potential ethical issues that arise whenever future developments, and particularly applications, are considered. Depending somewhat on the topic, I ask students to deal with the ethical implications of predictions they make about future developments. Some general

questions include:
- ◆ Can an application or development potentially do harm, as well as good, and how might psychologists and society deal with that possibility?
- ◆ Will certain groups be disadvantaged by limited access to improvements and how can that be prevented?
- ◆ What approaches should be used to ensure that a new application is safe and effective?
- ◆ What might happen if we go too far in our attempts to use scientific knowledge from psychology to solve individual or social problems?
- ◆ How can we ensure that the rights of the individual will not be violated by future developments in our field?
- ◆ How can we be certain that new research techniques are ethical?

Conclusion

Scientific futurism is obviously only one of many potentially useful pedagogical techniques and is best used as just one aspect of an overall effort to teach psychology effectively. As pedagogy, it is a thinly veiled attempt to garner student interest and thereby focus attention on the material to be learned. Beyond pedagogy, it provides the student with a glance into the likely future of psychology and promotes critical thinking, creative reasoning, and an appreciation of the importance of grounding progress in sound scientific logic and knowledge.

Recommended Readings and References

Buss, D. M. (1995). The future of evolutionary psychology. *Psychological Inquiry, 6*, 81-87.

Gibson, E. J. (1994). Has psychology a future? *Psychological Science, 5*, 69-76.

Halpern, D. F. (1996). *Thought and knowledge: An introduction to critical thinking* (2nd ed.). New York: Erlbaum.

McClelland, D. C. (1996). Does the field of psychology have a future? *Journal of Research in Personality, 30*, 429-434.

McKeachie, W. J. (1994). *Teaching tips: Strategies, research, and theory for college and university teachers* (9th ed.). Lexington, MA: D. C. Heath.

Smith, B. D. (1998, January). *The scientific crystal ball: Teaching the psychology of the future.* Paper presented at the meeting of the National Institute on the Teaching of Psychology, St. Petersburg Beach, Florida.

Smith, B. D., Levine, V., & Wilken, J. (1998). *Instructor manual to accompany psychology: Science and understanding.* Dubuque, IA: McGraw-Hill.

Smith, M. B. (1994). Human science—really. A theme for the future of psychology. *Journal of Humanistic Psychology, 34*, 111-116.

Sperry, R. W. (1993). The future of psychology. *American Psychologist, 50*, 505-506.

Chapter 24

Science Across the Psychology Curriculum

Rick Wesp
East Stroudsburg University
Nancy Koschmann
Elmira College

P sychologists are sometimes sensitive to popular perceptions of psychology as less than a real science. To our delight, however, on a recent questionnaire distributed to our classes we discovered that students gave psychology high marks as a science. Yet we were puzzled by the assumptions many of these same students still held: that *Cosmo*'s latest reader poll accurately reflects North American sexual practices; that more violent crimes are committed during a full moon; that housework is shared equally in a majority of modern marriages. Clearly there are significant incongruencies between what students believe and what they understand.

In this column we review methods we use to encourage students to become better scientists and develop in them an appreciation for a scientific approach. We suggest incorporating an approach that integrates more scientific thinking in existing courses by:

◆ Showing students that psychology is a body of knowledge derived from the application of scientific methodology,

◆ Involving students in scientific discovery and evaluation, and

◆ Helping students identify as scientists/psychologists.

In short, students need to witness science, practice science and, ultimately, become (think like) scientists as they explore behavior.

Seeing Psychology as Science

Define Science

To be better scientists, students must understand what science means. For many of our students, psychology is a science because it includes set

This article first appeared in the May/June 1998 APS Observer.

definitions, distinct categories, and technology (that is, fancy lab equipment). Yet most of us believe it is the process that makes our work scientific.

Definitions such as "[science] means the enterprise of explaining and predicting—gaining knowledge of—natural phenomena, by continually testing one's theories against empirical evidence" (Diamond, 1987, p. 35) can be useful as a starting point. But we have found that the best way to get students to reflect on the nature of science is to assign them the task of determining whether or not psychology actually is one. An assignment to design a scientific psychological study sends students into the library researching definitions and out gathering evidence. A common student approach has been to gather opinions about whether psychology is a science. We initiate our post-exercise discussions by asking questions such as "Did you learn whether psychology is a science, or whether people think it is?" and move to the broader questions about what constitutes science.

Describe the Actual Research Behind the Facts

Computer simulations, classroom demonstrations or lectures can expand on how data which underlie theories were gathered. For example, giving a lecture on Piaget's stages of cognition that details his methods—his baby diaries, notes, and the problems generated—leaves students with a fuller understanding of how systematic observation and testing can serve to round out a theory.

Demonstrate the Investigative Process

Students enjoy real-life detective stories such as Stephen Jay Gould's *The Mismeasure of Man*, which depicts the process by which scientific questioning and subsequent reexamination of evidence led to a radically different conclusion than originally posited. Many of the brief video Teaching Modules drawn from WNET's *The Mind* series (Worth Publisher, 1990) clearly illustrates the interrelated questions that guide the sequential steps of science. Films can demonstrate research: for instance *Rock-A-Bye Baby* shows a variety of approaches used to examine maternal deprivation and the more recent *Cross Cultural Approaches to Cognition* with Jerome Kagan records actual research in different cultures.

Discuss Your Own Research

Share the process by which you developed testable hypotheses from your particular interests in the field. Describe your methods, provide anecdotes that illustrate procedural or methodological issues, and present your findings.

Doing Psychology as a Science

Expose Students to Doing Science Early in Your Course

Start out the first day with a question, the answer to which must be gained through scientific inquiry in order to focus the students on the scientific process. We model the processes of generating hypotheses, constructing research instruments, interviewing or observing participants, analyzing and charting results, and brainstorming possible interpretations of the data. In one useful first day research project we replicate cognitive research on level-of-processing. Half the class counts the vowels in a list of words while the others search for synonyms. After a few intervening tasks, we compare memory under the two conditions and show that deeply processed information is better recalled. This class experiment demonstrates how psychologists investigate questions about how we learn, shows a method of science, and allows for a discussion of the application of such research to studying for the course.

Teach Topics with Broad Appeal

Bernstein (1994) suggests beginning introductory courses with a scientific examination of psychic phenomena; we also have found alcohol use, attitudes on sex, witchcraft, adjustment to college life, relationship variables, and campus violence to work well. For example, one class identified a list of college adjustment difficulties, voted as to which one they thought was most commonly experienced, then surveyed other students about their adjustment problems. Survey results demonstrated that their assumptions did not match empirical evidence.

Regularly Involve Students in the Practice of Science

Throughout the introductory course we encourage students to continue their application of the scientific method by surveying sleep patterns (states of consciousness) of class members or roommates, charting sibling position and correlating it with a personality trait (personality theory), or doing an interview on attitudes toward cheating (moral development). We typically begin with a small classroom survey and progressively bring students into active research.

Use Easily Accessible Research Settings

Students can observe behavior in dorm rooms, libraries, supermarkets, parks, passing vehicles, other classes or even on TV or in movies. We successfully use our college dining facility as a real-life laboratory where students can practice their new research skills. For example, students have made simple observations (what foods are taken), correlations (food portion size with amount of exercise), and introduced manipulations (will diners sit at a table where books have been left?). Athletic events offer data related to cognitive processes and sports psychology; for instance, students have evaluated the effectiveness of different practice techniques on performance of intramural teammates. Such environments are a rich source of interesting behavior, require no departmental financial support, and do not have to be set up in advance. Some studies might require institutional review board approval.

Discuss Research Ethics in Practical Terms

Ethical issues related to research are best discussed at the moment of research design; we have found that reading a list of ethical principles at the end of the research chapter is far less effective than having students create their own list, compare it with the one in the text, and then use the final list to guide them in evaluating the appropriateness of their own or classmates' studies.

Accept Errors and Problems

Learning from mistakes is also a crucial part of the scientific process. Our best student of the past few years will never forget to carefully label her data after failure to do so resulted in several wasted days of data collection. In another case, students studying helping behavior asked fellow students for a quarter for a phone call only to find that few of their classmates carried change. The experience showed them the subtle complexity of planning a study.

Seeing Oneself as a Scientist

Make Psychologists Real

Old movies remain useful: our students delight at the children's behavior in *The Child Watchers*, and enjoy seeing what famous researchers and authors looked like when they were younger . . . or alive. Biographical reflections of research careers like those in Brannigan and Merrens' (1993) *The Undaunted Psychologist* are effective reading assignments. Sites on the Internet allow students to examine research interests of psychologists at other institutions or you can invite researchers from other campuses to talk about their work and set up brown bag lunches where faculty and students can discuss their own projects.

Relate Scientific Inquiry to Students' Lives

We ask if they or anyone in their family had been a participant in a research project; sometimes we design one for the whole class so that all of us will be part of scientific history. Anything is grist for the mill: parents who had controversial medical treatment or a sibling who attended Headstart. Thus we focus the class on interesting and relevant topics, while making the point that science is relevant to all.

Introduce Students to Professional Organizations

Take students to conferences where they will see, hear and meet active people in the field. Encourage students to join professional organizations and subscribe to journals and newsletters, such as the APS *Observer*. Students can follow the activities of organizations such as the American Psychological Society.

Provide Students with Opportunities to Present Their Research

Hold a mini-conference where students present their semester's work either as a paper, a demonstration or poster. The sight of a classroom encircled by posterboard displays of charts and graphs, photos of the research in process, short write-ups in large print, and even video playbacks creates an enormous sense of accomplishment in the students (and in us, too!). These in-house opportunities can result in presentations at undergraduate conferences, Psi Chi poster sessions, local symposiums, or specialized meetings.

General Implementation

We have discovered that the above takes little extra time and effort, but it has made better scientists/psychologists of our students and increased our enthusiasm for teaching. Four hints for implementation are:

Identify Activities in Advance

Prior planning ensures that we introduce the elements of science in a logical manner. We choose activities and assignments that clearly demonstrate specific scientific concepts and then include these in our syllabus, careful to structure the assignments and activities from simple to complex tasks. In the introductory course, for example, assign a methodology or scientific concept on which to focus in conjunction with each content chapter.

Use Alternate Teaching and Grading Procedures

Consider assignments that do not require significantly more grading time and might be more authentic and effective in evaluating performance. Most examinations call for facts, but it is possible to develop other means of evaluation that are more active, rely less on rote learning, take into account the tentative nature of research conclusions, and are more time-effective. For example, have students outline as part of their exams possible methodological procedures to test a particular hypothesis. Have groups demonstrate experiments they have reviewed in the literature. A final pass/fail paper analyzing all the brief science activities and demonstrations included in the course also works well to encourage students to attend to these activities.

Introduce Cooperative Learning

We routinely require cooperative research projects, paragraph-length summaries of observations by student pairs or triads, and group interviews in class. Cooperative projects reduce the number of individual student projects you will need to plan and grade and group members can often work together to resolve problems without your assistance. Additional time working on projects with the groups is a more productive use of our time. Brief oral reports by randomly selected students will maintain motivation and check for quality. Students in upper level courses can cooperatively develop and conduct research with and design projects for students in introductory courses.

Don't Do Everything at Once

Try adding a few activities each time you teach a course, discarding or fixing those that were ineffective or too time consuming.

Conclusions

When a course is focused on facts that have already been discovered, students have little need to understand science and its methods. By emphasizing the process of science, we can develop an inquisitive approach that will lead students to search out and question the facts. Most faculty include many of our suggested activities, but we are suggesting that these activities become the focus rather than an afterthought. We found that by simply raising, over and over, questions about the processes underlying scientific discovery, articulating the need to challenge conclusions, and modestly increasing students' opportunities for empirical testing, we sensitize them to the scientific foundation of psychology and increase their ability to apply scientific procedures. And we watch our students become psychologists!

Recommended Readings and References

Bernstein, D. (1994). Tell and show: The merits of classroom demonstration, *APS Observer*, *7*(4), 24-25, 37.

Brannigan, G., & Merrens, M. (1993). *The undaunted psychologist*. New York: McGraw-Hill.

Diamond, J. (1987). Soft sciences are often harder than hard sciences. *Discover*, *8*(8), 34-39.

Halonen, J. (1996). On critical thinking. *APS Observer*, *9*(4), 28-29, 31.

Ware, M. L., & Johnson, D. E. (Eds.). (1996). *Handbook of demonstrations and activities in the teaching of psychology*: Vol. *1*. Introductory, statistics, research methods, and history. Mahwah, NJ: Erlbaum.

Chapter 25

Increasing Student Interest In Psychological Theories

Marianne Hammerl
Heinrich-Heine University

A ttracting and maintaining students' attention when teaching them basic psychological theories is not easy. Students tend to be more interested in practical, real world relevant topics and show little passion for the underlying theoretical concepts. Additionally, many students have difficulties in understanding scientific theories and theoretical questions.

The Too Much and Too Heavy Syndrome

The problems become apparent in two areas: perception and interpretation. Problems of the first kind include students' difficulties in identifying and stating the essence of a theory, resulting from an inability to distinguish between major and minor points. Even when the key points are identified, problems of the second kind can arise in the form of a lack of competence with a scientific point of view. That is to say, many students who are enthusiastic about the content of a special theory are not able to control their enthusiasm and evaluate the content according to scientific criteria.

What Can Be Done?

To alleviate these problems, instructors should: stress the usefulness of psychological theories; emphasize the relevance of psychological theories to everyday life; give support in understanding and in evaluating psychological theories, including their strengths and weaknesses; and show the benefits of proper application of theories.

In this column, some suggestions are offered that might help achieve these teaching goals. The following guidelines were developed and tested in introductory courses in theories of social psychology. However, they are easily applied to other types of psychological theories, for instance to theories of learning or personality.

This article first appeared in the January 1997 APS Observer.

Demonstrate the Need for Good Theories

Quoting Kurt Levin's famous maxim "There is nothing so practical as a good theory" is not a bad start, but letting students experience the need for good theories, which are an essential part of science, may be better. Why not start a new course with an *opening quiz* asking students for their predictions of the outcomes of some situations? For example: Are people who receive more than they deserve pleased or displeased? Do people who fear something want to be alone or with others? Perhaps our students can answer such questions accurately, but they will not be able to explain why their answers were correct. Students will discover that their common sense knowledge is helpful for predictions of behavior, but without understanding they will be unable to change or control behavior. Once convinced of the usefulness of psychological theories, students need help in understanding them.

Place Theories in a Common Framework

After discussing a theory in detail, including its failures and modifications, students sometimes become confused and unable to see the key points anymore. To clarify these points it is very helpful to present each theory within a common framework or system. One such framework consists of a system that identifies the input variables (In), the mediating process (Med), and the output variables (Out) described in the theory.

◆ The input variables represent the conditions that are producing the effects the theory under discussion describes.

◆ The mediating process represents the type of basic process (i.e., cognitive and/or motivational) that is supposed to be the underlying mechanism. In the context of learning theories, it is common to speak of the intervening process or variables.

◆ The output variables represent the resulting effects predicted by the theory when the input variables are present.

For instance, the theory of psychological reactance is a broad theoretical approach to the question of what happens when a person's freedom is threatened or eliminated. It describes the influence of social pressure on human behavior and cognition. The theory states that when people feel their freedom of choice is threatened, they experience unpleasant arousal (i.e., reactance), which motivates them to restore their freedom. This theory can be presented in terms of the In-Med-Out approach as follows:

◆ Input variables:
  • Expectancy of freedom (necessary condition)
  • Importance of freedom
  • Threats to or eliminations of freedoms (necessary condition)
  • Number and proportion of freedoms threatened or eliminated
  • Implication for future freedoms

◆ Mediating process:
  • Psychological reactance (i.e., motivational state)
◆ Output variables:
  • Direct restoration of freedom
  • Direct exercise of the threatened freedom
  • Indirect restoration of freedom: restoration by implication
  • Increase of the attractiveness of the threatened or eliminated freedom
  • Denial of threat
  • Preservation of other freedoms

As the example shows, input variables include not only necessary conditions but also variables that influence the extent or intensity of the effect. In this example, the importance of the freedom is not a basic requirement for the arousal of psychological reactance, as it is in the case with expectancy of freedom, but high importance makes the development of psychological reactance more likely. Additionally, it can be seen that just as reactance can be aroused by implication (see one of the input variables), so can it be reduced (see one of the output variables). Without this structural help it may be difficult for students to understand and remember a theory.

Placing all theories into an identical system makes it easier to compare the different concepts; similarities and differences may become more apparent. The difference between Festinger (cognitive dissonance theory) and Bem (self perception theory), for instance, can be shown within this framework by pointing out that the same outcomes are expected (i.e., output variables are identical), but different underlying processes are assumed (i.e., the mediating processes are different). In a similar way, the differences between S-R behaviorism and S-O-R neobehaviorism can be demonstrated easily. In courses in personality theory, it may be interesting to discuss within this framework the famous Rogers-Skinner debate on the control of human behavior.

Use the Theory of the Week Approach

Naturally, when introducing a new psychological theory, the instructor gives examples of its practical applications in various areas of psychology. For instance, students often do not know that concepts of social psychology were adopted by clinical psychologists (e.g., attribution therapy) or that effective therapeutic methods (e.g., paradoxical injunctions) can be explained by theories of social psychology (i.e., theory of psychological reactance).

Additionally, the instructor should find and present examples that deal directly with everyday life. In this context, the following idea, which can be called the *theory of the week approach*, has been useful. The students are instructed to see their world within the framework of the theory to which they were just introduced. For one week, the students are asked to try to interpret their current experiences (usual and unusual events) on the basis of this theory. Additionally, they are asked to search for past experiences that might be explainable by the theory under discussion. In a course in personality theories, for example, students can be asked to prepare a brief description of a currently famous person or a well known historical figure in terms of the personality theory under discussion. Depending on the course schedule, this idea is certainly modifiable to a theory of the day or month.

In the following class meeting, the students' examples should be discussed. Students are always astonished at the number of everyday life situations that fit into an actual theory. Reported examples may cover a wide range of situations: advertising, literature, songs, jobs, close relationships, or private thoughts.

There are always some reported examples that do not match exactly with the theory. However, these mistakes are useful for recapitulating the basic concepts of the theory. When discussing, for instance, the theory of psychological reactance, there are occasional reports best explained by the concept of frustration and do not appear to exemplify threatened freedom. Often, these erroneous examples are useful in demonstrating the different input variables of the theories.

Try the Best Theory Approach

Many theories of psychology are very convincing at first sight. Nevertheless, there are differences in their scientific relevance. Students need help differentiate between good and poor theories. In this context, the following suggestion, which can be called the *best theory approach*, has turned out to be useful.

During the first class meeting of a course, scientific criteria for evaluating a theory are gathered and discussed. Although instructors are free to choose their own criteria, there are some characteristics of a good theory that everyone considers to be important. For instance, whether a theory is testable, comprehensive, and empirically valid are always mentioned. Psychology courses differ with respect to whether value for future research or personal significance, for instance, are criteria for a good theory. The chosen criteria form the theory test stand, on which each theory is evaluated.

Criterion by criterion, the theory under discussion is evaluated by means of a rating scale to determine to what degree each criterion is satisfied. Depending on the course, this rating scale may be a 5- to 10-point scale. The criteria ratings are then summed. Near the end of the course, the theories are ranked according to their summation scores. The theory that is placed first is nominated as the best fitting theory. The criteria chosen for the theory test stand and the resulting ranking are then discussed. The merits and shortcomings of each theory are carefully considered, and, if necessary, a modification to the ranking is made. An important lesson learned by students is the realization that one best theory does not exist and that there are several good theories addressing different aspects of the same topic. Taking this into account, the class determines its favorite theory; and by the way, students learn quite a lot about scientific criteria.

The Feeling the Progress Approach

By involving your students in the activities described above, it is likely that you will increase their interest in and understanding of psychological theories. As a last step, ensure that your students become aware of the progress they have made. For that reason, you should repeat the opening quiz. Now, the students will: (a) be correct (again) in their answers, (b) feel more confidant that they gave the correct answer, and (c) be able to explain the correct prediction by referring to the corresponding theory or theories. They may also notice that their knowledge about theories enables them to deal with a huge amount of data by being more able to organize and evaluate the information.

Conclusion

These five teaching tips may be helpful in teaching psychological theories. I have found that increasing student interest can lead to a better understanding of theory and vice versa. Additionally, the improved interaction between students and instructors may increase our enthusiasm for teaching psychological theories.

Recommended Readings and References

Bell, P. (1978). "Psychology is good": True/false? *Australian Psychologist, 13*, 211-218.

Eysenck, H. J. (1985). The place of theory in a world of facts. In K. B. Madsen & L. P. Mos (Eds.), *Annals of theoretical psychology: Vol. 3.* (pp. 17-72). New York: Plenum Press.

Goodson, F. E., & Morgan, G. A. (1976). Evaluation of theory. In M. H. Marx & F. E. Goodson (Eds.), *Theories in contemporary psychology* (2nd ed., pp. 286-299). New York: Macmillan.

Gray, P. (1993). Engaging students' intellects: The immersion approach to critical thinking in psychology instruction. *Teaching of Psychology, 20*, 68-74.

Marx, M. H., & Hillix, W. A. (1987). *Systems and theories in psychology* (4th ed.). New York: McGraw-Hill.

Chapter 26

Using Evolution by Natural Selection as an Integrative Theme in Psychology Courses

Peter Gray
Boston College

Many who teach the introductory course bemoan the enormous breadth and diversity of our field. How, we ask, can we present psychology in an organized fashion, not as just a hodgepodge of facts and theories? One answer: Use evolution by natural selection as an integrative theme. No other concept can tie all of psychology together as meaningfully. Here are some thoughts about how to use the evolutionary theme in an introductory or more advanced psychology course.

Early in the Course, Explain Clearly the Concept of Evolution By Natural Selection and its Relevance to All of Psychology

Many students hold misconceptions about evolution that can interfere with their ability to apply the concept as the course progresses. Some conceive of evolutionary *fitness* in terms that go beyond the survival and reproduction of genes. Some believe that species can be arranged on an evolutionary ladder, that *lower* species are on their way to becoming humans, or that evolution is guided to meet future conditions or higher moral purposes.

One way to help students overcome such misconceptions is to elaborate on examples of evolution that have been observed and documented in our time, such as the evolution of beak thickness in finches on the Galapagos Archipelago, which has been studied for many years by Peter and Rosemary Grant (1991). Over prolonged years of drought the finches evolved thicker beaks, which could crack the harder seeds available, and over years of heavy rains the same species evolved thinner beaks, efficient for eating the softer seeds the rains produced. What was fit in one situation was not fit in the other. In no case did the species anticipate a change in climate by evolving characteristics to meet it in advance, and we know of no mechanism by which that could happen.

This article first appeared in the May/June 1996 APS Observer.

Ask "Why" Questions Throughout the Course and
Categorize Answers as Proximate or Ultimate Explanations

The relevance of evolution to all of psychology can be made clear by pointing out that psychology is the study of behavior and that all behavior is produced by biological mechanisms built through natural selection. The mechanisms of sensation, perception, motivation, emotion, learning, memory, reasoning, and language are products of natural selection, as are all of the mechanisms that make us cultural animals, underlie our social behavior, and allow us to develop personalities. This fact allows us to take a functionalist perspective in every realm of psychology. The psychological processes, traits, and tendencies that characterize our species as a whole came about because they promoted the survival and reproduction of our ancestors' genes.

For every universal human characteristic introduced in a course, we can ask "why" questions. Why does our visual system exaggerate the physical contrast in patterns of light? Why do people everywhere sleep about eight hours of 24, usually at night? Why do children everywhere, when they have a chance, play in certain predictable ways? Why does essentially everyone have the capacity to feel depressed, given certain conditions, or anxious, given others? By asking such questions and discussing students' tentative answers, we can help students understand the distinction between proximal causation (the immediate inducers of behavior) and ultimate causation (the evolutionary advantage served by the behavior-producing mechanism). Such questions often lead to lively debate in which students conclude that the two kinds of explanations are compatible with one another and serve different purposes.

Use Functionalist, Evolutionary Accounts as Frameworks for
Organizing Behavioral Facts, and Use the Facts, to Test the Accounts

Suppose, in response to the question of why humans sleep about eight hours per night, your students suggest more than one plausible evolutionary answer. The sleep pattern might have evolved as a mechanism to restore tissues that wear out from the activities of the day (restoration theory); to keep individuals quiet and hidden at night, when they are most vulnerable to predators and other dangers (protection theory); to conserve energy during the part of each 24-hour day when the individuals can do little else to promote their survival (energy conservation theory); or a combination of these.

With functional theories on the blackboard, the facts that you might want to present about sleep assume additional meaning. They are not simply curiosities but are data for testing theories. The fact that some people (with abnormally low sleep drives) sleep much less than eight hours per night without tissue damage is evidence against the restoration theory. Across species, differences in the amount and timing of sleep correlate with such factors as vulnerability to predation and amount of time that members must spend feeding, supporting the protection and energy conservation theories. Our knowledge of the physiological regulation of sleep—that sleep is controlled by a circadian clock linked to the day-night pattern of light and dark, and not by any known correlate of tissue damage—provides further evidence for the protection and energy conservation theories and against the restoration theory.

When facts are presented to support or refute a theory, students learn more than facts; they learn how psychologists use facts to test theories. The lesson is more compelling if students have developed the theories themselves, and in my experience, students become quite ingenious at developing plausible functional theories after a little practice.

Use Evolutionary Accounts to Help Students Overcome the Pathology Bias

Many students equate psychology with the study of psychopathology, and, in fact, psychology courses do often emphasize pathology at the expense of function. For instance, introductory presentations of social psychology typically focus on the harmful consequences of conformity, obedience, and concern for approval. Similarly, students often learn about the so-called negative emotions (such as anger, jealousy, fear, and shame) primarily as pathologies. But if these are universal human tendencies, they almost certainly served life-promoting functions to our ancestors. To overcome the pathology bias, we and our students can contemplate the potential evolutionary value of such tendencies before attending to the harmful consequences they sometimes have.

As an example, consider the bedtime protest of young children, which in our culture is often discussed in pathological terms as evidence of spoiling. Why do young children resist going to bed? Some students may suggest that the resistance is not so much to going to bed as to going to bed alone in the dark. Children talk about fear of the dark and fear of monsters hiding in the closet. In hunter-gatherer days, being alone in the dark was undoubtedly dangerous to a child (the monsters were real), and children who protested this condition and drew adult attention were more likely to survive. Such an analysis is supported by cross-cultural data. Present-day hunter-gatherers believe that putting a child to bed alone is an act of child abuse, and in cultures where children sleep with a parent or grandparent, bedtime protest is absent (Konner, 1982).

Ask Students to Critique Psychological
Theories from an Evolutionary Perspective

All of the grand theories in psychology, even those that place greatest weight on the role of environment or culture in shaping behavior, are implicitly theories of human nature. As such, they should be at least compatible with the theory of evolution by natural selection. We can ask students (as a written assignment or in a small-group discussion): Are a theory's basic premises compatible with evolution by natural selection? How might each premise be understood as promoting survival and reproduction? How might a theory be modified to make it more compatible with evolutionary theory, yet consistent with the facts used to develop the theory?

At a minimum, such exercises lead students to identify and think about the basic premises of each theory, and at best they lead to reasoned arguments involving evidence and suggestions for further research.

Describe the Limitations of Evolutionary, Functionalist Accounts

The evolutionary perspective, like any other broad perspective in psychology, has limitations. Functional, evolutionary accounts of specific human tendencies are easy to develop as theories but not always easy to test with facts. Some universal human traits may be side effects of our behavioral machinery rather than directly selected adaptations. Depending on conditions, our learning mechanisms can produce behaviors that are irrelevant or even contrary to survival and reproduction. These and other limitations—all made famous through the writings of Stephen Jay Gould—can be hinted at early in the course and then clarified in the exercises and discussions described above, as the course progressed. Evolutionary theory is not a royal road to understanding in psychology, but it is the best general guide we have.

Use the Evolutionary Perspective to Explain the Entwinement of Nature and Nurture

At one time psychology tended to treat instincts and learned actions as separate behavioral categories, but today—largely due to the influence of the evolutionary perspective—most psychologists realize that learning and instinct are inseparable. Evolution has not endowed us with one or two all-purpose learning mechanisms, nor with many rigid, unmodifiable behavior patterns. Rather, evolution has endowed us with many behavioral biases, or tendencies, each of which may have its own mechanism of modifiability (learning) built into it. The laws by which we learn about food, about the movements of objects in three-dimensional space, about other people's minds, and about the grammar of our native language are all apparently different from one another. The behaviors and mental activities through which we explore, assess, and thereby learn in each domain of our world are themselves instincts.

From an evolutionary perspective we can ask why different learning mechanisms have different characteristics, and we should expect to obtain answers in terms of their survival and reproductive value. The same mechanism that is well designed to help us learn whether a potential food is healthful or poisonous, based on the aftereffect of eating it, is not well designed to help us learn whether a new word should be treated as a verb or a noun. The evolutionary perspective provides us and our students with a powerful tool for understanding and thinking about all processes of learning.

When Humans are Compared to Other Species, Discuss the Evolutionary Rationale for the Comparison

Knowledge of evolution helps students understand and appreciate psychological research with nonhuman animals. From an evolutionary perspective, two kinds of similarities can exist across species. Homologies are similarities due to common ancestry, and analogies are similarities due to convergent evolution. Homologies necessarily involve common underlying mechanisms, but analogies do not. Psychologists who wish to learn about mechanisms of human behavior by studying other animals usually focus on characteristics that are homologous to those in humans. Analogies are of less value in the study of mechanisms, but they provide clues about ultimate function. Species that are analogous in some characteristic can be compared to see what other characteristics they share or what environmental pressures they face in common, to test theories about the value of that characteristic.

In his Nobel lecture, Konrad Lorenz (1974) contended that his main contribution was to clarify the distinction between homologies and analogies in behavior and to show the different values of studying each. I have found that sharing Lorenz's insight with students helps them overcome their confusion as to how and what psychologists can learn about humans through studying other species.

Use the Evolutionary Perspective to Foster Critical Thinking

All of the just-described applications of evolutionary theory involve critical thinking. They all ask students to generate evolutionary plausible answers to "why" questions.

A Final Word of Advice

If you haven't previously employed the evolutionary perspective in your course, start gradually. Make students aware of the perspective and apply it in ways with which you feel most comfortable. If it works, go a little further next time you teach a course. Don't use the perspective in ways that seem artificial or strained to you; in that case they will certainly seem so to students. This approach has worked well for me, and I believe it will improve the academic survival of both you and your students.

Recommended Readings and References

Buss, D. M. (1995). Evolutionary psychology: A new paradigm for psychological science. *Psychology Inquiry, 6*, 1-30.

Barkow, J. H., Cosmides, L., & Tooby, T. (Eds.). (1992). *The adapted mind: Evolutionary psychology and the generation of cultures.* Oxford: Oxford University Press.

Grant, P. R. (1991, October). Natural selection and Darwin's finches. *Scientific American, 265*, 82-87.

Gray, P. (1996). Incorporating evolutionary theory into the teaching of psychology. *Teaching of Psychology, 23,* 207-214.

Konner, M. J. (1982). *The tangled wing: Biological constraints on the human spirit.* New York: Harper & Row.

Lorenz, K. Z. (1974). Analogy as a source of knowledge. *Science, 185,* 229-234.

Spelke, E. (1994). Initial knowledge: Six suggestions. *Cognition, 50,* 431-445.

Chapter 27

Teaching Psychology from a Cross-Cultural Perspective

Roseanne L. Flores
CUNY-Hunter College

I t's your first teaching assignment and you have been asked to teach an introductory psychology course. You ask a colleague to look at the syllabus that you have agonized over for weeks to get the right balance among subject areas. She examines the syllabus, nods in approval and, just when you think you've been given the go-ahead, points out that nowhere in your syllabus have you referred to culture. You begin to feel faint and point out that the study of cultural issues would be a separate course. Besides, the textbook includes some references to culture, you know little about other cultures, and even if you did, how would that change the material you teach?

Or maybe you have taught for many years, and feel that introducing discussions of cultural factors into your course description would not substantively change the content. Or perhaps you believe culture is important, but to do it any real justice you would have to take a course yourself.

Whoever you are and whatever your experience with cultural issues, this column is for you. My purpose is to provide some helpful tips on incorporating culturally-relevant material into our psychology courses.

Culture and Psychology

What is culture and why is it important for the field of psychology? Although scholars disagree about how to define culture, most consider it to be a sociopsychological phenomenon that embodies people's shared beliefs, customary practices, attitudes, and values. Cross-cultural research is the study of human behavior across diverse cultural conditions.

Since the beginning, psychology has sought to study human behavior devoid of culture and context. It has attempted to create theories and obtain facts that extend across all cultures. The problem, however, is that principles that appear universal from one cultural perspective do not always extend across cultures. As psychology has come to recognize the impact of culture on human behavior, approaches to studying psychological phenomena have gradually begun to change. However, notwithstanding these

---

This article first appeared in the November 1997 APS Observer.

changes, instructors have been slow to incorporate culturally-relevant material into the classroom.

Understanding the Student Population

As the student population continues to change from one that was once homogeneous and embraced Western concepts to one that encompasses diverse individuals from virtually all areas of the world, there is a growing discontent with studying human behavior from a single cultural perspective. For example, while the Westernized approach to psychology emphasizes individualism and the development of universals that extend across all cultures, many students come from traditions that embrace a more collectivist approach to understanding human behavior.

Students from Asia, Latin, and African cultures have observed patterns of behavior different from the Western ideal. Many Asian children are taught that respect for adults/authority, familial responsibly, and advancement of the group are very important, whereas children from Western cultures are often taught the opposite: adults/authority can be questioned, families are important but one is responsible for oneself, and the advancement of the individual is primary (Kim & Choi, 1994).

Therefore, if one compared Asian children to their Westernized peers using the Western model as the norm, Asian children would be perceived as lacking some important social, emotional and cognitive skills. However, these same children would appear competent from the perspective of their own cultures' expectations.

To ensure that students appreciate the impact of such cultural differences on human behavior, instructors need to incorporate information into their courses that encompasses a broader view of the interdependence between culture and individual, and provides an understanding of the ways culture shapes human behavior.

Choosing a Textbook

Choosing a textbook is probably the most obvious, important, and easiest step the instructor can take to include cross-cultural material in the course. But what should instructors look for? Should a text be chosen that attends to culture throughout or should supplementary materials be used to enhance the current text? The answer depends partly on the instructor's expertise.

Experts in cross-cultural issues may find a single textbook limiting, and may choose to supplement with classics in the field [e.g., Dansen's (1977) *Piagetian Psychology: Cross-Cultural Contributions*; Whiting & Whiting's (1975) classic *Children of Six Cultures: A Psychocultural Analysis*; or Sapir's (1949) text *Culture, Language, and Personality*].

For the novice, choosing a textbook that extensively incorporates cross-cultural material may be best. For example, instructors wishing to introduce cross-cultural material on human development might consider either

Life-Span Development (Santrock, 1997) or *The Development of the Child* (Cole & Cole, 1996). Both textbooks pay special attention to differing sociocultural worlds, and examine how gender and ethnic diversity affect psychological processes. Those with more general interest might consider *Psychology: The Context of Behavior* (Santrock, 1993) which discusses the influence of context in many areas of psychology.

Supplemental Materials

Culture and Psychology (Matsumoto, 1996) is a wonderful supplement with cultural material relevant to any traditional introductory psychology textbook. The author assumes the student is grounded in the traditional psychological literature and therefore can critically think about alternatives to classic explanations. Matsumoto skillfully demonstrates how culture permeates a wide variety of psychological issues such as perception, cognition, language, definitions of intelligence, health, emotion, and work, and cites many studies that show the discrepancies between traditional and cross-cultural interpretations of research.

For example, when we examine the traditional method of asking people to solve problems involving mechanical devices in laboratory settings, Westerners often exhibit more advanced problem solving skills than their non-Western peers (Cole, Gay, Glock, & Sharp, 1971). However, if we look closely at the research, we find that perhaps Western peoples do better on problem solving tasks involving machines because they come from highly technological societies where even the youngest individuals are continually exposed to technology. Examples throughout the text guide the student to consider alternative perspectives as well as traditional approaches to topics in psychology.

Another supplementary textbook, which provides a wealth of information about culture and psychology, is *The Culture and Psychology Reader* (Goldberg & Verdoff, 1995), a compendium of articles that examine culture from historical, scientific, and practical perspectives. It could be used as a primary text for a specific course on culture and psychology, or in conjunction with more specialized texts such as Matsumoto's *Culture and Psychology*.

Good supplemental materials that specifically address cultural issues and enhance any course include Ekman (1984), Gauvain and Cole (1993), Greenfield & Cocking (1994), and Light and Butterworth (1992). These resources offer a collection of works concerning human development that examine social, emotional and cognitive issues from a cross-cultural perspective. All could be used to strengthen either a developmental or an introductory psychology course.

Instructors can also use videotapes that examine human behavior within different cultures. When selecting a videotape, make sure it adequately represents the area under study from a cultural perspective. For example, if you are studying health care and the elderly, you want your videotape to reflect health care in various cultures and its effects on the aging process. Tapes that might enhance an introductory psychology course include *Childhood: A Journey* produced by Daniel Wilson. There are several tapes in the series that provide a close-up look at children from around the world.

Teaching Strategies

Introduction of Theory

One way to enhance a course that incorporates cultural information is to introduce theories that depart from the more traditional Western approaches. Vygotsky's theory on language and thought and Valsiner's theory, which examines the impact of the physical and social environment on development, encourage students to view human behavior from a cultural perspective.

Student Projects

There are many student projects that can be designed to incorporate cross-cultural issues into a course.

◆ If you have a diverse student population, allow students to interview members of their families about various cultural practices, for example, eating and feeding practices in infancy. This method was adopted from a course designed by Patricia Greenfield on culture, race, and ethnicity taught at the University of California-Los Angeles. After completion of the interviews, students can be asked to compare their data and to relate these practices to theories they have studied during the semester.

◆ Have students conduct small research projects that allow interpretation of results from various cultural perspectives. For example, students could perform a traditional Piagetian task, such as conservation of mass, and attempt to explain their findings from different cultural perspectives.

◆ Assign students to small groups that include persons from different cultural backgrounds, choose a psychological phenomenon, and study it from the various cultural perspectives represented in the group. Then students should report on what they have learned, not only from published materials but also from their interactions with one another.

◆ Have students write papers about social issues such as the influence of race, gender and culture on the development of the self. Students could then be asked to discuss their papers in small groups.

Conclusion

Incorporating culture into psychology is not easy but it is necessary to study human behavior adequately. The aforementioned suggestions are in no way exhaustive, but they are beginnings toward the inclusion of more relevant cross-cultural information into psychology classes. Although no course can include everything, the intent of psychology is to examine human behavior, and we should strive to give as complete a view as possible to our students. That means inclusion of culturally-relevant information.

Recommended Readings and References

Bornstein, P., & Quiana, K. (Eds.). (1998). *Teaching a psychology of people*. Washington, DC: American Psychological Association.

Berry J. W., Poortinga, Y. H., Segall, M. H., & Dasen, P. (1992*). Cross cultural psychology: Research and applications*. New York: Cambridge University Press.

Cole, M., Gay, J., Glick, J. A., & Sharp, D. W. (1971). *The cultural context of learning and thinking: An exploration in experimental anthropology*. New York: Basic Books.

Cole, M., & Cole, S. (1996). *The development of the child* (3rd ed.). New York: W. H. Freeman.

Ekman, P. (1984). Cross cultural studies of emotion. In P. Ekman (Ed.), *Darwin and facial expressions: A century of research in review* (pp. 169-222). New York: Gardner Press.

Dasen, P. (Ed.). (1977). *Piagetian psychology: Cross cultural contributions*. New York: Gardner Press

Gauvian, M., & Cole, M. (Eds.). (1993). *Readings on the development of children*. New York: Scientific American Press

Goldberg, N. R., & Veroff, J. B. (Eds.). (1995). *The culture and psychology readers*. New York: New York University Press.

Goodnow, J. J., Miller, P., & Kessel, F. (Eds.). (1995). *Cultural practices as context for development*. San Francisco: Jossey-Bass.

Greenfield, P., & Cocking, R. (1994). *Cross-cultural roots of minority child development*. Hillsdale, NJ: Erlbaum.

Kim U., & Choi, S. (1994). Individualism, collectivism and child development: A Korean perspective. In P. Greenfield & R. Cocking (Eds.), *Cross-cultural roots of minority child development* (pp. 227-257). Hillsdale, NJ: Erlbaum.

Light, P., & Butterworth, G. (1993). *Context and cognition: Ways of learning and knowing*. Hillsdale, NJ: Erlbaum.

Loeb Adler, L., & Gielen, U. P. (Eds.). (1994). *Cross-cultural topics in psychology*. Westport, CT: Praeger.

Looner, W. J., & Malpass, R. (Eds.). (1994). *Psychology and culture*. New York: Allyn & Bacon.

Matsumoto, D. (1996). *Culture and psych*ology. Pacific Grove, CA: Brooks/Cole.

Santrock, J. (1993). *Psychology: The context of behavior*. Dubuque, IA: Brown & Benchmark.

Santrock, J. (1997). *Life-span development* (6th ed.). New York: McGraw-Hill.

Sapir, E. (1949). *Culture, language and personality*. Berkeley, CA: University of California Press.

Triandis, H. C., Lambert, W. W., Berry, J., Brislin, R., Draguns, J., Lonner, W. & Heron, A. (Eds.). (1981). *Handbook of cross-cultural psychology*. Boston: Allyn & Bacon.

Whiting, J., & Whiting, B. (1975). *Children of six cultures: A psychocultural analysis*. Cambridge, MA: Harvard University Press.

Part 6

Writing

Chapter 28

Why Not Make Writing Assignments?

Barbara F. Nodine
Beaver College

I begin this column by throwing down the gauntlet to faculty regarding writing instruction: Your students should write in all of their psychology courses. Exam writing is not sufficient; there should be a variety of written assignments. When I make these statements, faculty typically explain that though they are conscientious teachers, they cannot follow these prescriptions because:

◆ "My classes are too large."
◆ "I don't have time to read and grade all those papers."
◆ "Students are bad writers, so writing assignments are an unfair burden on both faculty and students."

These responses reflect faculty misconceptions based on old-fashioned, narrow ideas about writing. This column will refute these beliefs and offer a pedagogically-sound conception of how teachers might go about incorporating writing assignments in psychology classes.

Faculty should be as responsible for assigning various writing activities as they are for the decision about what content courses make up the major. Our graduates should be able to interact with the course material they are learning, in writing as well as in speaking and reading.

This column will describe a scheme for thinking about writing assignments to guide faculty in incorporating writing into the psychology major.

Writing-to-Learn Activities (Expressive Writing)

Writing activities can be defined in terms of the purpose of the writing and its intended reader(s). Expressive writing is written for oneself for the purpose of understanding a concept or topic. Thus, written reflection on material allows writers to clarify their own understanding of it.

This type of writing can and should be integrated into a lecture class as a form of active learning. For instance, a lecture might be stopped for three minutes, during which time students are asked to do free writing, that is, writing nonstop, without lifting their pens from the page and without concern for spelling or sentence structure. The writing could be in response to a question, such as *What is the best explanation for forgetting?* or *How do you*

This article first appeared in the November 1998 APS Observer.

think parents feel when told their child is handicapped?

Purpose

The purpose of expressive writing is for students to react to the content, to gather their thoughts about ideas being presented to them, and to incorporate someone else's language into their own. The ideas presented in lecture will be more accessible and memorable and better integrated into their thinking.

Often writing activities that ask students to react, summarize, or answer a question are a good beginning for a class discussion. Too often, faculty assume that they are having a class discussion when a few students are talking and the rest are on hold, waiting for this distraction to end and lecture to resume.

When the class discussion is preceded by a short writing interval all students are engaged, not just those few who always participate. Thus, without equipment or handouts, faculty can turn every lecture period into active learning for all the students.

Evaluation

Faculty sometimes misunderstand this type of writing assignment, believing that if they ask students to write they must collect and evaluate the writing. On the contrary, the whole point is for the student to use the writing for self-discovery.

If it was a graded assignment, the purpose would be diverted and students would no longer use this opportunity to incorporate the ideas into their own kind of thinking, but would feel that they had to repeat the teacher's language as they do when writing a test answer.

On the other hand, if instructors would like students to have some evaluation of what they wrote, they could ask volunteers to read, or ask students to pair up and share their writing. Remember, the point is to get thoughts on paper where they can be reviewed and reexamined. A review of what they wrote in the context of another person's reaction, not necessarily the faculty member's, should stimulate student thought.

Various Forms

There are numerous variations of writing-to-learn activities. A particularly adaptable form is to ask students to list three of something (e.g., effects, causes, implications, relevant theories, titles for a paper, titles for a graph) and then select the one that is clearest, best, most important, or even the most unbelievable or ridiculous. That way, students generate a number of alternatives and select from among them, rather than reaching immediate closure on the first answer that comes to mind.

Journals or Logs

Another frequently used expressive learning technique is journals or logs. Students are asked to write reactions to required readings or other course activities on a regular basis and often the instructor reads those journals, responding to them, but not grading them. Again, the purpose is to encourage writing that uses the student's language and ideas for reflecting, remembering, and accentuating the important thoughts.

Learning-to-Write Assignments (Transactional Writing)

We are all familiar with transactional writing; it is manifested in the journal articles we read, the textbooks from which we teach, and the term or research papers we assign. Transactional writing is written to convey information to a public audience, so it contrasts markedly with expressive writing. The student writer of a transactional piece might be describing the results of an experiment, or summarizing literature on a particular topic.

Students majoring in psychology are engaged in learning to write as beginning psychologists. Formal papers, of various types, should be assigned and students should have the opportunity to experience and understand the process of writing such papers through drafts and revisions that are ungraded. The lack of a grade during the drafting process allows students to explore their topics. Grading should come at the end of the process when the students complete their work. Thus, teacher responsibilities for these assignments include the design of the paper assignment, provision of a structure for the students, and a process of evaluation. There are several types of formal papers, so the teacher's instructions will vary with the assignment.

Laboratory Report Paper

The ubiquitous lab report has the clearly defined structure of the journal research article. Students often have some difficulty learning to use that structure because initially they are unable to distinguish what material belongs in each section, even though they understand the research project they have conducted.

Understanding how to write the parts of the research paper helps students understand the research process and become better readers of research articles. But writing this paper is more than getting the form correct; it is about exploring a topic, connecting thoughts, analyzing concepts, and presenting all of that thinking in a style that the writer expects the audience to read with understanding.

Term Paper

There is always the term paper. We assign it at every level of the major, setting expectations differently for freshman than for seniors. The best feature of a term paper assignment is that it allows students to explore topics in which they have an interest. Faculty should make part of the assignment a statement of the purpose of the paper. For instance a term paper might be described as one in which a thorough exploration of a topic addresses a controlling question or thesis statement. An analogy to a *Psychological Bulletin* article might be made and/or a good example of a student paper might be provided.

◆ Faculty should indicate length of the paper.

◆ The type of reference material should be defined: primary sources, number of sources, etc.

◆ The assignment should describe the audience for whom the paper is being written, usually a peer in the class for which the paper is assigned.

Assigning students to write for an audience with more experience or educational background than they have (such as the head of a clinic or the editor of the *Annual Review of Psychology*) puts them at a disadvantage. Students don't know what terms or ideas need to be contextualized for that audience. When writing for a peer audience, they understand and can meet the expectations and address the background level of those readers. Faculty assignments and expectations for the term paper will differ, depending on the level of the course and the centrality of the paper to the course goals.

A teacher of Senior Seminar would be unhappily surprised with a paper written on the same topic or at the same level as a minor writing requirement for students in Introductory Psychology. Faculty expectations for student papers are sometimes implicit and faculty become better teachers by making those expectations explicit.

Other Learning-to-Write Papers

You might assign a critical thinking/evaluation paper in which the student takes one journal or newspaper article and evaluates it by criteria taught in the course. Another option is case study papers, in which a description of a patient, novel, short story, or movie can be provided for students to analyze from the perspective of what they have learned in a particular course.

Interviews of people different from themselves with questions generated from the course content are enriching activities that can be transformed into a paper.

Teaching the Writing Process

In assigning learning-to-write papers, faculty should teach students something about the writing process. They could be given guidance on how to select and shape a topic, how to begin the first draft, and how to revise and edit. Heuristics, such as writing the introductory paragraph after the first draft is completed, help students understand that writing a paper is a recursive process, not a linear one.

Sometimes requiring the submission of an outline is a valuable step in the process. This step forces the student to conceptualize the whole paper. The negative effect of an outline is that students may follow it slavishly as they write, overlooking connections and creative alternatives to the outline, which was developed at an early stage of the paper preparation. People in composition studies are divided on the value of outlines.

One way to ensure that rewriting occurs is to ask that a minimum of one to three drafts be handed in with the final paper.

Ideally faculty should read a paper's first draft, not grading it because that might discourage the student from taking risks on a draft. Short of that, scanning the draft briefly in a student's presence or arranging a peer review session in class are beneficial activities. Faculty should provide questions that emphasize the peer readers' description of what they read, more than their evaluation for a peer review session. What does the reader think is the main point of his/her peer's paper? What organization does the reader use? Are the main points explained fully? Is the introduction engaging?

Faculty *Shoulds* in Teaching Writing

Rather than assume that students cannot write adequately, or that they should already know how to write a paper, we should assume that students are beginners and that our writing assignments should teach them something. It is a faculty member's responsibility to teach the assignment, not just grade it, by:

Defining the paper's purpose.

Defining the audience for a paper.

Offering some guidance on the process of writing the paper.

Defining plagiarism and the importance of citations.

Providing a model of a student paper.

Providing feedback.

Departmental Writing Decisions

Departments should define how their curriculum will build the writing skills they want their majors to have as they graduate. What types of writing should be taught? Each department should answer the following questions:

Should psychology majors be required to complete General Education composition class(es) or writing intensive class(es) during the first year or two, or as soon as possible after the major is declared?

How much experience should a student have using writing-to-learn assignments?

For what range of audiences should a student have experience writing?

◆ What purposes and forms of learning-to-write papers should a student be taught?

◆ How much rewriting experience should be provided?

◆ What sequence of writing experiences in psychology, from first through senior year, will best bring a student to the competency level sought?

I am probably preaching to the choir, and readers may not need to be convinced that writing is a valuable skill for students to acquire. I hope they believe that it is a skill that is developed gradually during the college years. Resistance sometimes occurs when faculty are urged to teach writing, perhaps because they believe that they (faculty) haven't the special knowledge of their peers teaching composition.

I have argued that much of the writing that faculty could assign does not even need to be graded—it simply needs to be made part of the way students learn psychology.

Secondly, our expectations should be taught to students, instead of making the assumption that they should already know these things. Simply showing them a good model and telling them about its merits would be good teaching.

Third, faculty should define the several types of writing that their department expects of graduating psychology majors. With these efforts, we will have a greater pride in our graduates.

Recommended Readings and References

Davis, B. G. (1993). *Tools for teaching*. San Francisco: Jossey-Bass.

Davis, M., & Hult, R. E. (1997). Effects of writing summaries as a generative learning activity during note taking. *Teaching of Psychology, 24*, 47-49.

Fulwiler, T., & Young, A. (1990). *Programs that work: Models and methods for writing across the curriculum*. Portsmouth, NH: Boynton/Cook.

Hettich, P. (1990). Journal writing: Old fare or nouvelle cuisine? *Teaching of Psychology, 17*, 36-39.

McKeachie, W. (1994). *Teaching tips: Strategies, research, and theory for college and university teachers* (9th ed.). Lexington, MA: D. C. Heath.

Nilson, L. B. (1998). *Teaching at its best: A research-based resource for college instructors*. Bolton, MA: Anker.

Nodine, B. F. (Ed.). (1990). Psychologists teach writing [special issue]. *Teaching of Psychology, 17(1)*.

Chapter 29

Raiders of the Lost Reference: Helping Your Students do a Literature Search

J. Frederico Marques
University of Lisbon-Portugal

Just as the character Indiana Jones had to use the library before beginning his adventures, college students also must use the library for their academic projects. However, unlike Dr. Jones, who always finds the right references before his treasure hunt, student searches don't always result in the same success.

Usual complaints are that students don't understand what kind of literature search is expected or where to start; they don't know how to get the best results from the search tools and resources available; they only find superficial information or are submerged in too much information; and they find it hard to evaluate both when to stop the literature search and the quality of the work done so far.

Providing guidance for literature searches is essential in order to teach college students—especially in their first years—to maximize the results of this kind of work during their initial academic projects. This column summarizes some of the points that I have found most helpful to students doing literature searches as they begin their own academic adventures.

Getting Students Started

Be Certain Your Students Know How to Use a Library

Students need to be familiar with library organization and available resources. You can ensure that students know how to use a library by referring them to the proper library services and requiring that they receive this training before working with them. Absent such training, a special program can easily be prepared with your library. Especially for first year students, a *guided tour* with a few practical exercises on the several services and tools that the library provides (e.g. catalogs, reference publications) is useful and librarians generally welcome this collaboration.

This article first appeared in the July/August 1998 APS Observer.

Define the Topic Area

Work with students in selecting, narrowing, and defining a topic area. Time spent on this task is critical for a successful review. Try to make the topic interesting and manageable. Avoid topics that are too broad or involve many esoteric sources.

Help Students Develop Realistic Time Frames

Students often have unrealistic expectations that they can finish a literature review in one or two sessions. We should moderate these expectations and ask students to evaluate the time they spend so that they can become more proficient in their searches. An early assignment might be to have students submit logs describing their searches, the amount of time spent doing them, and the results.

Reading Only Abstracts Is Taboo

Students sometimes assume they need only to read the abstracts of source material (e.g., articles, technical reports, material from databases). It is important to warn them that this strategy is unacceptable, and only sufficient to select articles for further reading. Although citation of abstracts may be necessary if the article is unattainable, the rule of thumb is that students should read the entire article if they cite it.

Teach Students How To Take Notes

Taking good notes is important so that the work done will be useful in successive sessions or for future projects. Students need to be told to take detailed notes both of what they have searched and of the content of each source to be used. Source details include a complete reference, methodology, important findings, statistics used, major strengths and weaknesses of the research, implications for future research, and any comments the student has. Note taking encourages students to read articles more carefully than when they only use a highlighter. Complete note taking also is important to avoid plagiarism, and students should be warned against copying material without crediting the authors. Also, advise students to duplicate lengthy reference sections in important sources to save work at a later date.

Understanding the World of Scientific Communication

A considerable number of first-year students (and sometimes more advanced students) have a limited or erroneous perception of the context of science communication and publication. The following teaching tips may be helpful.

Present Students With Different Types of Communication—Students need to be informed about different forums of scientific communication such as workshops, symposia, posters, or publications (e.g. monographs, different types of books and different types of journals and articles). This information assists them in becoming more knowledgeable consumers of scientific literature and in understanding which sources are the most useful.

Emphasize Journal Articles—At this preliminary stage in a literature review it is crucial to show students that articles published in the scientific journals are the primary source of scientific knowledge and that they should always search for and emphasize these sources in their academic projects. One of the reasons for poor or superficial literature reviews is basing a search solely on books or general manuals.

Help Students Evaluate Their Sources—Students usually know that articles can provide more recent information and data than most books and other sources, but they are unfamiliar with peer-review processes to which articles (but not books) are subjected. Presenting the general process of publication and the difference between highly selective journals and other publications is important in assisting students to evaluate sources.

Differentiate Between Classic and Out-of-Date Sources—Another important point is the life span of an article. Students have particular difficulty in understanding the difference between outdated and classic (older but still relevant) references. Presenting examples of the kind of information that can be more rapidly outdated (e.g., data) versus the content of classic scientific publications (e.g., theory, methodology, famous findings) and then discussing them is a good strategy to explain these differences.

Defining Objectives

Most faculty find defining objectives for their literature searches to be an obvious task, although we do not always state explicitly what we are seeking. Students have to learn to define their objectives as a function of the nature of the project their search is supposed to support. Some find this difficult, and begin their searches without a definite idea of what to look for.

Have Students List Their Objectives

Requiring students to list their objectives and discuss them in relation to the nature of their project (i.e. preparing a class presentation, writing a research report) is particularly helpful for several reasons. First, it allows us to show students that different kinds of searches can be made. Second, it is an opportunity to convey our expectations of what has to be done while letting students participate in that decision. However, minimum requirements and evaluation criteria should always be clearly stated (e.g. how many books and journals, journal level, time span for articles). Finally, creating such lists prepares students to understand and define what they must do for future projects.

Identify Technical Terms For A Search

One defining characteristic of any literature review is the subject or subjects that set the scope of the search. In this context we should convey the importance of using the appropriate technical terms and how to find them using special dictionaries, such as the *Thesaurus of Psychological Index Terms* in the field of psychology or the *Thesaurus of ERIC Descriptors* in education. It is easy to explain the organization of these reference dictionaries and exercises can be provided to familiarize students with their use.

Structure the Task to Assist Struggling Students

Literature searches are time consuming tasks that can unnerve and stress unmotivated and struggling students. Although all students need structure, for these students it is especially important that we clearly state our requirements and evaluation criteria and establish defined tasks and goals (e.g. first week: find out the names of the journals related to the subject and begin selecting references; second week: hand in 20 references and identify the five most important).

This structured approach, using simple incremental steps, will help both types of students develop skills for later use in projects that interest them more, and build the simple skills that literature searches require. Never hesitate to provide a student with explicit and detailed structure.

Doing the Search

Some students find themselves lost at this stage even though they know what they are looking for.

Start Out The Old Fashioned Way

I call this going straight to the heart. More satisfactory results are often obtained when students begin their searches in recent texts or in general manuals, or handbooks of topics in psychology, that by themselves are insufficient for many projects, but give an overview of the area and an indication of where to look for more specific references.

Next, have students investigate review journals such as the *Annual Review of Psychology* (which has a useful cumulative subject index) and the *Psychological Bulletin*. These are good starting points for students, as they supply extensive analyses of the literature that provide other relevant references.

Refer your students to *Contemporary Psychology*, the only book review journal in our field, and its annual subject index.

Third, students can read relevant journals, examining the more recent volumes directly or through their indexes or tables of contents and backtracking references found in specific articles.

Fourth, have students talk with knowledgeable colleagues and follow up on their suggestions. One advantage of nonelectronic searches is access to older references that may be important.

Don't Start With Computer Databases and Tools

While a matter of faculty preference and style, I advise having students become directly involved with sources. Students often become lost when they begin their searches using computer databases of abstracts (e.g. PsycLIT) where a general request provides too many irrelevant references and a very specific request does not provide enough information. For most undergraduate academic projects, this is probably a poor strategy.

Helping students to do more direct and focused searches is more important than providing extensive training on how to maximize results with these kinds of tools. Only after students have become familiar with the general area and terminology do they move to a second phase using computerized tools. When a very specific purpose (e.g. identifying all the works published by a specific author or completing a reference) arises, students can be encouraged to begin their searches with these computerized tools.

Extensive Searches—Getting to the Bottom of Things

For more advanced projects, or when the first kind of strategy does not fulfill its objectives, an extensive search can be advised, using computerized database and special reference books (e.g. PsycLIT, PsycINFO, ERIC, SSCI [Social Sciences Citation Index]). Don't forget about biological or biomedical data bases (e.g. Medline) when appropriate.

Explicitly Define the Project (Again)

Helping students with an in depth literature search requires a more individualized approach as different topics often lead to different strategies and tools. Understanding these needs and helping students to state them explicitly is also crucial when a literature review for a simpler project has been initially unsuccessful, or when engaging in a more sophisticated review.

Sometimes a literature search requires a reformulation and specification of the original and more general objectives. Restating the specific topic area guides students to better reference and database resources, and to search requests (e.g. defining and combining several key subjects) that are more likely to produce good results. Even if faculty are not familiar with the best databases for a given topic or how to use them, well planned requests help students get more focused assistance from librarians.

Use the Worldwide Web Carefully

The Web is also a source for more extensive literature searches. Students enjoy surfing the net but should be warned that the giant waves of information they get often contain only a few drops of relevant content. Assessing the quality of sites can also be difficult, since quality varies greatly. Students should be directed to search university, scientific/professional, journal, and publishing company based sites for quality information. The quality of discussion groups may be difficult to assess.

Encourage Use of Email

The Web and email have brought together researchers all over the world and have added students to the scientific community. While the old snail-mail attempts to contact researchers had a low probability of producing an answer, email has surely improved the odds. More advanced students especially should be encouraged to use email to contact relevant researchers with appropriate questions.

Obtaining Sources Not in Your Library

Students doing an extensive literature review may find citations for references that are unavailable online or in their library. Teach students about interlibrary loan procedures, traveling to nearby larger university libraries, and document purchases if necessary. Structure the literature review so that the first or second sweep is completed early enough so important sources can be tracked down if not readily available.

When To Stop

Students often need assistance in knowing when enough is enough. When they have read recent review articles, a series of publications by authors repetitively cited in the literature, the classic articles in a topic area, and have closely looked at relevant journals and references, students are usually done.

Conclusion

In helping students do literature searches, two aspects are important. First, we must understand that students' needs for literature searches are different from our own. Sometimes we teach students to use approaches to a literature search that are suitable for our research projects, but not necessarily for their academic work. Secondly, help students not only to practice, but also to evaluate the results of the different strategies and skills involved in literature searches. Only by doing this can students improve and become independent and proficient in this critical academic task.

Recommended Readings and References

Kelley-Milburn, D., & Milburn, M. A. (1995). CYBERPSYCH—Resources for psychologists on the internet. *Psychological Science, 6*, 203-211.

Reed, J. G., & Baxter, P. M. (1992). *Library use: A handbook for psychology.* Washington, DC: American Psychological Association.

Rosnow, R. L., & Rosnow, M. (1998). *Writing papers in psychology* (4th ed.). Pacific Grove, CA: Brooks/Cole.

Sternberg, R. J. (1993). *The psychologist's companion: A guide to scientific writing for students and researchers* (3rd ed.). Cambridge: Cambridge University Press.

Chapter 30

Improving Your Students' Writing: Arts and Drafts

Mitchell M. Handelsman
University of Colorado–Denver

Margie Krest
University of Colorado–Boulder

More and more psychology instructors are having students write multiple drafts of research papers. This process leads to better final papers and is closer to what psychologists do when they write their own scientific work.

However, faculty members are often frustrated by the enormous amount of time needed to comb through and respond to rough drafts. Likewise, students become frustrated and overwhelmed when their papers are returned with a mass of red ink, with every extraneous comma circled, and with each page littered with multiple occurrences of "AWK," as if the paper were annotated by a tropical bird.

Assumptions

This column provides instructors with advice on how to improve the scientific writing of their students. We start with two assumptions. First, writing well is not so much a matter of correct grammar as it is a matter of expressing ideas well. Indeed, grammatical and stylistic problems often arise from unclear thinking about one's ideas.

Second, early drafts of research papers demand different types of comments than do final versions. Responses to early drafts should be supportive, helping students formulate and develop their ideas. Only later should stylistic and grammatical concerns become a focus of attention.

Our basic approach is to limit the length and number of our responses to each paper while providing students with useful and substantive comments. We spend time helping students organize their thinking and convey their ideas rather than marking every dangling modifier, vague pronoun, or split infinitive. The result is a more efficient and effective process.

We have divided this column into two sections. First, we outline general guidelines for responding to drafts. Second, we outline the common problems in drafts and suggest ways to respond to these problems.

This article first appeared in the March 1996 APS Observer.

General Tips for Responding to Drafts

Focus on Ideas and Thinking

Grammar and writing style are less important at this stage. Our major role as instructors should be to help students develop and convey their thinking. We can expect students to take more responsibility for editing their own papers once they know what they want to say. Interestingly, grammar and style often improve markedly as students discover how to think about the issues addressed in their papers.

Adopt a Reader's Perspective

Share responses as a reader rather than as a critic. This will help students keep their audiences in mind and make your comments seem less punitive. For example, "I was confused when I read this; it could use more explanation," might work better than, "This is vague and poorly written." The former statement gives information about the experience of the audience and gives the writer direction, while the latter seems more negative and provides little direction.

Be Collegial

Teach students how psychologists work with each other by treating students as we (as scholars) treat colleagues. Good comments are ones that stimulate additional thought and productive conversations among students and between students and instructors.

Be Specific, Up to a Point

Some comments by instructors are so vague they provide no guidance at all. Others are so detailed they offer no opportunity for students to re-think their work. The goal should be to provide brief suggestions without rewriting the paper.

Anticipate Problems That Students Will Encounter

There are normal *developmental milestones* in the production of a research paper. Inform students that problems, such as the 10 listed below, are not errors or evidence of weak writing skills. Rather, they are normal and unavoidable aspects of the writing process. The process itself helps writers organize their thinking and solidify their understanding.

Forewarned that they are bound to make at least some of these mistakes, students may catch and correct them at earlier stages in writing. They may feel freer to take risks because they understand how impossible it is to write a perfect draft. They are also more likely to view resulting feedback on their drafts less as condemnation than as helpful guideposts.

Top 10 Problems

The Early Exaggeration

Many students portray their topics as the most important ever to confront humankind, or they approach the topic from such a broad perspective that they could hardly hope to cover adequately the issue even in a dissertation. For example, a paper about current student reactions to the words *politically correct* need not start with a comprehensive discussion of the history and disastrous effects of stereotypes. We need to help students understand that papers can contribute to the literature even when they address small parts of larger issues. Helpful feedback might be as follows: "My first impression was that this is a paper about stereotypes rather than a study of student attitudes. How about starting closer to your topic?"

Providing Partial Pictures

Students often take shortcuts and leave out important information, or they neglect to show how the information they do provide relates to their topic. For example, a student may report Smith's assertion that people often recover repressed memories in the late afternoon, but neglect to say whether this conclusion is based on theory, clinical experience, or empirical data.

Instructors often respond to this type of problem by marking "incomplete," or "rework." Or, they spend an inordinate amount of time actually filling in the missing content, an activity which is understandably very agreeable to students but which does not help them become better writers. We suggest more efficient yet informative responses such as "How does Smith support this assertion?" Or, we could make a statement that highlights the importance of the audience, such as, "Readers who have not read Smith's article may not understand the basis of this argument."

The Plethora of Particulars

Including too much information in drafts often leads to the opposite problem: Too much detail makes it hard for the reader to follow the discussion. In a case study, for example, the eye color of the client, or the number of years a therapist has been in her present location, are usually not germane. In this situation, a direct statement will suffice: "Omit these details that readers don't need." Or, simply, "Omit unnecessary details."

Data Dumping

Students often simply summarize and report what they have read, assuming that their grade will be based on the quantity of the material they present rather than on the quality of their thinking about that material. We have all encountered papers that are little more than a string of one-paragraph abstracts of each paper the student has found. An expression of curiosity rather than scorn may stimulate some thought: "I'm interested in how you relate these data to your thesis." Or, "How do these two paragraphs tie into each other, and into the rest of your paper?"

Strutting Sources' Stuff

A variant of data dumping occurs when students incorporate the conclusions of other authors, often by stringing together long quotations. In order to encourage students to do their own integration and interpretation, we might say, "You've read more than anyone on this topic; what sense do you make of the issues?" Or, "Paraphrase these quotations and explain their significance."

Excessive use of quotations may also indicate that students have lost their focus. In this case they may need only a gentle reminder: "Omit the quotations. How do the ideas relate to your thesis?"

The Petrified Position

Students often gather and present data from a narrow and rigidly held ideological position, and they may either misinterpret or ignore alternative information and perspectives. For example, students may adhere to a psychodynamic viewpoint while minimizing family systems or behavioral explanations either by omitting them or by treating them as mere variants of their initial perspective. As instructors, we need to remind students of the attitude that underlies research in general, and of the creativity and objectivity necessary for good thinking. Questions such as, "How would a family systems theorist interpret these data?" or, "What are the distinctions between behavioral and psychodynamic approaches?" may stimulate a fruitful discussion.

Focusing on the Flashlight

Consider a paper with the objective of applying ethical principles to a given problem. Students will often spend the majority of their paper merely defining the ethical principles they have studied in class and then impulsively proffer a solution devoid of an actual application of the principles learned. When students repeat but do not apply what they have learned, it is as if they take us into an uncharted cave but spend all their time describing the flashlight rather than the cave. We might respond, "I need less definition of the principles and more about *how* they apply."

The Conclusion Cliff

Students often jump precipitously from the body to the conclusion of their papers, and assume that the reader will intuitively understand their reasoning. After a careful summary of the literature on both sides of an issue, students might conclude, for example, that "serotonin indeed yields a better explanation than does norepinephrine" but provide the reader with no clue about how they moved from the conflicting set of studies to such a confident judgment. We need to encourage students to think more carefully, as well as to explain and convey their thought process to the reader: "I don't understand how you came to your conclusions. Your reasoning is the most interesting, creative, and important part of your paper! Please share your thinking with me."

The Ending Equivocation

While some students are busy jumping over the conclusion cliff and proving petrified positions, others are refusing to take any position at all at the end of their papers. They often fear making judgments or offering personal conclusions. We need to encourage them to take the risk: "After all your good analysis, I'd love to hear your personal conclusion; what is your judgment on the ethics of deceptive research?"

Stilted Style

Finally, there are times when the student's writing style does overcome substance and needs to be addressed. The temptation may be quite strong for us to rewrite sentences. A better option is to point out the *types* of errors that students make rather than take it upon ourselves to mark each one. For example, we might say, "Watch out for passive voice throughout the paper," or "You have a number of run-ons and sentence fragments." We thus place responsibility for finding and correcting grammatical errors on students; plus, we have 20 extra minutes and lots of extra ink to spend on our crossword puzzles or on rewriting our own papers.

Conclusion

By providing students with more productive feedback on draft versions of research papers, much of the frustration of both students and instructors can be avoided. The research paper should be a vehicle instructors use to help students think better and develop their own excitement and passion about psychology. When instructors are freed from responding to papers as grammarians, we can instill in students—through the writing process—more of the excitement about the ideas that attracted us to the teaching of psychology in the first place.

Recommended Readings and References
Krest, M. L. (1988). Monitoring student writing: How not to avoid the draft. *Journal of Teaching Writing*, 7(1), 27-39.
Nodine, B. F. (Ed.). (1990). Psychologists teach writing [Special issue]. *Teaching of Psychology*, *17*(1).

Sternberg, R. F. (1992). How to win acceptances by psychology journals: 21 tips for better writing. *APS Observer, 5*(5), 12-13, 18.

Tchudi, S. N. (1986). *Teaching writing in the content areas: College level*. Washington, DC: National Education Association.

Part 7
Teaching One-on-One

Chapter 31

Academic Advising for Undergraduates

Mark E. Ware
Creighton University

S ome individuals might question why a column on teaching would carry an article about academic advising. The simple answer is that much of our work as teaching faculty takes place out of the classroom; advising is one such activity. For example, in my more than 30 years as a faculty member, I have had to field a number of student comments and inquiries spanning academic, career, graduate school, and personal issues. Here are some examples from my students:

- I got a C in organic chemistry, and I've decided that I don't want to go to medical school. I think I'll major in psychology and become a clinician.
- I'm working 35 hours a week and getting Cs and Ds. I don't know what to do.
- I'll be graduating in December, and I'll need a job. How do I get one?
- I'm having trouble getting along with guys my own age. I was sexually molested when I was five years old. I've never told my parents or anyone else about this. Will you help me?
- I think I want to go to graduate school. How do I do that?
- I don't want to take experimental psychology next semester because I heard it was very hard. What should I take instead?
- Remember when you had the speaker who talked about suicide in Introductory Psychology? I'm worried because last summer I tried to kill myself twice. What should I do?
- I like psychology, but everyone says you can't get a job with a psychology major. Is that true?

Despite many administrators' widely publicized views about the importance of advising, surveys reveal low student satisfaction with advising. A faculty member at a large university even commented that advising was "at best an embarrassment and at worst a disgrace." The purpose of this article

---

This article first appeared in the May/June 1995 APS Observer.

is to identify some of the major goals of good advising, to discuss limits on advisors' knowledge and abilities, to elaborate on the variety of approaches to advising, to briefly discuss materials for advising, and to provide some rules for advising.

The Goals of Good Advising

Assist in Academic Success

Faculty find themselves in a position to communicate strategies for academic success, such as note taking, study skills, test taking, and time management. Statements at the beginning of the article illustrate the complexity of academic issues that students raise.

Support and Encourage Students

Advisors can also support and encourage students. The C student majoring in psychology as a liberal arts degree deserves as much encouragement as students whose aspirations, skills, and behaviors support post baccalaureate education as a means for achieving their career goals. A good advisor helps students *reach*, to consider courses of study or careers they might not otherwise.

Assist Students In Learning About Themselves

Advising is most effective when students are encouraged to examine their personal attributes. Advisors can encourage and direct students to identify their interests, values, skills, and aspirations. Such efforts can reinforce the principle that career advising consists of more than transmitting occupational information. More effective decision-making consists of comparing and contrasting information about one's self, one's major and the world of work.

Help Students Identify and Reach Their Academic Goals

Advisors from small liberal arts colleges to large public research universities agree that the questions they are most frequently asked are about (a) academic issues such as institutional policies and procedures, (b) career opportunities, and (c) post baccalaureate educational alternatives. Good academic advising provides accurate information to assist these students.

Students' entrance into a department's advising program usually begins with his or her declaration of psychology as a major. The mundane task of discussing class schedules is more important than many faculty realize. Good advising contributes to positive experiences in courses by insuring that students have prerequisites, that courses fit their educational goals, and that students have information about college policies, regulations, requirements for the degree, the major, and the minor. Moving systematically through general education requirements and using students' tentative career goals can provide meaningful rationales for selecting courses.

Think About and Identify Career Goals

Choosing and preparing for a career is a major developmental task for young adults and adults, and faculty advisors can assist students in this process. If advisors are familiar with the results from numerous psychology alumni surveys (e.g., McGovern & Carr, 1989) they can help answer the common question about what students can do with a psychology major. Furthermore, advisors can inform students about university career and placement office functions, or schedule talks by individuals from these offices.

Inform Students What They Learn As a Psychology Major

Advisors can supplement occupational information by identifying the types of skills that students can acquire while majoring in psychology such as: (a) writing coherent and well organized essays; (b) developing rapport at a group level; (c) learning to tolerate different values and attitudes; (d) collecting, recording, organizing, analyzing, and interpreting empirical data; (e) designing and conducting surveys; (f) understanding, evaluating, and generalizing research findings; and (g) using library resources or personal contacts to find information to solve a problem or answer a question. Identifying such transferable skills can markedly increase students' prospects for obtaining relevant and challenging employment.

Assist Students in Graduate School Application

Advising students about post baccalaureate education includes identifying alternative fields (e.g., education, social work, medicine, and law) and foundation courses for various programs. Encouraging students to seek a match between personal characteristics (e.g., values, interests, and skills) and characteristics of graduate programs increases their likelihood of success and satisfaction. Additional advising tasks include establishing a realistic timeline for completing applications for graduate school (including a goals statement), taking the GRE (or other standardized test), and selecting faculty to write letters of recommendation.

Limits to Advisors' Knowledge and Abilities

Faculty advising takes place in a context of departmental and campus-wide supports. One of the painful lessons I have had to learn and relearn is that I am not a guru—that I could not and should not try to advise students about all of the issues they raise.

Colleagues are among faculty's most immediate resources, one or more of whom may be called upon to help fulfill students' informational and developmental requirements. One of the most important advising skills I have acquired is making referrals. Faculty have a responsibility to make effective referrals to other faculty or student personnel specialists who can competently meet student needs. Depending on the school, such specialists are in offices of student affairs, psychological counseling, academic support services, or career development and placement centers.

Although faculty play a leading role in advising, they need not be responsible for the entire process. In the final analysis, faculty must find a personal comfort zone or limit of advising that reflects their training, skill, and experience. Beyond that limit, making an appropriate referral may be the best form of advising.

Approaches to Advising

One-on-One Advising

Traditional advising consists of one-on-one contacts between advisors and students. Although this method may be unsurpassed at individualizing the process, one-on-one advising is time consuming and inefficient for delivering generic information. Requiring advisees to read printed materials or to view videotaped materials before their appointments can increase the efficiency and effectiveness of one-on-one interactions.

Student Initiative

One of the most under-used approaches is that of giving students greater responsibility, especially for course scheduling and a program of study. One novel and effective technique consists of using computers to assist psychology majors to become more responsible for maintaining and revising their own advising files (Appleby, 1989).

Peer Advising

Another uncommon, but not unique, approach consists of peer advising. Peer advising programs have provided information about registration procedures, graduate school, job search strategies, and referral procedures. With thorough training and supervision, upper level undergraduate or Psi Chi students can provide a novel dimension to advising (Ware, 1993b).

Group Advising

Meeting in conversation hours with groups of students who have similar needs or interests is another advising approach. Examples include meetings to introduce students to the requirements for the major, to present psychologists or psychology alumni representing different careers, and to discuss strategies for getting into graduate school or the job hunt.

Academic Courses

Academic courses can constitute another form of group advising. Examples include courses for freshman to orient them to college life and for upper level psychology majors to aid them in career planning and decision making (Ware, 1993a). Other relevant educational opportunities include field placement experiences and programs in career guidance and college placement services.

Materials for Advising

There are a variety of materials that departments can develop or acquire to assist advisees. Many faculty have developed handouts and brochures for students seeking information about the academic, career, and post baccalaureate educational areas. Several individuals and the American Psychological Association have produced books and videotapes containing information about academic issues, careers, and post baccalaureate education in psychology (Ware, 1993b).

Rules for Advising

There are some simple yet important rules of thumb when advising. These include:

◆ Identify advising limits. Advisors should not coerce students, promote student dependence, or conduct therapy (Keith-Spiegel, 1994).

◆ Leave your office door open or ajar. Regardless of whether you or your advisee is male or female, it is good practice to advise *in public*.

◆ Give your advisee your undivided attention. If you must talk with a colleague briefly or answer your phone, let your advisee know you will be doing this.

◆ Schedule office hours when you will be available and when advisees will be relatively free. Scheduling office hours at 7AM or only in the evening is a disservice to your advisees.

◆ Be in your office or easily found during office hours.

◆ Urge your advisees to schedule an appointment with you. If an advisee schedules an appointment with you, find out what they want to talk about. This allows you time to think about the topic and obtain any necessary information, and you may have tasks you want the advisee to do before you meet.

◆ An advisee's failure to plan is not your crisis. If an advisee is upset, it is almost always not with you but with something else that has occurred. Do not overidentify with advisees. Keep your cool and focus on solutions to problems and how to proceed.

Conclusion

In this article, I tried to demonstrate that academic advising encompasses promoting academic success, supporting and encouraging students, assisting students to learn more about themselves, stimulating thinking about careers, and the like. The resources listed below constitute a starting point for developing skills for this important faculty task.

Although I recognize that the student population is heterogeneous and that such diversity (e.g., age, gender, and ethnicity) adds complexity to advising, the length of this article prohibits addressing those issues. Interested readers should check relevant sections in Ware (1993b).

Recommended Readings and References

Appleby, D. C. (1989). The microcomputer as an academic advising tool. *Teaching of Psychology*, *16*, 156-159.

Keith-Spiegel, P. (1994). Ethically risky situations between students and professors outside the classroom. *APS Observer*, *7*(5), 24-25, 29.

McGovern, T. V., & Carr, K. F. (1989). Carving out the niche: A review of alumni surveys on undergraduate psychology majors. *Teaching of Psychology*, *16*, 52-57.

Ware, M. E. (1993a). *Advising in the classroom: Teaching a career development course*. Omaha, NE: Creighton University, Department of Psychology. ERIC Document Reproduction Service No. ED 348-585.

Ware, M. E. (with Busch-Rossnagel, N. A., Crider, A. B., Gray-Shellberg, L., Hale, K., Lloyd, M. A., Rivera-Medina, E., & Sgro, J. A.). (1993b). Developing and improving advising: Challenges to prepare students for life. In T. V. McGovern (Ed.), *Handbook for enhancing undergraduate education in psychology* (pp. 47-70). Washington, DC: American Psychological Association.

Chapter 32

Students with Academic Difficulty: Prevention and Assistance

Ellen E. Pastorino
Valencia Community College

I t happens every year. In late August or September, armed with a syllabus, textbook, an idealistic outlook, and renewed energy after a summer hiatus, we prepare to impart our enthusiasm, curiosity, and lifelong love of learning to eager students enrolled in our psychology classes. We have spent five, ten, fifteen, or more years studying, teaching, and researching behavior. The students will recognize and appreciate this dedication and passion, and be oh so motivated to learn!

Unfortunately, after ten years of teaching, my experience and that of my colleagues with whom I have spoken, support the notion that students cannot always be characterized this way. Many students come to college ill-prepared to learn. They may be enrolled in remedial courses for reading, math, and/or English. They may have the necessary academic skills, but be unmotivated to learn and/or limited to concrete thought, or their expectations for college study and success may grossly underestimate the reality. What can be done to prevent students from being academically unsuccessful or at least to minimize the problem? What can we do to intervene when students experience academic difficulty in our courses?

Preventing Academic Problems

Course Expectations and Objectives

Your syllabus provides a road map for students, telling them what is important and what is expected of them. It is the professor's duty to clearly communicate this information on the first day of class. Students want professors to address basic course information such as requirements and expectations at this time. What is your attendance policy? How will attending class help students succeed? What content will the course cover? For example, students are often amazed to discover that they will be required to master concepts in biology, perception, and development when they are enrolled in a general psychology course. They are expecting to hear about

This article appears in the November 1999 APS Observer.

psychological disorders and therapy when only a fraction of the course may cover this content. Students also need to see the relevance of a psychology course to their lives. Explain why psychology may be useful to know and how it may apply to them.

Communicate to students what your tests and assignments will be like. How much studying will be required to do well? Do you have a clear grading policy? You may even consider incorporating a syllabus section on *How to Do Well in this Course*. After reviewing the syllabus, ask students to anonymously write at least three questions they have about the course. Collect their questions and assess them. What were they confused about? Do students still have any misconceptions about the course? Address these issues at the next class meeting. You may even consider giving students a quiz on syllabus content to ensure that they read it carefully.

Course Prerequisites

It is important that students start your course with at least the minimal skills necessary to do well. Have students met the course prerequisites? What are their reading and writing skills? Even though it is not a college prerequisite per se, I caution students who are enrolled in remedial courses that psychology will require the ability to comprehend abstract concepts and that correct English usage is required on any written assignments. If students lack these skills, yet still want to remain in the course, they now understand that the course work will require that they receive extra tutoring in these basic skills.

Selection of Textbook and Study Guide

Make sure students are aware of the correct textbook to purchase, especially when a standard textbook is not the norm. Is the textbook available at the start of the semester? Have you taken into account your students' reading level or any language barriers when selecting a textbook? Does the textbook provide relevant examples? Does it emphasize the same material as your lectures? Will you require the study guide? Does the study guide promote active learning and have questions that model the type of test questions that you are likely to give to students? Considering these issues is more likely to create a *goodness of fit* between the textbook, your students' academic skills, and course expectations and objectives.

Clarity of Assignments, Tests, Projects, etc.

Often students are upset with their performance in a course because they did not know what the professor was looking for in an assignment. Or they describe test questions as *tricky*. Or they say that they didn't know what material was going to be emphasized. You can do several things to minimize these complaints while at the same time making the students responsible for their learning.

Save representative student assignments and include them as examples for future students. Students are honored when you ask for a copy of their work! Break down research papers or projects into discrete steps, each with their own deadline. For example, students must turn in their sources for a research paper by a certain date. You then can give feedback regarding primary and secondary sources, or whether they have enough sources. This feedback will then assist students when they meet the next deadline of writing the introduction leading up to their hypothesis. At the same time it encourages effective time management.

Consider offering mini quizzes using the type of questions they can expect to see, and that highlight the material that will be emphasized on the exam. At the beginning of each course section, I distribute what I call *study objectives*. This two-page handout lists all the material I expect students to master for the upcoming exam (e.g., describe the functions of each part of the brain; compare and contrast Piaget's and Vygotsky's theories on cognitive development). It does not reflect what *could be* on the exam, but actually what *will be* on the exam. If it is on the handout, students can be certain that they will be tested on that information. Some of this material will be emphasized during class time, but several objectives direct students to those portions of the text that they will be required to master independently. By adopting this strategy, students know exactly what information they are responsible for learning.

Class Time

Many of us received minimal training on teaching in our graduate studies. We teach generations raised on fast paced media directed toward a short attention span. Given this situation, our teaching and presentation style are critical to student learning. It is necessary to speak at an appropriate vocabulary level, defining and reinforcing psychological terms at every opportunity. Have a clear organization and/or outline for each day's material. Cue students at the beginning of class with a brief review of the previous classes' theme, how that relates to the current course information, and summarize what has been covered at the end of the class period. Consider handing out an outline of your lecture, or putting it on the board (overhead) before class starts.

Relate the different subfields of psychology to each other so that students can grasp the big picture of psychology. For example, explain how psychoactive drugs or memory relate to the material on biology, or highlight classical and operant conditioning again when discussing emotions or attitude formation. In a general psychology course, I typically cover therapy as the last section in my course because it nicely brings together all the concepts of the course: biology, learning, perception, development, etc.

Whenever possible, illustrate concepts with demonstrations so that students can see psychology in action and apply it to themselves. Use examples relevant to them! How does their music relate to the content? How can their social world (friends, dates, jobs, family) relate to psychological phenomenon? If you feel that you are too old or too *out of it* to identify with your students, give them the opportunity to provide you with relevant examples from their lives.

Assisting Students with Academic Difficulty

You have followed all of the teaching tips previously described, give your first exam, and a large percentage of the students fail or only do marginally well, or most do well but one or two are really struggling. Now what? Don't despair! Don't throw up your hands, give up, and commiserate with colleagues on how students are so different today than yesterday. Nor should you reduce your expectations, curve grades, or *dumb down* your course. We can help students do better! However, faculty must be patient. There is always another student who needs help and when working with individual students change and progress are often slow.

Meet with students who are not academically succeeding and assess and discuss the following issues:

What Problems? Initial Assessment

You need to understand the circumstances of the person who needs help. What are his/her concerns or problems? The assistance needed by a first semester college student may differ from that of a junior or senior, who theoretically should already know how to do well in college. There are transfer students, nontraditional students, single-parent students, all of whom may need modifications in the type of assistance that is required. Getting to know the individual student may make it easier to address and pinpoint students' difficulties and put them within a context.

Are They Reading the Material and How Often?

Have students bought the required textbook and have they read the assigned chapters? Students are often amazed when they hear that they may need to read the material three or four times to comprehend it.

◆ Do students pre-read prior to coming to class?
◆ Do they briefly review the material that will be discussed?
◆ Do they actively read the material and have questions in mind as they read?
◆ Do they monitor their reading to ensure comprehension and reread the material after class to clear up any questions they have?
◆ Have they considered taking notes on their reading?

Employing these strategies enhances memory by engaging in the techniques of rehearsal, semantics, and distributed practice.

Review Students' Study Habits

Assessing students' study habits often pinpoints where improvement and practice may be needed.

◆ Are their notes clearly outlined and detailed?
◆ Do they review and organize them after class?
◆ Are they grasping the main concepts?
◆ Are they asking questions during class when something is not clear?
◆ Do they provide examples in their notes as cues for remembering?
◆ Are they using the study guide?
◆ Is the environment in which they are studying appropriate? Is it a quiet place free from distractions?
◆ Do they apply the principle of distributed practice by breaking up study sessions or do they attempt to cram for exams?

Active Learning

Assess what steps students are taking to actively learn the material. Simply reviewing their notes the night before the exam will not be sufficient to succeed.

◆ Do they use note cards?
◆ Have they outlined the chapters?
◆ Rewritten their notes?
◆ Can they organize a study group to discuss the material or at least pair up with a partner to teach each other the material?

Just discussing the material with friends or relatives will assist students in evaluating what they have comprehended and what they are still confused about. Suggest that they try to explain important concepts to one another.

Practice Tests

Practice tests help students monitor and assess their learning. They also prepare students for the types of critical thinking that will be required of them—thinking that may significantly differ from what was asked of them in high school. Study guides, other testbanks, old tests, and computer tutorials make it especially simple to offer students this opportunity with minimal effort. However, completing the practice tests is not enough. It is important for students to understand why they missed a question and why the answer they chose is not as accurate as the correct one. Students' mistakes direct them to the information that they need to restudy, reread, or ask questions about. Once they have relearned the material, then they can reassess their knowledge with another practice test. If they want to be more successful, they must practice, practice, practice! A sports analogy may be helpful. Students know practice makes them better at volleyball, basketball, soccer, etc.; the same principle applies to studying.

Campus Resources

The first campus resource that is available to students is you! Being available during your office hours communicates to students that it is important to you that they do well. However, if you know that a student wants to talk to you about strategies for improving his/her performance in your class, a process is necessary for establishing the appropriate atmosphere. Make an appointment with the student in a quiet setting where each of you will have the other's undivided attention.

Many campuses also have additional resources to assist students having academic difficulty. Tell students in person or on papers if you believe that they could use this type of help. Of course, this means that you must be aware of not only what resources, but the quality of student resources that are available. Tutorial assistance in writing and or reading labs may be available and student organizations such as Psi Chi or a Psychology Club may have tutors for psychology courses. If test anxiety or stress is a problem, students often can receive assistance through counseling services or campus workshops. It also is a good idea to get feedback from students on their evaluation of these services after they have used them. Over the long term, this increases your familiarity and knowledge of what will be most helpful to the student.

Commitment to College

There is a positive correlation between student attendance and student performance. Therefore, students need to be committed to attend classes regularly if they want to succeed. A negative correlation between number of employment hours and student performance also exists. Students who work a considerable number of hours may not have the time or energy to do well in college. Does the student view college as a full time job? Maybe they should. Typical students spend 15 hours of their week in class, and can expect to devote 25 hours of time outside of class studying. Emphasize the time demands and dedication necessary to succeed in college.

◆ Why is the student in college?
   How many credit hours are they taking?
   What courses are they taking concurrently?
   How many hours are they working?
   What priority have they given to their psychology course?
   How many classes have they missed?
   How much time do they spend socializing or partying?
   Do the answers to these questions reveal a realistic work load?

By reflecting on these issues, students are given the opportunity to rethink their commitment to a college education. Some may need to hear that it is okay for them to consider not going to college at this time in their lives.

Realistic Increments for Improvement

Many students do take me up on these challenges, buckling down and studying for the course, and are disappointed when on the next exam they don't get an "A." However, students need to be given realistic expectations for improvement. One student after actively studying went from a 45 on the first exam to a 70 on the second exam, but was disappointed with this outcome. We sat down and examined the 25 point difference in performance and how the strategies that she used made the difference between failing and passing the exam.

It also is important to respond to and encourage any improvement that does occur. One student, after failing two exams and finally seeing me and incorporating many of the techniques discussed, scored an 80 on the third exam. We were giving each other high fives when he got the news!

In the endeavor to prepare and assist students in succeeding in college, faculty often experience the same frustrations that students do. Don't be discouraged, expect to be frustrated, but do not give up. Be patient. By using these tips you better prepare students for all of their college studies, not just for psychology. Your feedback and extra time might make the difference between a student giving up on the dream of a college education and persevering and succeeding.

Recommended Readings and References

Appleby, D. (1994). How to improve your teaching with the course syllabus. *APS Observer, 7*(3), 18-19, 26.

Bernstein, D. (1994). Tell and show: The merits of classroom demonstrations. *APS Observer, 7*(3), 24-25, 37.

Davis, B. G. (1993). *Tools for teaching*. San Francisco: Jossey-Bass.

Galliano, G. (1997). Enhancing student learning through exemplary examples. *APS Observer, 10*(4), 28-30, 37.

McKeachie, W. J. (1994). *Teaching tips: Strategies, research, and theory for college and university teachers (9th ed.)*. Lexington, MA: D.C. Heath.

Mealey, D. L., & McIntosh, W. D. (1995). *Studying for psychology*. New York: Harper Collins.

Nilson, L. B. (1998). *Teaching at its best: A research-based resource for college instructors*. Bolton, MA: Anker.

Chapter 33

The Value of Collaborative Scholarship With Undergraduates

Stephen F. Davis
Emporia State University

The classroom is the sole forum for teaching. Or is it? In the eyes of many faculty, especially new faculty, teaching takes place inside the classroom. A carefully planned class, well-crafted lectures, and, more recently, multimedia presentations are their focus.

But teaching can, and should, extend beyond such confines. Specifically, faculty-student research collaboration offers a rich forum of many opportunities for teachers to practice their craft and students to learn outside the classroom. The pivotal element in such collaborative scholarship is the gradual process of professional growth shown by our students. While this growth can bring many rewards for them, faculty also accrue genuine rewards from such collaboration.

Students Benefit from Collaborative Scholarship

In addition to the potential for academic credit, there are a number of professional activities and scholarly skills developed in student-faculty collaboration. Because their activities and skills are basic to the successes of more advanced students, their early development is important to students just beginning their training in psychology. My students have engaged in a variety of such activities beneficial to their education. These rewarding experiences have included:

◆ Preparing and completing an experiment; conducting literature reviews through electronic and/or traditional print media; evaluating and refining experimental designs; gathering and analyzing data; and preparing APA-style papers.
◆ Formally presenting research results.
◆ Publishing a journal article.
◆ Attending professional meetings and student research conferences, including initiating the beginnings of a professional network.
◆ Participating in research which, in turn, facilitates admission to gradu-

This article first appeared in the January 1995 APS Observer.

ate school (Keith-Spiegel, 1991; Smith, 1985)

Faculty Benefit From Collaborative Scholarship

Research collaboration with students is also beneficial for faculty. Faculty benefits include:

◆ Witnessing student professional growth and development—perhaps the richest reward.

◆ Facilitating reviews of the current literature in selected research areas. This keeps one current in a variety of areas outside one's specialty area.

◆ Keeping analytic skills and deductive processes fine-tuned and active through the design and conduct of research.

◆ Generating useful research data.

◆ Maintaining and expanding professional networks through attendance at conventions. This benefit is especially true of student research conferences where one can meet other student mentors.

◆ Enhancing one's effectiveness as a teacher through active involvement in research. Unless teachers closet themselves and keep their work a secret, how can it be otherwise?

Collaborative Research: Doing and Teaching

Research Ideas

Collaboration, as it exists in my laboratory, may be unique in one sense: Most of the research ideas are student generated. It took me a little while to learn that not all of my student researchers shared my strong interest (much to my surprise) in the effects of animal odors in enclosed runways; and some were assertive enough to propose research projects they wanted to conduct.

My initial reactions to their *unorthodox* proposals probably were less than encouraging. After all, what could be as important as rat smells? Thankfully, a few hardy souls persisted, and several of their proposals came to fruition. Our animal research projects diversified. Our agenda began to include human research on topics such as Type A personality, fear of death, the impostor phenomenon, locus of control, level of self-esteem, irrational beliefs, and mate selection.

In recent years a number of teaching-oriented projects addressing topics such as academic dishonesty, chapter versus unit test, student/teacher expectations, and the training of teaching assistants have become components of our research agenda.

General Structure

I attempt to involve students in professionally meaningful ways as early as possible in their collegiate career. The students' initial assignments and responsibilities are elementary and basic. For example, students in animal labs first learn accepted practices of animal care and maintenance. Likewise, students conducting human research projects first code data sheets or learn to make computer entries. As initial projects are completed, additional ones involving increased training and responsibilities are undertaken. Having long accepted the value of *peer teaching* (McKeachie, 1986), much of the training is done by advanced students.

This interactive and supportive milieu creates an atmosphere in which students feel free to contribute to the design and implementation of experiments. By the time students are working on their second or third project, they are able to provide meaningful input and begin actual data collection.

As student researchers assume additional responsibilities, they also begin to participate in the training of new recruits and the cycle perpetuates itself. A key to collaboration as we practice it is gradual professional growth for all students involved.

Teaching Issues in Collaborative Scholarship

Although the general structure for collaborative research is rather straightforward, implementation can be challenging. Some of the skills you may expect to develop include:

Tolerance for ambiguity—There are multiple projects ongoing all the time, none go smoothly, and some seem to become studies in *applied chaos theory*. The faculty in charge must provide stability, wise and good advice, a cool head, and saintly patience. You are part scientist and part den mother.

The ability to give up controlling one's own time—A commitment to students means being available. For the faculty involved in collaborative scholarship it sometimes feels like you are on call 25 hours a day. The heater in the animal colony breaks down on weekends; rats escape at the worst of times; students run the last part of the experiment late on Friday afternoon and then need help. Although Type As may find relinquishing time control to be uncomfortable, it probably takes a Type A to effectively orchestrate collaborative research.

Being an obsessive's obsessive—Students find questions about APA writing style you never knew existed. The fantasies of being the *great teaching scientist* melt away under the minutia of conversions to metric measurement, exact placement of the manuscript page header, whether figures have page numbers, and how to construct an acceptable table.

Surviving endless meetings—If you are successful, students seek you out. It is not uncommon to be meeting with one small group of students and have several more queued up in the hall waiting to discuss another project.

Being a generalist—You can safely predict it is the topics you would never expect—and know the least about—that will most likely interest students for collaborative research projects.

Super listening skills—Being a generalist carries with it the responsibility of having (or developing) super listening skills. Don't lose potentially good research because you did not listen carefully or long enough to your students' ideas.

Hand holding at convention time—Do not forget how fearful the first paper or poster can be. The successes promoted by good practice and preparation will result in a decrease in future anxiety attacks, but a bottle of Pepto Bismol may still be a lifesaver just before presentation time.

The Question of Course Credit

Because these collaborative activities are not tied to regularly scheduled academic courses, this process sustains itself on a year-round basis. However, from the time they begin their research activities, students are informed they can receive course credit, via independent study.

To receive credit, the student must have worked in the laboratory for at least one semester and request credit during the regular enrollment period. During a conference on the student's progress, any previous credit awarded for research, and specific plans for the proposed credit are discussed.

Because academic credit can be awarded in 1-, 2-, or 3-hour blocks at my institution, the task of matching a project to appropriate academic credit is facilitated. Although it is arguable that the completion of normal research activities is sufficient to warrant course credit, I add an additional requirement. Students receiving course credit must prepare an APA format paper based on the designated research project. Ideally, this paper will be presented at a convention.

Funds and Equipment

You may have noticed that your own research requires some minimal level of support for facilities, equipment, and travel. Collaborative research is no different, and the discovery of this fact is another lesson for your students, Hence, it is advantageous to secure sources of funding, especially ones that are available on your own campus.

Although good research can be conducted without unlimited research funds and the latest equipment, these institutional grants really enhance collaborative projects. Don't be bashful. If you are conducting several collaborative projects, apply for several grants; such funds frequently are not expended during the academic year.

Conditions and Commitment Required

While collaborative research offers significant benefits, some cautions should be considered before students and faculty rush out to implement such programs. An overriding concern is the level of involvement one is willing to undertake. As described, my approach does not link research to a particular course or academic term; hence, students and faculty have to make extra time for these activities. We all can come up with numerous reasons why we "simply cannot" take an another responsibility. However, if collaborative scholarship is important, then one can and will find the necessary time. It is just a matter of priorities and good time management.

The enthusiasm of faculty research directors has a direct influence on the number of students who choose to work under their direction. High enthusiasm and drive equate to a larger number of student researchers. While one's laboratory may have "humble beginnings," it does not take a long time for the word to spread; an active and productive research operation serves as a magnet for aspirant students. The time may come when the size of your research group must be limited. My own group has ranged from six to 34 students. The current size of 14 appears to be optimal for my temperament and the diversity of our projects.

Where to Find Out More:
Opportunities for Undergraduates to Present Research
Examples of state and regional student conferences:

◆ Southern Undergraduate Psychology Research Conference
◆ Arkansas Symposium for Psychology Students
◆ ILLOWA Undergraduate Psychology Conference
◆ Mid-America Undergraduate Psychology Research Conference
◆ Great Plains Students' Psychology Conference
◆ Michigan Undergraduate Psychology Paper Reading Conference
◆ Minnesota Undergraduate Psychology Conference
◆ Carolina's Psychology Conference
◆ Delaware Valley Undergraduate Research Conference
◆ Lehigh Valley Undergraduate Psychology Research Conference
◆ University of Winnipeg Undergraduate Psychology Research Conference

Information concerning these conferences appears regularly in *Teaching of Psychology* and the *Psi Chi Newsletter*.

Student Sessions Sponsored by Psi Chi:

◆ Psi Chi (the National Society in Psychology) sponsors student sessions at all six regional meetings, as well as the APS and APA annual meetings.

Publication Opportunities for Undergraduate Students:

◆ *The Journal of Psychology and the Behavioral Sciences*
◆ *Modern Psychological Studies*
◆ *Journal of Undergraduate Studies*
◆ *Psi Chi Journal of Undergraduate Research*

Recommended Readings and References

Keith-Spiegel, P. (1991). *The complete guide to graduate school application: Psychology and related programs*. Hillsdale, NJ: LEA.

McKeachie, W. J. (1994). *Teaching tips: Strategies, research, and theory for college and university teachers* (9th ed.). Lexington, MA: D. C. Heath.

Smith, R. A. (1985). Advising beginning psychology majors for graduate school. *Teaching of Psychology, 12*, 194-197.

Part 8
Faculty and Student Integrity

Chapter 34

Dealing with Problem Students In the Classroom

Sandra Schweighart Goss
University of Illinois at Urbana–Champaign

Problem students run the gamut from merely annoying, through disruptive, to "unbalanced." Some are very bright and some are struggling. Some are only a problem for you; others are a problem across the campus.

Dealing with problem students is often difficult for new faculty, and experienced faculty as well. In this column I will describe the more common types of problem students, some alternative approaches to dealing with them, and then summarize some tips that come from classroom management research and classroom experience.

Types of Problem Students

The *Everything Always Happens to Me* Student

This type of student is common. She has the best intentions, but some external force always interferes with her completion of course requirements. She shows up to the exam an hour late complaining that she dozed off or her alarm failed, even if the exam is at 7PM. She cannot turn her paper in because the printer jammed as she was printing it 15 minutes before class. In other words, this is a friendly and well meaning student who is often bewildered by all of the "bad luck" that interferes with her good intentions.

Dealing with this type of student is made simple with some advanced planning. At the beginning of the semester consequences for missing exams or turning in papers late should be explicitly stated in writing, thus making all students accountable for their behavior. It is also important to guide such students into appropriate workshops or seminars on topics such as time-management and organizational skills.

The *I Don't Agree With You* Student

We occasionally have a student who challenges almost everything presented. Research in classroom management shows that high-achieving students challenge the teacher through the material rather than through non-cur-

This article first appeared in the November 1995 APS Observer.

ricular confrontation or by acting out. Before identifying a student as a problem, be sure that the student is questioning your authority and not the material. Stay rational and objective, and analyze the content of the student's criticism.

Successfully coping with a challenging student is especially important early in the term when interactions between teacher and student *ripple* through the classroom (Kounin, 1977). A teacher MUST intervene to maintain student respect and an educational classroom climate. The class will become irritated that the student is disrupting the flow of the lecture and "wasting" time.

The first intervention is often a soft reprimand in class, or talking to the student alone outside of class. Focus on the student's impact on the rest of the class since the student may be unaware of classmates' reactions. It is equally important to convey that you are interested in his comments and would be happy to talk with him during office hours. Most often this takes care of the problem.

If the soft-reprimand does not work, you may have to ignore the student in class. This can often be done gracefully by saying something like, "I see your hand, Jack, but let's give someone else a chance."

The *Quick to Anger* Student

Handing back exams and quizzes can be one of the most difficult aspects of teaching. Students who did not perform well often become either quiet and withdrawn or angry and belligerent.

A good way to deal with student complaints about quiz/exam items is to have a written policy on challenging items. Colleagues and I have developed a one-page form, available to all students when quizzes and exams are returned. The form simply states "On Question___ on Form___ I believe that answer___ should also be considered correct because" with a space to state the argument. At the bottom of the form there is a statement, "I found supporting evidence on page ___ in the textbook." Having these forms available, and carefully reading those that are submitted, makes a tremendous difference in classroom climate.

Having standard procedures that acknowledge that students may have a different, but valid, perspective allows students to try to resolve their disputes reasonably. Decisions concerning their arguments are almost universally accepted by the students.

I have a similar policy when handing back papers. When the paper is assigned, students receive a scoring grid indicating what I will be looking for in the paper and how many points are available for each grading category. The grid also has space for comments. By referring to the completed scoring grid, students can easily see in which areas they performed well and where their paper fell short.

When papers are returned, I tell students that I will reread any paper that they think was unfairly graded, but only after they have both read through their paper and responded to my comments. Usually I have requests to reread two papers out of 60, and occasionally the student was correct and I missed something the first time I read the paper. Even when the grade does not change, I write additional comments in response to their questions and the matter is usually resolved amicably.

Occasionally a *quick to anger student* will be so irritated that he will confront you verbally. Although rare, this can be extremely disconcerting. However, there are some ways to help defuse a confrontation.

Try to talk with the student in private. In class you must be nonemotional; encourage the student to see you after class. Once in private, allow the student to have his say without interruption. This is exceedingly difficult, especially if the student is saying things that you believe are untrue, but interrupting at this stage usually accomplishes nothing. The student may not yet be ready to listen and may become even more angry if interrupted. During this stage I listen, nodding my head and maintaining eye contact. Eventually the student will run out of steam. Wait until you are sure the student is finished. At this point the student may even be a bit sheepish. Now you can acknowledge the student's anger and calmly summarize what he said. In most cases this procedure allows a rational discussion of the complaint.

The *I'm Not Here* Student

At the opposite end of the spectrum is the student who attempts to draw no notice to herself, does not volunteer in class, and does not challenge the teacher regarding poor grades. These students worry me because they often succeed in becoming invisible, going through the first year (or more) of college without making personal contact with any instructor. I try to remedy that by making nonthreatening contact with as many students as possible. With such a student I try to start a dialogue, often written at first. I write a note on her papers, exams, or error sheets. I tell her she did well on the assignment, that she is doing better on quizzes now, or I ask her to see me during office hours if she is not doing well. I learn her name and say "Hi" in class. I also have my email address on my syllabus and encourage all students to send me questions or comments. I still have an email correspondence with a student who was in my class three years ago and barely said two words in the classroom.

I do not worry about getting such students to participate in class, although it appears that small group work gets them more involved. If I can let the quiet student know that at least one instructor knows who she is, then I feel I have succeeded.

The *Unbalanced* Student

Rarely, you will have a student with a serious emotional problem. Even if you are a clinician, it is important NOT to deal with such a student alone but to involve your department, colleagues, and campus resources.

The first step is to speak privately to the student, to be sure the student is aware of the problem and is receiving help. However, if the student is engaging in inappropriate classroom behavior, it is important to keep the class on-task—not allowing the student to take control. This may involve ignoring the student, moving the student's seat, or having a colleague sit in on your class who can provide support, feedback, and help if intervention is necessary. It is not fair to the rest of the students to have the classroom constantly disrupted.

Find out how your campus assists such students. At minimum, you need to contact its mental health professionals and make sure that the student is receiving appropriate help. You can also use such resources for information about the best way for you to cope with the troubled student. At maximum, you might need to have the student removed from your class.

Some Teaching Tips

By keeping these tips in mind the number of unexpected, unpleasant interchanges should be greatly diminished. However, not all problems can be anticipated and there will be situations that require you to react on the spur of the moment.

The Best Defense is a Good Offense

Anticipate areas of conflict and establish procedures for dealing with such conflicts BEFORE they occur. Such rules and procedures should be written, in your syllabus or in the directions for individual assignments. Having established procedures for dealing with everyday problems such as contested exam/quiz items, late papers, missed exams, and class attendance, can minimize students' uncertainty, and provide a feeling of empowerment and participation in decisions.

It goes without saying that these rules and penalties should be applied equally to all students. Do NOT make rules you are not going to enforce and do NOT make exceptions.

Stay Adult

Maintain your adult/professional demeanor. Be an active listener and do not interrupt when the student presents the problem. This will go further to defuse the situation than anything else you can do or say.

Deal with the Problem at an Appropriate Level

Do not be afraid to involve your colleagues or departmental administration when the problem is beyond your ability to handle alone. For example, dealing with an "unbalanced" student requires knowledge of the campus/department rules and support from colleagues. On the other hand, do not overreact to student behavior. Remember that students who are truly baiting you derive no pleasure if you are not duly perturbed. Adjust the intervention to meet the challenge at the appropriate level and intervene immediately when necessary.

Talk to Your Colleagues

Faculty tend to develop classroom policies in a vacuum, but it is helpful to talk to teaching colleagues about what has and has not worked for them. This need not be restricted to colleagues within your department.

Recommended Readings and References

Eble, K. (1988). *The craft of teaching* (2nd ed.). San Francisco: Jossey-Bass.
Kounin, J. (1977). *Discipline and group management in classrooms*. Huntington, NY: Krieger.
McKeachie, W. (1994). *Teaching tips: Strategies, research, and theory for college and university teachers* (9th ed.). Lexington, MA: D. C. Heath.

Chapter 35

Cheating: Preventing and Dealing With Academic Dishonesty

Donald H. McBurney
University of Pittsburgh

S omeday it will happen to you. A student will turn in such an excellent, well-written paper that you seriously doubt its authenticity. Or, during a test, you will look up and find a student copying from another student. The sinking feeling that immediately weighs in on you could be overwhelming as you realize you must decide how to deal with a suspected or actual case of cheating.

If it hasn't happened to you yet, either you are new at the game, you have your head in the sand, or you have been incredibly lucky. Or, perhaps you have created a situation in which cheating is unlikely. Studies show that about 40 percent of students cheat in a given term.

An Ounce of Prevention

Communicate Policies on Cheating

My institution requests all instructors to state their policy on cheating in the syllabus. Believe it or not, students have argued that they should not be punished for cheating because they were never told they couldn't do it. State clearly when students may cooperate and when they must work independently. Students who have been encouraged to use programmable calculators in math courses may naturally expect that they can use them in your class. (Many calculators permit considerable amounts of text to be stored in their memories. Either design the test so that calculators are not necessary, or insist that they push the erase button to delete text memory.)

Relate With Your Students—Avoid Adversarial Relationships

Students may cheat because they feel alienated from the system. Let your students know that you respect them and expect the best from them. I believe students are less likely to cheat if they feel they know and like the instructor. Learning and using students' names in class may have a beneficial side effect of reducing cheating.

This article first appeared in the January 1996 APS Observer.

Teach Students What Plagiarism Is So They Can Avoid Doing It

The nature of cheating depends on the assignment. Written assignments run the risk of plagiarism. Some instructors may be surprised to learn that students sometimes plagiarize unintentionally because they do not know enough about what constitutes scholarship. Before giving written assignments, it is a good idea to discuss how to credit other people's work. Some departments promulgate written guidelines on plagiarism.

We will discuss later what to do when you suspect cheating. But one technique that is particularly suited to written assignments is to ask a student whom you suspect of plagiarism to explain something in the paper in other words. More sophisticated techniques include blanking out key words and asking the student to fill in the spaces.

Structure Writing Assignments So Students Cannot Use Others' Work

Having informed students what plagiarism is, you should structure the timing of the assignment in such a way that plagiarism becomes less likely. Several weeks before the final paper is due ask the students for a statement of their topic. Next ask for a preliminary list of references that they intend to consult. Then have them turn in a tentative outline. Any changes you may suggest at these stages will make it more difficult for them to turn in a paper previously prepared by someone else. The only clear case of plagiarism I have experienced occurred with a student who had missed several weeks of class and skipped these stages. Your guidelines should suggest that they keep all drafts of their work, notes, printouts of computer searches, etc. They should photocopy the first page of every article or book cited in their reference list. This way they can't cite papers they haven't at least laid eyes on. Some faculty also inform students that they keep a record of all papers written, or the papers themselves, for the preceding five years.

Take Control of the Test Situation

Arrange the classroom situation to suit the nature of the test. You may want students to sit in every other seat, take assigned seats to break up groups of would-be cheaters, or leave the front row open for latecomers, etc. Some instructors number all tests and have students leave completed tests face down on the desk. Then they may be picked up in order, and papers of suspected cheaters can be compared for similarities. (Be aware that papers can be similar if students study together. But hearing boards that review suspected cases of cheating can be skeptical of purely statistical evidence.)

I require students to reverse baseball caps because the bill makes it harder for you to monitor their gaze. (I do not ask for their removal: A student may be taking chemotherapy, or just having a bad hair day.)

You should resist their complaints to the contrary and efforts to put you on the defensive. You do not need to explain why they should follow your instructions. You may instruct a student who is behaving suspiciously to sit elsewhere without making an accusation or justifying yourself.

Opinions vary on how faculty members should dress. But I make a point to dress in a businesslike manner on test day because I believe it is important to convey to students that they should take the situation seriously and the professor's appearance can make the point without making them uncomfortable.

How you manage the testing situation depends on factors such as the type of test, class size and whether you reuse the same test for different classes or across semesters. Because I seldom reuse tests, for example, I generally do not need to count the booklets as I pass them out, nor do I need to recover them. But once a student has left the room, I do not permit that student to reenter. In large classes, I use alternate forms of the exam (e.g., same items appear in three different orders) so that a student looking at a classmate's answer sheet is not helped by doing so. Simply changing the order of pages is not nearly as effective as scrambling items within pages.

If your class is large enough that you don't know all students, require them to show picture ID and sign their test (as well as print their name on the test). Be sure to have additional proctors in large classes. I try to have help in classes larger than 75, about one for every additional 100 students.

Be Prepared

After teaching for 30 years I thought I knew all the tricks students used. Then one term I was confronted by two new ones. So I sat down and compiled a list of over 40 different ways to cheat, and about the same number of ways to prevent cheating. I am sure there are more. My point is that we need to keep a very large number of variables and contingencies in mind on test day.

For example, what would you do if you entered your classroom and saw "Professor X's test has been canceled" written on the blackboard and many of the students had left? Suppose the fire alarm goes off in the middle of the test. Suppose students go to leave the test and find the doors locked by computer. Then, when you use the emergency phone to call campus security you are advised that the only way to unlock them is to pull the fire alarm. Imagine running out of test booklets because the secretary miscounted. All of these have happened in my experience.

During the test, the student can cheat in two basic ways: refer to contraband materials or get help from another person. I have already mentioned the use of programmable calculators. Students occasionally wear earphone tape recorders to tests. I require them to give me the cassette. Less technologically sophisticated but effective is hiding written material under clothing, which is awkward to prove for obvious reasons.

A student receiving help from neighbors is probably harder to detect. Folklore tells of the power wedge, *whereby a group of students arranges itself in the pattern of* geese in flight with the one who knows the material in the lead position. Signaling methods can be ingenious; the M&M method indicates the correct alternative by the color of the candy. A simpler method is to point to the question with the pencil as if studying it and touching left ear for *a*, knee for *b*, etc. Be on the lookout for students who appear to be doing an impression of a third base coach.

One of the most clever methods includes a student bringing a friend who is not in the course to sit next to him or her. The friend takes an exam and works on it as if a registered student. The actual student copies the answers from the ringer. When they are done, the ringer can either walk away and leave the test at the seat or turn it in with a fake name. Alternatively, the ringer can walk out with the test, which could also wind up in a fraternity file.

When a Student Cheats

Know and Follow Your Institution's Procedures

My institution has a written set of guidelines on dealing with cheating. Be familiar with your institution's policies and know what steps are available to you before an incident arises. Have the students read the guidelines so they become familiar with the alternatives and processes set forth.

Settling Matters Informally

Generally, you should first try to settle the matter informally. But you and the student need to know how to proceed if the student denies the charge, or refuses to accept your proposed penalty. If you are lucky enough to settle the matter informally, be sure to get the student to sign a statement admitting the offense and accepting the penalty. You should file this statement for possible future use and send a copy to the department chair or the dean. This student may be a repeat offender requiring more serious action.

Settling Matters Formally

Some cheating incidents will require resolution through formal institutional processes. Be aware of deadlines and what information must be submitted. Write memos to your file on incidents of cheating that you witness. Write down details of the case such as who sat next to the student. Have TAs or proctors write statements on what they witnessed. Get signed statements from all parties, including the student, if he or she confesses. In brief, keep a paper trail.

The Legal System and Cheating

We live in a litigious society and many situations that were once dealt with informally now wind up in court. The best way to avoid a lawsuit is to know and abide by your institution's policies and procedures. Many faculty look the other way when they see cheating because they believe that it is necessary to have evidence that would stand up in a court of law, or they believe the procedures are too bureaucratic, and they do not want to deal with them.

Courts will generally not get involved in a case if the student has been accorded due process, which is a less stringent criterion than having to follow legal rules of evidence and procedure. Due process has been accorded when the student has had an adequate opportunity to be heard, established rules and procedures have been followed, the student has been assumed innocent until proven guilty, and the burden of proof has been placed on the institution.

Keep A Sense Of Humor

Finally, do not take yourself too seriously. One instructor (probably fictitious) was trying to get the last stragglers to turn in their final exams. He announced that he would not accept any more papers after a certain time. Still, one student kept on working. When she ignored his final ultimatum, he refused to accept her paper. She walked up to the desk, looked him in the eye, and said, "Do you know who I am?" Thinking that she might be the daughter of a trustee, he warily said, "No." Whereupon, she slipped her paper into the middle of the pile, squared it up, and strolled out. Sometimes there is nothing we can do.

Recommended Readings and References

Department of Psychology, Bishop's University. (1994). *Guide to academic honesty (avoidance of plagiarism)*. Lennoxville, Quebec: Author.

Hill, G. W. IV, & Davis, S. F. (1998). *How can we promote academic honesty?* Retrieved April 20, 1999 from the World Wide Web: http://www.psychplace. com/editorials/academic/academic1.html

Kibler, W. L., Nuss, E. M., Paterson, B. G., & Pavela, G. (1988). *Academic integrity and student development: Legal issues and policy perspectives.* Asheville, NC: College Administration Publications.

McBurney, D. H. (1992). *How to cheat in college (and how you might get caught).* Unpublished manuscript, University of Pittsburgh.

McKeachie, W. J. (1994). *Teaching tips: Strategies, research and theory for college and university teachers* (9th ed.). Lexington, MA: D. C. Heath.

Singhal, A. C., & Johnson, P. (1983). How to halt student dishonesty. *College Student Journal, 17,* 13-19.

Chapter 36
Treating Students Differentially: Ethics in Shades of Gray

Arno F. Wittig, David V. Perkins, Deborah Ware Balogh, Bernard E. Whitley, Jr., and Patricia Keith-Spiegel
Ball State University

S ome instructors' classroom behaviors are clearly inappropriate and unethical, regardless of any provocation. The angry professor who hit a student who came to class late, the irritated professor who announced in class that most of the students had the IQ of a nail, and the racist professor who suggested that African Americans and Hispanics should not enroll in her classes because they could not keep up with Anglos deserved, and received, strong sanctions. Differential behavior outside the classroom, as illustrated by the professor who gave afternoon oral exams to his male students in his office and evening exams to his female students in his apartment, is also clearly unacceptable. Although detecting and policing such behaviors can be difficult, there is little doubt in these cases that acceptable academic standards of conduct have been breached.

Our concern here is with classroom-related situations that are often not clearly addressed in professional ethics codes or extant departmental policies, but still may harm some students in overt, subtle, or indirect ways. These are the *gray areas* that we presented in our casebook (Keith-Spiegel, Wittig, Perkins, Balogh, & Whitley, 1993, currently in revision). Even though the ethically correct response may not leap out when such ambiguous incidents occur, acting fairly and with the intent to do no harm are the best guides for ethical behavior.

Since our casebook was published, we have been amazed at the number of additional examples with unclear features that instructors have sent to us. We have selected four cases, all variations on the theme of dealing with the unique needs of specific students. In situations such as these, policy or other guidelines are usually nonexistent, yet, if mishandled, the student-in-question or other students in the class may be unfairly disadvantaged. We end each discussion point with a teaching tip for the reader.

This article appears in the July/August 1999 APS Observer.

Case #1. Unintentional Inequity

Professor Heartalk starts her Wednesday class by saying, "Students, we have the good fortune to have A. Ward Winner, the outstanding author, visiting our campus next week. His works fit perfectly with the theme of this course. I am assigning you to attend his talk next Tuesday evening at 7PM in Speakers' Hall, then to write a reaction paper, due on Friday, that will be worth 30 points."

Good use of a campus activity? Innocent enough? But how should Professor Heartalk respond after class when a student explains that attending the talk is impossible because of a work commitment? Does Professor Heartalk have the right to assign attendance at an evening speaker when the class is scheduled to meet at 2PM on Mondays, Wednesdays and Fridays? On the one hand, if the student attends she jeopardizes her employment, and her job is essential to remaining in school. On the other hand, if the student does not go to the talk, the loss of 30 points may jeopardize her class grade. What if, instead of work, a student is a member of an athletic team with an important practice scheduled that night? Or has a conflicting night class?

Heartalk's assignment certainly appears to present an ethical dilemma, at least when applied to some students. Some students are being forced to make a decision that will have consequences regardless of what they choose to do. Apparently, nothing prohibits the professor from expecting students to attend the talk, giving no consideration to their other obligations.

What resolution might be sought? In our opinion, every teacher has responsibilities that go beyond the obvious, such as pedagogical competence. In dealing with gray area concerns, we believe that professors should strive in every instance to do no harm. They should be vigilant and actively attempt to avoid or prevent situations that, through acts of commission or omission, might wrong one or more students. They must respect the autonomy of others, accept the responsibility for the welfare of their students, and treat all students with fairness and equity.

Reconsider Case # 1. Although attending the visitor's talk may be encouraged (e.g., perhaps the student's work schedule can be rearranged), Heartalk must recognize that her class is just one part of her students' total college experience. Employment, extracurricular activities, and family obligations are among the other important aspects of a student's life that may prevent attendance at class excursions.

Fairness implies that Heartalk should provide an alternate experience that any non-attender can complete for the same credit. Heartalk might select a reading from the speaker's works and ask for a report on it. Or, it may be possible to have the talk videotaped. Failure to provide such alternatives to students with legitimate reasons for missing the talk violates fairness or equity standards and certainly creates the potential for harm.

Of course, there remains that fuzzy area of deciding what activities are considered *legitimate* enough to warrant a no-penalty excuse. Should a student be extended the opportunity for an alternate experience when the reason is a conflict with a fraternity or sorority meeting? What about the student who says, "I'll have to miss my favorite TV show and I don't own a VCR! Can't I do something else instead?" Does it matter if the favorite TV show is *South Park* as opposed to a one time only broadcast of an opera?

Teaching Tip: Define legitimate reasons for missing class in the syllabus and on the first day of class.

In Heartalk's case, the impact may be overt and measurable, but many cases present subtle or indirect influences. Several other examples of actual incidents illustrate the range that may be expected.

Case #2. Uncommunicated (Unpublished) Policies

A distraught student tells Professor Niceguy that her boyfriend since grade school broke up with her two days ago. She has been crying steadily, and cannot concentrate on her studies. She begs to postpone taking tomorrow's exam and for an extension on a written assignment. Niceguy grants both, adding, "Don't tell anyone that I am letting you do this."

We may all sympathize with the collapse of a first-love relationship of such long duration and understand the trauma involved. Yet, Niceguy must have at least subconsciously recognized that giving extra time is potentially problematical or he would not have admonished the student to keep their agreement a secret. No doubt other students who do not ask for help also have occasional sympathetic circumstances that interfere with their ability to perform their best on time.

Setting attendance and deadline rules that allow no exceptions is unfair to students with a serious illness or other emergency. Niceguy has no strict policy. But, he operates informally and covertly by picking whose excuse requests he will honor from among those assertive enough to approach him. As such, he may do more harm than the excessively strict instructor because at least in the latter case the students all know the rules.

Teaching Tip: Set a formal policy in your syllabus, and allow yourself the right to consider unusual exceptions on a student-by-student basis.

Let us now look at an increasingly common type of special need involving our growing number of nontraditional students.

Case #3. Capricious Decisions

During class, Kara Keepintouch's cell phone rings. She answers, mumbles a couple of responses, then packs her things and leaves. Professor Disrupted is furious and starts the next class by mandating a new policy — absolutely no cell phones or noisy beepers are allowed in the classroom.

Kara raises her hand and explains that she is a single mother whose child is in a day care center. The cell phone made it possible for the center to contact her and inform her that her daughter was sick. Must she turn off the phone? How can he enforce the rule? What rights does Disrupted have?

The classroom is expanding in diversity, creating many new dilemmas related to the needs of nontraditional students. Professor Disrupted may be able to compromise. She might ask Kara to switch to a silent beeper, or to sit by the door and quietly excuse herself if needed. This respects this student's legitimate needs, while at the same time preserving the rights of the other students to an undisturbed class.

The dilemma that often arises is where the line is drawn in making adjustments to meet a single student's needs, especially if there is a chance that other students could be disadvantaged by the accommodation. What if a student cannot find child care on a particular day and brings the young child to class, or if the grade school holiday calendar does not match with the college calendar? In a recent online debate among teaching psychologists, it was clear that opinions varied from welcoming young children under such emergency conditions and viewing toleration of their presence as honorable, to absolute condemnation of using a classroom as emergency day care on the grounds that the learning atmosphere is usually compromised to the detriment of everyone else in the room, including the bored or fussy child.

We may cautiously conclude that the instructor's attitude about children in the classroom is an important factor. The instructor who is comfortable with the situation will probably also be far more effective in maintaining a good environment for the other students. If one chooses to allow children in the classroom on occasion, we advise coming to a clear understanding with the parent that should the child be unable to remain quiet and relatively unobtrusive, both must leave.

Teaching Tip: Do not make capricious decisions, consult with your colleagues, and look for creative *win-win* solutions for contemporary problems.

Teaching Tip: Weighing the needs of the individual AND the needs of the group often results in fairness. Be flexible.

The final case is similar to the first in that all students are required to engage in a certain activity. This time, however, the activity itself and how it impacts differentially on students is at issue.

Case #4. Intrusive Requirements

Sincerely convinced that *body markers* are indicators of good health, Professor Disclose requires a journal for his seminar class in Psychology of Health. For 10 days students must record all the food, drink, and drugs they ingest or use, all instances of urination and defecation, any nausea or vomiting, menstrual periods, any sexual activity including erotic or wet dreams, and any cold or flu-like symptoms. Disclose says he will collect and evaluate these journals once they are completed. Connie Servative refuses to complete the journal, claiming it would violate her rights of privacy, while Cokey Caine simply plans to fictionalize the entire assignment.

Again, the variety of sensitivities among contemporary students requires us to examine assignments that may be delicate, controversial, or overly intrusive. We have heard of assignments that are of highly questionable pedagogical value and possibly even risky. For example, one instructor required her class to visit night clubs in a dangerous neighborhood and write a paper analyzing observations of the denizens of these establishments. Professor Disclose's assignment is not necessarily useless or dangerous, but the degree of self-revelation is excessive, especially for more modest students or those with something to hide. At the very least, Disclose should have offered an alternative assignment requiring equal effort without censure to those who found this assignment unappealing.

We believe that in almost all circumstances, students should not be required to write about deeply personal matters; the probability of emotional harm or loss of dignity is simply too great. Further, there are things about our students that we simply have no right to know. In those few cases where sensitive revelations are pedagogically justifiable, students should be forewarned and given opportunities to find an alternate class should they choose not to participate.

Teaching Tip: Think through the nature and potential consequences of course assignments before the course begins and be extremely cautious about assignments requiring students to disclose deeply personal matters.

Conclusion

Gray areas regarding differential treatment of students exist in abundance, yet they often provoke little or no *overt* reaction from students or colleagues, even though the potential for harm can be substantial. In a national survey of psychology educators (Tabachnick, Keith-Spiegel, & Pope, 1991), however, the majority of the respondents believed that bending rules for selected students was unethical despite the fact that two-thirds of the respondents admitted to doing this on at least rare occasion. Students also perceive instructors who do not provide a *level playing field* as highly unethical (Keith-Spiegel, Tabachnick, & Allen, 1993).

We have no desire to stultify teaching innovations. Nor are we interested in recommending standards as if *one size fits all*. However, the application of underlying principles of fairness, equity, respect for our students' autonomy, and, above all, doing no harm will assist instructors to evaluate the integrity of dealings with specific students.

Recommended Readings and References

Brookfield, S. D. (1990). *The skillful teacher*. San Francisco: Jossey-Bass. See especially Chapters 2 (Developing a Personal Vision of Teaching) and 12 (Building Trust with Students).

Costanzo, M., & Handelsman, M. M. (1998). Teaching aspiring professors to be ethical teachers: Doing justice to the case study method. *Teaching of Psychology, 25*, 97-102.

Grauerholz, E., & Copenhaver, S. (1994). When the personal becomes problematic: The ethics of using experiential teaching methods. *Teaching Sociology, 22*, 319-327.

Keith-Spiegel, P., Tabachnick, B. G., & Allen, M. (1993). Ethics in academia: Students' views of professors' actions. *Ethics and Behavior, 3*, 149-162.

Keith-Spiegel, P., Wittig, A., Perkins, D., Balogh, D. W., & Whitley, B. E. (1993). *The ethics of teaching: A casebook*. Muncie, IN: Ball State University.

Kitchener, K. S. (1992). Psychologist as teacher and mentor: Affirming ethical values throughout the curriculum. *Professional Psychology, 23*, 190-195.

Koocher, G. P., & Keith-Spiegel, P. (1998). *Ethics in psychology* (2nd ed.). New York: Oxford University Press.

Tabachnick, B. G., Keith-Spiegel, P., & Pope, K. (1991). Ethics of teaching: Beliefs and behaviors of psychologists as educators. *American Psychologist, 46*, 506-515.

Chapter 37

Ethically Risky Situations Between Students And Professors Outside the Classroom

Patricia Keith-Spiegel
Ball State University

T he classroom is only one of the places where students learn from professors. Office hours, school-sponsored educational and social events, professional meetings, the coffee lounge, and even hallways provide opportunities to educate students. Professors advise, supervise, mentor, encourage, and collaborate with students. Most of these activities occur outside the classroom.

Psychology teachers who are readily available to students should be praised for their dedication. They usually deserve it. Graduate students, especially, may enter into very friendly relationships with their professors, often involving interactions in a variety of situations. Ethically risky situations lurk close by, however, because multiple roles in the context of unequal power create a potential for exploitation. When the formalities of the classroom are not operative and decorum is relaxed, both students and faculty may begin to blur boundaries. This may create misunderstandings and ill-fated consequences for both students and faculty. New faculty, emerging from close roles and relationships with their professors, may be especially vulnerable to boundary blunders with their own undergraduate students.

While there has been a fair amount of discussion in the literature of both predictably harmful behaviors and clear-cut policy violations, my colleagues and I became intrigued with the lack of published literature about the ethically risky and gray areas involved in teaching students, especially undergraduates. In response, we created a casebook from which most of the examples in this column are derived (Keith-Spiegel, Wittig, Perkins, Balogh & Whitey, 1993).

Outside Influences on Grades

Teachers are gatekeepers with power to label students as *bright, mediocre*, or *dumb*. Although it is assumed that grades reflect actual academic

This article first appeared in the September 1994 APS Observer.

performance, we found that 60 percent of a national sample of 482 teaching psychologists admitted, on an anonymous survey, that how much they liked (or disliked) students influenced their grading, at least on one occasion.

Subject evaluations are often based on observation and interactions occurring outside the classroom. For example, students who give positive feedback on lectures, drop by for pleasant chats, or express an interest in our research may receive an enhanced "score" in the subjectivity zone between actual academic performance and the assigned mark.

Students who show disrespect or who are insensitive may be affected in the opposite direction. We are all human, but we are also called upon to issue grades based on objectively derived criteria. This may require deliberate vigilance, perhaps even including mechanisms that blind us to students identified during the grading process.

Reference Letters

A frequent situation where subjective evaluations play a legitimate role is reference letters. Often, observations upon which these judgments are based occur outside the classroom. While in the men's room, a professor overheard one of his best students refer to him as "pompous dweeb." When that student later asked for a letter, the professor refused. We may quibble about whether the professor was overly sensitive to an otherwise deserving (and possibly unusually perceptive) student. Yet, in the final analysis, professors are not required to write anyone a letter. But, because letters may be pivotal factors on students' lives, we have an ethical obligation to inform students of the subjective information we may choose to, or be requested to, divulge, and any idiosyncratic criteria we may employ when evaluating a student's interpersonal style or character.

Research Assistance for Academic Credit

On many campuses financial support for student assistants is low or has disappeared altogether. The requirements for professors to produce scholarly work for the purposes of promotion and tenure, however, have remained constant or increased.

Giving students academic credit for research assistance is an increasingly popular practice. As long as students are learning to do research, are carefully supervised, and receive credit in proportion to their contributions, a mutually advantageous partnership can be created. Ethical issues arise if the professor takes credit for students' work, is not properly attributing credit to students, is sloppy in supervision and therefore generating possibly invalid data, or assigns only tedious tasks that result in minimal learning.

Mentoring to a Fault (Paternalism)

A professor spends considerable time, by personal choice, counseling and encouraging the best students in the department into the graduate programs and careers he thinks are in their best interest. But students have complained that the professor becomes upset, even to the point of withholding support, if his advice is challenged or ignored.

Students may sometimes see us as parental figures, but we may fail to realize that these feelings can be reciprocated and the result can be extremely inappropriate. If strong feelings emerge when advising a student, or if coercive tactics are being used (e.g., holding a letter hostage unless certain decisions are made), it is time for a *boundary check*.

Excessive Mentoring (Dependence)

A gifted senior, with very high grades and GRE scores, is encouraged by her professor to remain as a non-degree student for another year rather than go directly to graduate school. He explained that they could continue their research program and that he could write her a stronger letter. This situation strongly suggests that the professor has developed a dependency on the student and is exploiting her naivete.

An extra year can be beneficial, but this is typically because some deficit hampers the student's chances of moving forward, such as a too-low GPA or lack of research experience. Losing good students to graduate programs or professional employment elsewhere goes with the territory of a teaching career and should be one of our goals.

Office Hour Availability

When students often found "No Office Hours Today" on their professor's door and complained about it, the professor replied that he had other things to do and often no one came by anyway. Aside from the fact that this may be a violation of the university's policy, erratic office hour patterns deprive students of important learning opportunities. This professor's attitude also communicates that students are less important than everything else he does. (The occasional missed office hour is a part of life, but advance warning should be given whenever possible.)

Inconvenient office hours raise similar issues. A professor who holds them from 6-7AM and 5-6PM and who defends the practice by declaring, "If students *really* want to see me they can figure out how to get there" suggests insensitivity. Although the professor may be within her rights to hold office hours at odd times, her underlying motivation insinuates a preference to avoid students.

Counseling Students on Nonacademic Matters

A teary-eyed student asks for advice about her unwanted pregnancy. After asking a few questions, the professor recommends an abortion. When do professors cross the line in terms of advice? We are encouraged to counsel about professional development and career options, and personal circumstances are often intimately involved.

Interaction with student advice seekers is a common experience for the teaching psychologists. However, the kinds of issues that would be suitable for consideration in psychotherapy are not, in most instances, appropriate for advising sessions. We might listen for a while, but referral to the counseling center or some other resource is highly recommended.

Holding Classes or Other Activities Off-Campus

Class meetings held in professors' homes and field trips to interesting places greatly enhance learning. But there can be a darker side, usually more legal than ethical, to using off-campus learning sites. A professor held a seminar meeting in her own home, a gesture that included enticing refreshments. Upon leaving, a student slipped on a soda drink spill and broke his ankle. He sued for negligence. That this meeting was a required experience was made an issue with the court. University policy and perhaps legal counsel should be consulted before planning off-campus events.

Shared Interest After Hours

Our teaching ethics group at Ball State wrestled with the scenario of professors and their students who enjoyed the same thing after hours in the same place, which, in small college towns could be the only place. Such settings might include the tennis court, golf range, aerobics class, gym, church, and so on.

When large groups are together, focusing on something else (e.g. a temple service), no ethical problems would normally arise. However, in one-on-one settings the preferable arrangement is to avoid teaming up with one's own student in any regular basis, especially if the students are undergraduates in the major, the activity is competitive, or if other students are somehow disadvantaged by the arrangement. More insidious possibilities also exist. What if a cut-throat-on-the-court professor constantly loses tennis matches to a student in his statistics class? Will some form of retaliation against the student appear during the grading/evaluation process?

Professors Who Like to Be With Students

Some professors enjoy students' company and can frequently be found chatting with them about nonacademic matters. Colleagues may be concerned that professors who spend a great deal of purely social time with students are crossing a boundary between professor and chum.

If professors who can be found socializing frequently with students on campus are fulfilling other academic duties and are usually available to all students that come by (as opposed to a favored in-group), no ethical issues necessarily pertain. However, if a professor has no other independent social life, this is not healthy for the professor, and it presents potential ethically precarious situations for the unwitting students upon whom such a professor is emotionally dependent.

Gossip

On Friday afternoons, some students and faculty hit the village spots or relax in campus lounge areas and strike up idle conversation. Two topics of mutual interests are other students and other faculty. Students may remark that a professor is a poor lecturer, flirts with other students, or gives unfair exams. Or students may begin to talk about peers and reveal private matters that professors probably do not want to know but that could affect their perceptions. "John plagiarized his term paper for Dr. Racimora's class last year." Or, "Jenny smokes dope on the weekend." It becomes the professor's responsibility to monitor what is going on, draw boundaries, and change the direction of the conversation when appropriate.

Attending Students' Events

"Can you come to my party next Saturday night?" is not an unusual invitation, particularly to younger faculty. Sometimes the occasion is a milestone or rite of passage (wedding, graduation, senior recital, etc.). There is probably nothing inherently unethical about attending student events, unless this association in some way leads to an advantage—or the appearance of an advantage—for some students as opposed to others. This, however, can be very tricky. If a professor attends one student's extracurricular event, another student could be disappointed if a similar invitation is refused.

Faculty members are far less exposed if the student-oriented events they attend are university sponsored and/or other colleagues are present. Standards of good taste, decorum, and reasonable sobriety should be maintained.

Students at Conventions

Student attendance at professional meetings facilitates their professional development. But beware. Conventions are often set in a grand hotel, and liquor is typically readily available. In one case, a professor and several students had drinks at the social hour and began joking about the department "back home." The professor divulged inside information about the strife currently raging within the faculty. By morning, the professor was filled with regret. Yet, despite begging the students to keep quiet, the stories quickly circulated.

Conclusion

Exemplary professors care about their students' achievement and their academic development as much as they do about their own work and advancement. They interact with their students outside the classroom, and are reasonably available for assistance in understanding the subject matter as well as for advising. Ironically, in the process of being helpful and available to students, more complicated roles are created and these require vigilance and sensitivity to avoid the risks of exploitation or misunderstanding.

Recommended Readings and References

Blevins-Knabe, B. (1992). The ethics of dual relationships in higher education. *Ethics and Behavior, 2*, 151-163.

Hogan, P. M., & Kimmel, A. J. (1992). Ethical teaching of psychology: One department's attempts at self-regulation. *Teaching of Psychology, 19*, 205-210.

Keith-Spiegel, P., Tabachnick, B. G., & Allen, M. (1993). Ethics in academia: Students' views of professors' actions. *Ethics and Behavior, 3*, 149-162.

Keith-Spiegel, P., Wittig, A. F., Perkins, D. V., Balogh, D. W., & Whitely, B. E. Jr. (1993). *The ethics of teaching: A casebook.* Muncie, IN: Ball State University.

Tabachnick, B. G., Keith Spiegel, P., & Pope, K. S. (1991). The ethics of teaching: Beliefs and behaviors of psychologists as educators. *American Psychologist, 46*, 506-515.

Contributors

DREW C. APPLEBY chairs the Psychology Department at Marian College in Indianapolis, Indiana, where he has been on the faculty since 1972. He received his PhD in experimental psychology in 1972 from Iowa State University. Appleby founded and was the first Director of Project Syllabus (sponsored by Teaching of Psychology, Division 2 of the American Psychological Association).

PHILIP BANYARD is associate senior lecturer in psychology at The Nottingham Trent University-United Kingdom, where he teaches introductory and applied psychology courses, in particular health psychology. He is also the chief examiner for an advanced level psychology course (which is a national qualification for students that forms the basis of their entry requirements for university). He has been teaching psychology in Nottingham for 20 years and still can't believe his luck that he gets paid for doing something that he enjoys. Mind you, he doesn't let his boss know about this. He follows the local football team (Nottingham Forest) and their continuing bad form brings some balance and some hard earned misery into his life.

BARNEY BEINS began programming and using Apple II computers for pedagogy more than 15 years ago. He received his BA from Miami University (Oxford, Ohio) and his PhD from the City University of New York. His current work includes editorship of the "Computers in Teaching" section of the journal *Teaching in Psychology*. He is a fellow of the APA and secretary of its division on the teaching of psychology. He is a professor of psychology at Ithaca College.

DOUGLAS BERNSTEIN was director of the introductory psychology program at the University of Illinois from 1984–1998. He chairs the program committee for the National Institute on the Teaching of Psychology and organizes the annual APS Institute on the Teaching of Psychology, which takes place prior to the APS Convention each year.

RICHARD R. BOOTZIN is professor of psychology at the University of Arizona. He has been a faculty member for 30 years, at Northwestern University and the University of Arizona. He has been a coauthor of widely adopted textbooks in Abnormal Psychology and Introductory Psychology.

STEPHEN F. DAVIS is a professor of psychology at Emporia State University (Emporia, KS), where he has been on the faculty since 1979. He received his PhD in experimental psychology from Texas Christian University. Davis was National President of Psi Chi and has published more than 175 articles and presented over 550 convention papers with student coauthors.

RUSSELL A. DEWEY, of Georgia Southern University, earned his undergraduate and doctoral degrees in psychology (cognition and instruction) at the University of Michigan, where he coordinated "Psychology as Natural Science" and won an Outstanding Teaching Fellow award. In 1981 he was elected Professor of the Year at Georgia Southern University. He is a specialist in teaching large introductory psychology classes.

STANFORD C. ERICKSEN received his PhD from the University of Chicago in 1938 in experimental psychology. He was professor and chairperson of the Department of Psychology at Vanderbilt University and is currently emeritus professor of psychology at The University of Michigan where, in 1962, he was the founding director of the Center for Research on Learning and Teaching. His "Memo to the Faculty" series was widely read and after retirement in 1980, he continued these reports as "Update on Teaching" at the University of Florida.

ROSEANNE L. FLORES, a developmental psychologist, is an assistant professor with the Department of Psychology, Hunter College of the City University of New York. She received her PhD from the Graduate School and University Center of the City University of New York. Her primary interests are in young children's understanding of temporal knowledge as embedded in cultural historical contexts, and the impact of poverty on children's language and cognition. She teaches courses in developmental and general psychology and has given workshops to graduate students on teaching psychology to undergraduates.

GRACE GALLIANO is a social psychologist who has both learned and taught psychology in a wide variety of settings and institutions. She created several test banks and study guides in the psychology of women, and human sexuality, as well as introductory, social, and developmental psychology. She recently coauthored (with Curt Byer and Lewis Shainberg) the newest edition of *Dimensions of Human Sexuality*, published by McGraw-Hill. While she continues to love generating good examples at Kennesaw State University (just outside of Atlanta), she is actively at work on a psychology of gender text.

ANDREW GRAYSON is a senior lecturer in psychology at the Nottingham Trent University. He is an active researcher in the field of autism and communication disabilities. He has also researched and published in the area of students' everyday problems.

SANDRA SCHWEIGHART GOSS received her PhD in 1984 from Indiana University in educational psychology with a specialty in teacher behavior. She is director of the introductory psychology program at the University of Illinois at Urbana-Champaign. She is on the program committee for the National Institute on the Teaching of Psychology and is an active participant in departmental and campus programs on effective college teaching.

PETER GRAY received his PhD in the behavioral and life sciences at the Rockefeller University in 1972 and then joined the Boston College Psychology Department, where he has served as department chair, undergraduate program director, graduate program director, and has taught a wide variety of psychology courses. He is the author of an introductory textbook (published by Worth) and articles in physiological developmental and educational psychology.

JANE HALONEN received her PhD from the University of Wisconsin-Milwaukee in 1980. She is director and professor of psychology at James Madison University in Harrisonburg, VA. Halonen is past president of the Council for Teachers of Undergraduate Psychology. A fellow and president-elect of APA's Division 2, she has been active on the Committee of Undergraduate Education, helped design the 1991 APA Conference on Undergraduate Educational Quality and the 1999 Psychology Partnerships Project, and served as a committee member to develop standards for the teaching of high school psychology.

MARIANNE HAMMERL received her PhD in psychology at the Heinrich-Heine-University in Duesseldorf, Germany, where she is currently assistant professor. She teaches courses in social psychology, general psychology, and methods of psychology and has authored articles on human learning.

MITCHELL M. HANDELSMAN is professor of psychology at the University of Colorado-Denver. He is a 1995 recipient of the Teaching Excellence Award given by Division 2 (Teaching of Psychology) of the American Psychological Association.

G. WILLIAM HILL, IV, is a professor of psychology at Kennesaw State College. He is active in the APA Division on Teaching of Psychology, and has served as the chair for its program at the annual APA meeting. He founded the annual southeastern Conference on the Teaching of Psychology.

JAMES HILTON is an Arthur F. Thurnau Professor and the undergraduate Chair in psychology at the University of Michigan. Among the courses he teaches are introductory psychology, introductory social psychology, and experimental methods. He is a three-time recipient of the LS&A Excellence in Education Award at the University of Michigan as well as the recipient of the class of 1923 Memorial Teaching Award.

PATRICIA KEITH-SPIEGEL is the Reed. D. Voran Honors Distinguished Professor of Social and Behavioral Sciences at Ball State University. Her books include *Ethics in Psychology: Standards and Cases* (1985) and *Children, Ethics and the Law* (1991) with coauthor Gerald P. Koocher.

THOMAS J. KRAMER is professor of psychology at Saint Louis University. He teaches undergraduate courses concerning groups and teams that rely heavily on experiential learning.

MARGIE KREST is an instructor at the University of Colorado-Boulder in the Department of Environmental, Population, and Organismic Biology. She teaches courses in scientific writing.

JAMES H. KORN is professor of psychology and associate graduate dean for teaching at Saint Louis University. His current research studies how we become teachers and learn to teach psychology.

NANCY KOSCHMANN team taught and conducted research with Rick Wesp at Elmira College for over 10 years. Both were awarded the College's Josef Stein Award for Excellence in Teaching. She continues at Elmira College and teaches courses in human development and counseling

MARGARET A. LLOYD is professor of psychology at Georgia Southern University and a recipient of that institution's Award for Excellence for Contributions to Instruction. She is a past president the Society for the Teaching of Psychology (APA's Division 2) and currently serves as the director of the Society's Office of Teaching Resources in Psychology. She is the author of *Adolescence* (1985) and coauthor (with Wayne Weiten) of *Psychology Applied to Modern Life* (1994). She has served as the chair of the psychology departments at Suffolk University (1980-1988) and Georgia Southern University (1988-1993).

NEIL LUTSKY is professor of psychology at Carleton College in Northfield, Minnesota. He received a BS degree in economics from the University of Pennsylvania and his PhD in social psychology from Harvard University. He has served as a consulting editor of the journal *Teaching of Psychology* and as the 1998-99 President of the Society for the Teaching of Psychology.

J. FREDERICO MARQUES is assistant professor at the Faculty of Psychology and Education, University of Lisbon, where he finished his PhD in general psychology with a specialty in cognitive psychology (categorization and memory processes). He teaches introductory classes in experimental methodology and has done several workshops on literature searches for first year students and for more advanced psychology students.

JOHN KIHLSTROM is a professor in the Department of Psychology at the University of California-Berkeley and a member of Berkeley's Institute of Cognitive Studies and Institute of Personality and Social Research. He has taught the introductory psychology course almost every year since 1980, along with other large-enrollment courses in personality and in consciousness.

DONALD H. MCBURNEY (PhD, Brown University, 1964) has proctored exams and read term papers for more than 30 years, first at the University of Tennessee, and now at the University of Pittsburgh where he is professor of psychology. He works in sensory processes and perception, specializing in psychophysical work on taste and smell. He is the author or coauthor of *Research Methods* (4th ed.), Brooks/Cole, 1998; *How to Think Like a Psychologist*, Prentice Hall, 1996; and *The Evolved Mind: Psychology from an Evolutionary Viewpoint*, Prentice-Hall, forthcoming.

LEE I. MCCANN received his PhD from Iowa State University. He is a professor of psychology at the University of Wisconsin Oshkosh, coeditor of the *APS Observer* Teaching Tips column, and a consulting editor for *Teaching of Psychology*. He is coauthor (with Baron Perlman) of *Recruiting Good College Faculty: Practical Advice for a Successful Search*, and presents workshops on teaching related topics. His research interests include social transmission of diet preference in rats and intraspecies communication in fish..

SUSAN MCFADDEN is coeditor of the APS *Observer* Teaching Tips column. A Rosebush professor at University of Wisconsin Oshkosh in the Department of Psychology, she has taught psychology for 27 years. Her courses include Introductory Psychology, Adult Development and Aging, and History of Psychology.

MARIANNE MISERANDINO received her BA. in psychology from the University of Rochester, a PhD in social-personality psychology from Cornell University, and completed a post-doctoral fellowship in human motivation at the University of Rochester. Her commitment to teaching is evidenced by her work as news editor, reviewer, and frequent contributor to the APA journal *Teaching of Psychology*. In 1995 she wrote the *Instructor's Resource Manual* to accompany *Social Psychology* by Robert S. Feldman. She is currently an assistant professor of psychology at Beaver College. Her research interests include the impact of perceived competence and autonomy on the motivation of elementary school children.

JAMES S. NAIRNE is professor of psychological sciences at Purdue University. He received his PhD from Yale University in 1981 and he has been teaching introductory psychology ever since.

BARBARA F. NODINE is a professor and chair of the psychology department at Beaver College in Glenside, PA. She was guest editor for a topical edition of *Teaching of Psychology* on writing and has consulted on writing across the curriculum at dozens of universities. She was editor for an issue devoted to writing of topics in learning and learning disabilities and has done research on children's ability to compose stories. In 1996, she was the recipient of the Society for the Teaching of Psychology Award for Teaching Excellence.

JOHN C. NORCROSS is a professor of psychology at the University of Scranton and a clinical psychologist in part-time practice. His most recent books include the third edition of *Systems of Psychotherapy: A Transtheoretical Analysis* (Brooks/Cole, with James Prochaska), *An Insider's Guide to Graduate Programs in Clinical Psychology* (Guilford, with Tracy Mayne and Michael Sayette), and the *Handbook of Psychotherapy Integration* (Basic Books, with Marvin Goldfried).

JOSEPH J. PALLADINO, professor of psychology at the University of Southern Indiana, is the founder of the Mid-America Undergraduate Psychology Research Conference and the Mid-America Conference for Teachers of Psychology. He is past president of the APA Division on Teaching. Steve Davis and he have written *Psychology*, an introductory textbook published by Prentice Hall (1995).

ELLEN E. PASTORINO is a professor of psychology at Valencia Community College in Orlando, Florida. She received BS degrees in psychology and history from Emory University and her PhD in school psychology from Florida State University. She has authored test banks, instructor's manuals, and student study guides. She is presently coauthoring (with Susan Doyle) a new introductory psychology textbook to be published by Harcourt Brace.

BARON PERLMAN is editor of the APS *Observer* Teaching Tips column. A University and Rosebush Professor at the University of Wisconsin Oshkosh in the Department of Psychology, he has taught psychology for 25 years.

JAMES V. RALSTON has used computing technology for more than 20 years in the service of science, education, and business. He received a BS from Tulane University, a PhD from SUNY-Buffalo (aka the University of Buffalo), completed post-docs at the University of Hawaii and Indiana University, and taught at Ithaca College for five years. He is currently a manager in the E-Business Operations at Sprint PCS in Kansas City, MO.

CATHERINE HACKETT RENNER is an assistant professor in the department of psychology at West Chester University. She received her PhD in Experimental Psychology in 1985 from Ohio University. She has interests in the design and analysis of research studying judgment and decision making in applied settings.

MICHAEL J. RENNER is an associate professor in the department of psychology at West Chester University. He received his PhD in Biological Psychology in 1984 from the University of California, Berkeley. He has interests in animal behavior and cognition, and studies curiosity in a variety of species in laboratories and zoos.

LEE SECHREST is on the faculty at the University of Arizona. He has been teaching—and making up examinations—for 43 years in classes ranging from introduction to psychology to statistics to personality. A primary focus of his interests and work has always been research methods, including measurement.

BARRY D. SMITH is professor of psychology at the University of Maryland, College Park, where he has also been Acting Chair of the Department and Director of Undergraduate Studies. The recipient of the Distinguished Teacher/Mentor Award, he has regularly taught introductory psychology, as well as graduate and undergraduate courses in personality, statistics, research design, and clinical biopsychology. He conducts psychophysiological research at the university and in laboratories at the National Institutes of Health (NIH) Clinical Center in Bethesda, Maryland. He has authored and edited several books, most recently *Psychology: Science and Understanding* (1998), published by McGraw-Hill.

ROBERT J. STERNBERG is IBM Professor of Psychology and Education in the Department of Psychology at Yale University. He is editor of *Teaching Introductory Psychology* and coauthored *Teaching for Critical Thinking* with Louise-Spear Swerling. He has taught introductory psychology for about two decades.

MARK E. WARE is a professor of psychology at Creighton University in Omaha, Nebraska, where he has been since 1965. In 1972 he received a PhD in psychology from United States International University in San Diego. Ware was associate editor of *Teaching of Psychology* (1985-1996); he is a fellow of APA and an APS Charter Fellow.

MICHAEL WERTHEIMER obtained his PhD in experimental psychology from Harvard in 1952. He taught courses on the history of psychology more than 50 times. His publications include *A Brief History of Psychology* (3rd ed.) (1998) (4th ed. in press). A former president of APA's Division 26 (History of Psychology), he became professor emeritus at the University of Colorado in 1993.

RICK WESP team taught and conducted research with Nancy Koschman at Elmira College for over 10 years. Both were awarded the College's Josef Stein Award for Excellence in Teaching. Rick teaches a variety of general experimental psychology courses. He is now at East Stroudsburg University.

ARNO F. WITTIG (PhD, Ohio State University, 1964) is professor of psychology and dean of the Honors College at Ball State University. He specializes in sports psychology research, concentrating on gender differences and psychological rehabilitation from injury. He and the other authors of this chapter (David V. Perkins, Deborah Ware Balogh, Bernard E. Whitley Jr., and Patricia Keith-Spiegel) are a team, since 1992, studying ethical issues in higher education. All are members of the Psychological Science Department at Ball State University.

TODD ZAKRAJSEK received his PhD from Ohio University and is currently an associate professor of at Southern Oregon University in Ashland. He has authored both an introductory psychology student study guide and instructor's manual. His current research interests pertain to effectiveness of instructional methods and factors related to student learning.

Index

THE AMERICAN PSYCHOLOGICAL SOCIETY

Founded in 1988, the American Psychological Society (APS) is the nation's leading organization dedicated solely to scientific psychology. APS's mission is to promote, protect, and advance the interests of scientifically oriented psychology in research, application, and the improvement of human welfare. APS's membership includes the world's foremost psychological scientists and academics. Members cover the entire spectrum of basic and applied psychological science and all of the subdisciplines. All APS efforts are dedicated to the advancing of the scientific discipline of psychology and the "giving away" of psychology in the public interest.

THE *APS OBSERVER*

The premier newsletter for the field of psychological science, the *APS Observer* informs APS members—as well as public-policy makers, the media, libraries, and nonmember subscribers—of noteworthy events, activities, news, and opportunities affecting (and affected by) psychological science.

The *Observer* offers a host of information that is invaluable to the academic, research, and applied psychological community. Informative news articles discuss issues such as important national trends, public policy, and research related matters of direct relevance to the discipline of psychology and its application, in addition to news about the Society itself, and detailed and practical "how to" information (such as the Teaching Tips columns that make up this book) for psychological scientists in all stages of their careers.

For information on APS membership, publications, programs and features, contact the APS Office.

The American Psychological Society
1010 Vermont Avenue, NW ◆ Suite 1100
Washington, DC 20005-4907
Phone: 202-783-2077 ◆ Fax: 202-783-2083
Email: aps@aps.washington.dc.us
www.psychologicalscience.org